County Books.
£4·99-10%
1-7-99

Jerry Bacfosread 1-10-99

RAF
FIGHTER SQUADRONS
IN THE BATTLE OF
BRITAIN

1. **RAF Fighter Command Sector and Group Boundaries**

Key

——— Group boundaries

- - - - Sector Boundaries

Wick

Turnhouse

Usworth

No. 13 GROUP

Catterick

Church. Fenton

Kirton-in-Lindsey

No. 12 GROUP

Digby

Coltishall

Pembrey

Wittering

Duxford

Debden

North Weald

No. 11 GROUP

Filton

Northolt

Hornchurch

No. 10 GROUP

Middle Wallop

Biggin Hill

Kenley

Tangmere

St Eval

RAF
FIGHTER
SQUADRONS
IN THE
BATTLE OF BRITAIN

Anthony Robinson

Brockhampton Press

First published in Great Britain
in 1987 by Arms and Armour Press Limited, Artillery House,
Artillery Row, London SW1P 1RT

This edition published in 1999 by Brockhampton Press,
a member of Hodder Headline PLC Group

ISBN 1 86019 907 0

British Library Cataloguing in Publication Data:

Robinson, Anthony, *1947–*
RAF fighter squadrons in the Battle of Britain
1. Great Britain. *Royal Air Force*—History   2. Britain, Battle of, 1940
3. Fighter planes—History
I. Title
940.54´21   D786

Jacket illustration by James Goulding.

Edited and designed by DAG Publications Ltd.
Designed by David Gibbons; edited by Michael Boxall;
typeset by Typesetters (Birmingham) Ltd; printed and bound
in Great Britain by Creative Print and Design (Wales), Ebbw Vale

CONTENTS

LIST OF MAPS

INTRODUCTION

During the 46 years since the Battle of Britain was fought, numerous books have been written about this, the first decisive engagement in the history of warfare to be fought in the air. My Bibliography, which is a selective rather than complete list, includes no fewer than 56 titles. What need is there for a further addition to this already vast literature on the Battle? The reason is simply that none of the previously published works deals adequately with the Battle from the perspective of the RAF fighter squadrons. And, since the squadron was the basic combat formation in RAF Fighter Command, an understanding of the conditions under which these units fought is essential to a proper appreciation of the course of the Battle. Indeed the operational effectiveness of the fighter squadrons was a factor of such crucial importance that it transcended even the abilities of brilliant individual pilots and the tactical and strategic skills of the senior commanders in deciding the outcome of the fighting.

On paper, at least, each fighter squadron appeared much the same, having an established strength of sixteen aircraft and 26 pilots which enabled it to maintain a standard combat formation of twelve fighters in the air. Yet in reality every squadron differed quite considerably in character and effectiveness. Many units fought under serious handicaps. Some were unlucky and suffered serious casualties within days of entering combat and so had to be withdrawn before they had a chance to show their mettle. Others had to fight with inadequate equipment. The RAF's standard fighter tactics were antiquated and ineffective. None of the British fighter pilots could match the Luftwaffe's veterans of the Spanish Civil War in length of combat experience. Under such conditions, the successful RAF fighter squadrons were those that were able to improvise effective tactics in the heat of battle. Much of course depended upon effective tactical leadership, but this did not always come from the squadrons' nominal commanders. In relating the operational histories of eight of the squadrons heavily engaged in the Battle, I have tried to explore further these significant themes of tactics and leadership.

Another important factor to be considered is the human element. No author writing about RAF Fighter Command in the Battle of Britain can ignore the courage and skill shown by the pilots engaged, nor fail to be awed by their willingness to accept battle daily against impossible odds. One of the surviving participants, Squadron Leader G. H. Bennions, DFC, has concisely and movingly expressed the magnitude of their achievements. He writes: 'At no time during the Battle did we have more than 650 aircraft or 1,200 pilots in Fighter Command as a whole and, in the No. 10 and No. 11 Group areas rarely more than 400 aircraft with 600 pilots. Out of the 1,200 pilots who were in action during the Battle, 500 were killed and 500 wounded. A tremendous sacrifice of and by some extremely nice people.' The arduous and anonymous toil of the groundcrews in keeping the aircraft serviceable also deserves high praise. That they feature so little, either collectively or as individuals, in the histories of the Battle is indicative of the selfless nature of their contribution.

The basis for my research into the operational histories of the RAF fighter squadrons in the Battle of Britain has been provided by the official records held in the Public Record Office at Kew. The documents I have consulted are listed under 'Manuscript Sources' in the Bibliography. I have also greatly benefited from reading the published work of earlier writers on the Battle. Surviving members of the eight fighter squadrons with which I deal in detail have been most generous in providing me with their recollections and information from their personal records. Without their help this book would have been much the poorer. I am most grateful to Air Commodore H. A. Probert, MBE, MA, the Head of Air Historical Branch, Ministry of Defence, and to Wing Commander N. P. W. Hancock, DFC, of the Battle of Britain Fighter Association, for their assistance in contacting these participants. I would also like to thank the undermentioned for their unfailing help and courtesy during the preparation of the book:

H. C. Baker Esq.; Squadron Leader A. C. Bartley, DFC; Squadron Leader R. A. Beardsley, DFC; Squadron Leader G. H. Bennions, DFC; Wing Commander R. J. E. Boulding; Squadron Leader B. H. Bowring; Wing Commander D. G. Cox, DFC, AE; Wing Commander B. J. Jennings, AFC, DFM; Fight Lieutenant Jan Kowalski, DFM; Squadron Leader H. S. Newton, AFC; Group Captain E. N. Ryder, CBE, DFC and bar; Wing Commander H. M. Stephen, CBE, DSO, DFC, AE; Group Captain F. B. Sutton, DFC; Air Commodore J. M. Thompson, CBE, DSO, DFC, AFC; Wing Commander G. C. Unwin, DSO, DFM; Squadron Leader F. Usmar; Squadron Leader R. W. Wallens, DFC; Squadron Leader G. H. A. Wellum, DFC; Wing Commander I. B. Westmacott, DFC; Group Captain A. R. Wright, DFC and bar; Flying Officer C. E. Hampshire; Wing Commander M. H. Constable-Maxwell, DSO, DFC, MA; Flight Lieutenant M. H. Mounsdon; Squadron Leader W. J. Pilkington-Miksa, VM, KW, DFC; B. Coopman, Esq; No. 56 Squadron RAF; No 85 Squadron RAF; Captain W. Milewski, Keeper of Archives, The Polish Institute and Sikorski Museum; RAF Station Biggin Hill.

December 1986   Anthony Robinson

THE BACKGROUND

The British fighter forces that met and defeated the full weight of the Luftwaffe's attack on the United Kingdom in the summer of 1940 constituted the cutting edge of what was the most advanced air defence system anywhere in the world. Yet the Battle of Britain proved to be a very different conflict from that which the pre-war architects of RAF Fighter Command had envisaged and planned to fight. The major fear of the 1930s was that of the knock-out blow from the air: a series of swiftly executed, devastating bombing raids on Britain's population centres, which, if successful, would paralyze the nation's will to fight right at the outset of hostilities. Consequently the RAF's fighter squadrons were trained and equipped to deal with massed raids by bombers operating from their bases in Germany and therefore flying considerably beyond the range of single-engined escort fighters.

In the event, however, the threat of an immediate knock-out blow proved to be illusory. In 1938 Luftwaffe staff planners had examined the feasibility of a bomber offensive against Britain and had concluded that without bases in the Low Countries no effective action could be taken. This view was confirmed by a second staff appreciation drawn up in the spring of 1939, but the German victories in the Low Countries and France in May/June 1940 gave the Luftwaffe the airfields it needed to mount an air attack on the United Kingdom and set the stage for the Battle of Britain. Contrary to the expectations of the RAF's fighter commanders before the war, the German offensive would be carried out by the full might of the Luftwaffe's tactical air forces and not just by the medium bombers and their long-range fighter escorts of twin-engined Messerschmitt Bf 110s. The attacking force would therefore include substantial numbers of Messerschmitt Bf 109E single-engined fighters. The Bf 109E was technically on a par with the

10

RAF's Supermarine Spitfire Mk I and it was significantly better than the Hawker Hurricane Mk I which equipped the greater part of the RAF's fighter force.

The increased weight of the attack and the feasibility (hitherto hardly considered by the RAF) of the Germans' providing their bombers with single-engined fighter escort over Britain were not the only unexpected features of the forthcoming assault. The siting of the RAF's fighter airfields, radar stations and various other elements of the command and control system had been orientated towards an attack coming from over the North Sea. Suddenly, in the early summer of 1940, the direction of the main threat had shifted southwards and westwards to the Channel coast. It was not Britain's cities that were the primary target for air attack during the initial stages of the campaign, but RAF Fighter Command itself. In the German view, once the British air defence forces had been eliminated, the fall of the United Kingdom would inevitably follow.

The general outline of the events which made up the Battle of Britain is well known and can be briefly summarized as:

Phase I (early July to 12 August 1940). Attacks on Channel convoys and coastal objectives such as ports, airfields and radar stations in southern England. Light but widely scattered night bombing attacks.

Phase II (13 August to 6 September 1940). The main focus directed to RAF airfields. From 24 August onwards the size of the bomber formations is reduced and their fighter escort correspondingly increased, with the objective of bringing the RAF's fighters to battle. The bombers released from daylight missions are switched to night attack.

Phase III (7 September to late September 1940). The daylight bombing offensive switches to London. Night attacks intensify, opening the Blitz of 1940–1.

Phase IV (Late September to December 1940). Daylight fighter sweeps at high level, accompanied by fighter-bomber raids. Heavy night bombing raids.

A word of caution is necessary about the practice, which in general is perfectly valid, of arranging the events of the Battle into phases;

in fact, no hard-and-fast divisions can be made. The Luftwaffe's tactics were infinitely varied and in Air Chief Marshal Sir Hugh Dowding's words: 'these phases indicated only general tendencies; they overlapped and were not mutually exclusive'.

Blow-by-blow narrative accounts of the Battle can be found in such standard references as *The Narrow Margin* by Derek Wood and Derek Dempster (Hutchinson, 1961) and B. Collier's *The Defence of the United Kingdom* (HMSO, 1957) by anyone wanting more detailed information on the course of the fighting. The purpose of this book is not to cover the same ground again, but rather to examine the problems of tactics and leadership encountered by the RAF's fighter force when it was pitchforked into a battle which in many ways, was very different from that which it had expected to fight. Deficient in the tactical skills necessary for fighter-versus-fighter combat, often inadequately trained and even to some extent inappropriately equipped, the RAF fighter squadrons had perforce to make good these shortcomings as best they could in the heat of combat.

Under such conditions, a great weight of responsibility fell to the squadron commanding officers and to their flight commanders. Consequently the quality of the RAF's tactical leadership was a matter of vital importance. In some instances this leadership was poor, as Fighter Command's Commander-in-Chief, Air Chief Marshal Sir Hugh Dowding, acknowledged in his Dispatch on the Battle of Britain. He pointed out that some of the worst losses of the Battle had been caused by the mistakes of inexperienced squadron commanders. He recommended that in future promotions to the command of fighter squadrons be made from among those officers who had proved their abilities as flight commanders. If it were necessary to promote an officer from outside Fighter Command, Dowding thought he should fly as an ordinary member of the formation until he had gained the experienced to lead it.

Because the RAF's fighter tactics evolved during the Battle of Britain on an *ad hoc* basis at squadron level, it is necessary to look in detail at the experience of individual units in order to understand how they developed. In the following chapters of this book, the combat records of eight of the fighter squadrons heavily engaged in the fighting are described and analyzed. Before examining the detailed picture of the air battles at squadron level, however, it is essential to describe briefly the overall organization of RAF Fighter Command. It is impossible to appreciate the conditions under which the RAF fought the Battle of Britain without some knowledge of the Command's strength, organization and deployment, the characteristics of its aircraft and, most significantly of all, the workings of its crucially import command and control systems. And since the fighter tactics of the Battle had to be built upon the foundations of the RAF's peacetime doctrines, however unsure they had been shown to be, these too need to be described and assessed.

RAF Fighter Command was formed on 6 July 1936 under Dowding's command. It superseded the earlier Fighting Area which, up to that time, had been responsible for the home defence fighter squadrons as a subordinate command within the Air Defence of Great Britain. The latter command, which controlled all UK-based combat squadrons up until the mid-1930s, would have had an impossible task in overseeing the tremendous pre-war expansion of the RAF, so it was broken down into separate functional commands to control fighter, bomber, coastal and army co-operation squadrons. The formation of Fighter Command was not simply a matter of administrative convenience, but signalled an important shift in British air policy. Up until 1936 Britain had relied on the deterrent effect of its bomber forces to counter German rearmament, but it had then become apparent that the policy had failed. Sir Thomas Inskip, the Minister for Co-ordination of Defence, decided to postpone the planned build-up of the RAF's strategic bomber forces and instead to give priority to the needs of Britain's air defences.

During the earlier years of the inter-war period the home defence fighter squadrons had been very much the poor relations of the bomber force. Baldwin's famous dictum that 'the bomber will always get through' was no more than a faithful reflection of the Air Staff's thinking. Air Chief Marshal Sir Hugh Trenchard, the forceful and dogmatic architect of the peacetime RAF and Chief of the Air Staff from 1919 to 1929, had seen the air defence fighter squadrons as simply a sop to civilian morale. In his view, the only defence against air bombardment was counter-bombardment, and the fighters would not significantly affect the outcome of a future war. Dowding, who, as the Air Member for Supply and Research, had sanctioned the early development work on radar, was influential in challenging this conventional wisdom within the RAF. It was he who persuaded Inskip to reverse the RAF's traditional strategy of deterrence through the threat of counter-bombardment. His seniority within the service and determined character enabled him to press the case for the air defences in spite of the disapproval of such policies on the part of most senior RAF commanders. Indeed, Dowding was later to claim that much of his pioneering work in building up Britain's air defences was pushed ahead against the resistance of Air Staff inertia.

At the same time as the RAF's defensive strategy was being reassessed to meet the threat from Germany, so too were the air defence units being physically re-orientated. This was necessary because, when Britain's air defences were reconstituted after the First World War, the only possible threat was that represented by France's Aviation Militaire, then the largest European air arm and generally supposed to be the most efficient. As a consequence, the airfields of Fighting Area, Air Defence of Great Britain were sited to meet a bomber attack from across the English Channel. In the mid-1930s, it became necessary to redeploy the air defences to confront an air attack from the east. By an ironic twist of fate, the fall of France in 1940 brought about yet a further rearrangement of air defence installations: the right flank of the eastward-facing air defences had rested on the Solent, and hurried measures had to be put in hand to extend the coverage westwards.

It had been calculated that Fighter Command would require a minimum strength of 46 squadrons to deal effectively with the anticipated scale of bomber attacks from Germany. On the outbreak of war in September 1939, 35 of these squadrons were operationally deployed, together with the four fighter squadrons required for the Air Component of the British Expeditionary Force to be dispatched to France. An additional seven fighter squadrons, earmarked for the defence of the fleet anchorage at Scapa Flow, the defence of Northern Ireland and merchant shipping convoy protection, had yet to be formed. The German invasion of the Low Countries and France effectively invalidated the assumptions on which earlier calculations had been based, and a hasty reassessment showed that RAF Fighter Command would need a force of 120 fighter squadrons in order to defend the United Kingdom from the greatly increased threat. Such an expansion of the RAF's fighter forces was totally unrealistic and even a modest increase in strength of ten squadrons proved to be impossible to achieve at that time, largely because of the need to replace aircraft and pilots lost during the Battle of France and the air fighting over Dunkirk.

Fighter Command's actual strength at the start of the Battle of Britain (on 9 July 1940) was 58 fighter squadrons. Four of these units were in the process of forming or re-equipping and had not been declared operational on that date, and many nominally operational squadrons were inexperienced and in need of further training, while others were recovering from heavy losses suffered in the air battles of May and June. Six Fighter Command squadrons were equipped with the twin-engined Bristol Blenheim If which was of little use for dogfighting, and it was soon to become apparent that the Boulton Paul Defiant Mk I turret fighter, which equipped a further two squadrons, was little more effectual than the Blenheim. Therefore the brunt of the fighting would have to be borne by the nineteen squadrons equipped with the Spitfire Mk I and the 27 Hurricane units. All four non-operational squadrons were also equipped with Hurricanes and a further five squadrons were to be formed on this fighter during the course of the Battle. Although the Hurricane was well able to deal with German bomber aircraft, it was outmatched in performance by the Messerschmitt Bf 109E. So, on the face of it at least, all that the RAF had to take on the German fighter forces of rather more than 800 Bf 109Es on anything like equal terms were the nineteen Spitfire squadrons, with just under 300 Spitfire Mk Is on strength.

In the event, the Hurricane proved to be a rather more effective opponent of the Bf 109E than its shortcomings in performance might suggest. It was an extremely manoeuvrable aircraft and a good, steady gun platform, which made it more than a match for the Bf 109 in a dogfight, so there were many combats in which the Hurricane was able to hold its own against the theoretically superior German fighter. It was only when the Luftwaffe pilots avoided a turning dogfight and used the Bf 109E to its best advantage in dive and zoom tactics that the Hurricane was outclassed.

Wing Commander I. B. Westmacott, who flew Hurricanes as a flying officer with No. 56 Squadron during the Battle, has written: 'I had a great affection for the Hurricane although it had certain faults . . . It was an extremely strong aircraft and would take a lot of damage, while being easier than the Spitfire to repair.' Squadron Leader H. S. Newton, a sergeant pilot with No. 111 Squadron, had great confidence in the Hurricane as a fighter aircraft. He mentions in particular its Rolls-Royce Merlin engine, the lower wing loading than the Bf 109 (which gave greater manoeuvrability), the eight-gun armament and the pilot's armour protection as especially good features of the aircraft. In addition, he cites the advantages to the RAF pilots of fighting over their own territory and under the direction of ground control. By contrast, as he points out, the Luftwaffe fighter pilots knew that if they were shot down and survived they would become prisoners. They also had the constant worry of limited fuel, with the possibility of being forced down into the Channel during their return flight, and, unlike the RAF pilots, they received no information on the enemy's movements from ground control during their missions.

The supply of replacement fighter aircraft during the Battle was never a critical problem, thanks in large measure to the dynamic influence of Lord Beaverbrook at the Ministry of Aircraft Production, building on the sure foundations laid by Lord Swinton as Secretary of State for Air in 1935–8. Hurricane reserves reached their low point of 78 aircraft on 30 August 1940, while Spitfire reserves were lowest on 20 September with 38 aircraft available for immediate issue. RAF and civilian repair and salvage units substantially increased the reserves available from new production by recovering and repairing crashed and battle-damaged fighters. Between July and December 1940 they returned a total of 4,196 damaged aircraft to serviceable condition, and 35 per cent of all fighters issued to the squadrons during the Battle of Britain came from this source. While the provision of adequate fighter reserves was to cause many worries to the aircraft industry and repair organizations, the situation never reached a point where operational units were kept waiting for replacements, even during periods of heavy losses.

The output of trained pilots to replace casualties in the front-line units was an entirely different matter and proved to be one of Fighter Command's most vulnerable points during the Battle. Since it took about one year of training to produce an operational pilot, any expansion of the intake of pupil pilots could have no immediate effect on the problem. It is clear that the requirements for replacement pilots during periods of heavy fighting had been seriously miscalculated by the RAF planners before the war. RAF Training Command (which was divided into Flying Training and Technical Training Commands in May 1940) had proved to be rather an unenterprising organization, reluctant to compromise its justifiably high peacetime standards in the interests of emergency expansion. For example, some volunteer aircrew with worthwhile experience in civil aviation had been required to go back to square one and start their service flying training from the primary stage.

The Empire Air Training Scheme had been started too late to influence the pilot supply situation in the summer of 1940. The shortage of trained pilots was so critical that the Flying Training Schools could not even supply the full intake for the courses at the Operational Training Units (OTUs, formerly known as Group Pool Squadrons). Even had they been able to do so, the output from the OTUs would have been inadequate. In Dowding's words, 'the lack of flexibility of the training system, therefore, proved to be the "bottleneck" and was the cause of the progressively deteriorating situation of the Fighter Command up till the end of September'.

Once the RAF was engaged in the Battle of Britain, very little could be done to provide immediate remedies to the situation. The courses at the three OTUs were cut from four weeks to two weeks, but this measure provided little relief since the supply of pilots was too small to fill the exta places created, and it exacerbated the fighter squadrons' problems of assimilating and training pilots who were manifestly unready for combat when posted to the front-line units. An alternative to the Flying Training Schools as a source of pilot supply were the squadrons of Bomber, Coastal and Army Co-operation Commands which, with the Royal Navy's Fleet Air Arm, provided small numbers of volunteers for the fighter squadrons. The commanders of these formations were naturally reluctant to lose experienced aircrew and so relatively little use was made of this expedient. In any case, many of these pilots were temperamentally unsuited to fighter operations. The most substantial reinforcement of Fighter Command's front-line strength during the Battle came from the squadrons manned by Polish and Czech airmen who had made their way to Britain after the fall of France to continue the fight against Nazi Germany.

The RAF's senior commanders were initially somewhat doubtful about the value of these units, for although they were composed of trained pilots, few of the foreign airmen spoke good English and they were of course unfamiliar with Fighter Command's aircraft and operational procedures. Notwithstanding these reservations, a total of four such squadrons became operational during the Battle – No. 302 (Polish) Squadron, No. 303 (Polish) Squadron, No. 310 (Czech) Squadron and No. 312 (Czech) Squadron – and they proved that any doubts about their prowess in combat were totally unfounded. A further valuable reinforcement came from No. 1 Squadron, Royal Canadian Air Force, which operated Hurricanes as a unit of Fighter Command during the Battle.

Because the RAF's fighter squadrons usually operated over friendly territory during the Battle, any pilot who parachuted uninjured from his crippled aircraft could soon be returned to action. Dowding, ever the realist, thought that in these circumstances the Luftwaffe would be perfectly entitled to fire at RAF pilots coming down by parachute. Yet, with some exceptions, the German airmen behaved humanely, if quixotically, and broke off the attack once their opponents had abandoned their aircraft. Not all combats took place over land, and the early air fights of the Battle in defence of the Channel convoys showed the need for an air–sea rescue service. One was quickly improvised, although it had yet to achieve its full efficiency when the Battle ended. The

Luftwaffe which, unlike the RAF, had routinely to operate over the Channel throughout the Battle, proved to be better prepared to recover its airmen from the sea.

The implications of Fighter Command's chronic pilot shortage during the Battle of Britain were far-reaching. In the first place it inhibited the formation of badly needed new fighter squadrons. Secondly, it hampered the smooth operation of the rotation scheme, whereby exhausted units could be withdrawn to relatively quiet sectors and replaced by fresh squadrons from those areas. Finally, it severely circumscribed Fighter Command's tactics during the Battle by enforcing the absolute necessity for economy of effort in order to conserve the Command's meagre resources. The brunt of the fighting was borne by the twenty or so squadrons and 400 pilots of Air Vice-Marshal Sir Keith Park's No. 11 Group, which covered south-east England and the approaches to London. Under normal circumstances, each squadron in this Group would be required to fight on until such time as it was unable to muster an airborne strength of nine aircraft. On paper a Fighter Command squadron had an established strength of 26 pilots and sixteen aircraft. In fact, because of the pilot shortage, fresh squadrons had only twenty or so pilots, although they were issued with their full complement of sixteen fighters. The squadron would usually operate in the standard twelve-aircraft formation, until losses made this impossible. The time during which a fighter squadron could remain in action naturally varied according to the skill and good fortune of individual units. In general a period of between four and six weeks was the norm, although some squadrons suffered such severe losses that they had to be withdrawn after only a week of fighting. They would then rest and re-form in a quiet sector, where newly posted pilots could be given some badly needed additional training, before being fed back into the Battle.

In September 1940 this carefully planned system had to be abandoned when casualties became so serious that No. 11 Group squadrons needed to be replaced before any of the units resting and re-forming were ready to take their place. Dowding was then forced to adopt a far less efficient procedure, whereby all squadrons were categorized according to their operational commitments. Category 'A' squadrons were those stationed within No. 11 Group and on its immediate flanks, which were engaged in continuous heavy action. Category 'B' squadrons, of which there were only four, were maintained at full operational strength on airfields outside the No. 11 Group area, in order to provide a small reserve from which the Category 'A' squadrons could be reinforced or relieved if dire necessity made this unavoidable (two of the Category 'B' squadrons were in fact committed to action). Category 'C' squadrons were stripped of all but a handful of their operational pilots in order to reinforce the Category 'A' units and they then acted mainly as training units for new pilots, although they could and did engage small-scale raids by unescorted bombers.

The strain that this arrangement imposed on the pilots of Category 'A' squadrons was immense, with some units flying fifty to sixty hours on operations each day with no prospect of relief. All that Dowding could do to ease their burden was to insist that all pilots took 24 hours' leave each week. Thus, during the closing weeks of the Battle, its outcome depended on the resilience of 23

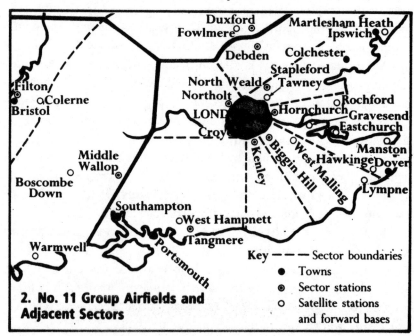

2. No. 11 Group Airfields and Adjacent Sectors

Key — — — Sector boundaries
● Towns
◉ Sector stations
○ Satellite stations and forward bases

hard-pressed fighter squadrons and the four units in immediate reserve. Such was the narrowness of the margin by which RAF Fighter Command won the Battle of Britain.

Fighter Command's basic organization into groups, sectors and squadrons proved to be well conceived. Although the practice of operating in squadron strength, rather than in wings several squadrons strong (to match the Luftwaffe's basic units, the Gruppe of 30 aircraft and Geschwader of 90 plus aircraft), was to be the subject of an acrimonious debate within the Command, the organization as it existed in 1940 withstood the test of battle. For most of the Battle of Britain, Fighter Command was divided into four groups: Nos. 10, 11, 12 and 13 Groups. No. 10 Group, under Air Chief Marshal Sir Christopher Quintin Brand, covered the West Country and was the latest group to be formed, becoming operational on 18 July 1940 as part of the measures to extend the British air defence coverage west of the Solent.

No. 11 Group, as it covered London and south-east England, was in the forefront of the Battle. Its commander, Air Vice-Marshal Park, had previously been Dowding's Senior Air Staff Officer at HQ Fighter Command and the two men worked well together and had absolute confidence in each other's abilities. Air Chief Marshal Trafford Leigh-Mallory, whose No. 12 Group covered the Eastern Counties and Midlands, was the chief critic of Park's tactics of operating in Wing strength and was eventually to replace him as Air Officer Commanding No. 11 Group after the Battle. The quieter areas of northern England and Scotland, well beyond the range of the Luftwaffe's single-engined escort fighters, was the province of No. 13 Group under Air Vice-Marshal R. E. Saul. As might be expected, No. 11 Group controlled the largest forces, the strengths of the four groups in mid-August being: No. 10 Group ten squadrons, No. 11 Group twenty-three squadrons, No. 12 Group sixteen squadrons, and No. 13 Group fourteen squadrons.

The groups were sub-divided into sectors, which comprised the main sector station, plus satellite airfields and sometimes forward-operating bases. No. 11 Group's sector stations were Biggin Hill, Kenley, Hornchurch, North Weald, Northolt, Debden and Tangmere. Each fighter sector was normally assigned between two and four squadrons, which it controlled through its operations room. The fighter squadrons, in addition to their complement of some twenty pilots and sixteen aircraft, included the groundcrew needed to maintain their aircraft. Each fighter was assigned an air-frame rigger and engine fitter, while other technical specialists, such as armourers, wireless, electrical and instrument mechanics, were attached to the flights. The squadron was divided into two flights, 'A' Flight and 'B' Flight, and when operating at full strength of twelve aircraft was further sub-divided into three-aircraft sections which were identified by a colour code. 'A' Flight comprised Red and Yellow Sections, 'B' Flight Blue and Green Sections. It was customary for a pilot to identify himself over the radio-telephone (R/T) and often in combat reports by his position in the formation. For example, Yellow 1, was leading the second section of 'A' Flight, with Yellow 2 to his right and Yellow 3 to his left. The Squadron itself was given a callsign to use over the R/T, so as not to reveal its identity in transmissions which would be monitored by the enemy. Examples included 'Dysoe' for No. 74 Squadron and 'Gannic' for No. 92 Squadron.

In the course of daily operations, each squadron when not actually airborne would pass through various states of preparedness. These were: Released (not required for operations), Available (take-off in twenty minutes), Readiness (take-off in five minutes) and Stand-by (take-off in two minutes), the latter condition requiring the pilots to sit strapped in their aircraft awaiting the order to 'scramble'. It was the heavy responsibility of the Group controllers, and ultimately the Group's Air Officer Commanding, to ensure that squadrons were ordered off in adequate strength and in good time to deal with incoming raids. The ever-present danger was that the Luftwaffe would launch a strong attack at a time when all squadrons were either returning to base at the end of an earlier engagement, or on the ground refuelling and re-arming.

In view of Fighter Command's limited strength in relation to its immense task, it was as well that it possessed an excellent command and control system which allowed its resources to be deployed with considerable economy of effort. That it did so was largely due to the forethought of its AOC-in-C, Air Chief Marshal Sir Hugh Dowding, who had taken an active interest in the problems of air defence since serving on the Air Council as Air Member for Supply and Research (later Air Member for Research and Development) during the early 1930s. It is a truism to state that Fighter Command's command and control system was the most advanced of its kind operating anywhere in the world; but, for all its innovative features, it did have certain limitations that were to affect the way in which the RAF's fighter squadrons fought the Battle.

Early warning of attack depended on radar (the present-day term is in fact anachronistic, for it was known as RDF in 1940), but once the enemy aircraft had crossed the coast the main responsibility for raid reporting passed to the Observer Corps. Information from both sources was passed to Fighter Command's control rooms, but first passed through a filtering process which would eliminate obvious errors. The operations room at HQ, Fighter Command was the only one to monitor the entire air defence picture for the United Kingdom and was responsible for overall co-ordination of the defences. It was the group controllers who decided which fighter squadrons were to engage particular enemy formations, but when this decision had been made, control of the actual interceptions passed to the sector controllers. They ordered the squadrons to take off and then, when they were airborne, passed instructions to them by R/T to bring them into contact with the enemy. Once the raiders were in sight, the fighter formation leader (often, but not invariably the squadron's commanding officer) signified by the code-word 'tally-ho' that he was taking over responsibility for the attack. The sector controller would monitor the course of the fighting by listening in to the R/T transmissions and at its end would direct the squadron back to base.

The great strength of the British air defence system lay in its ability to direct the fighter squadrons against enemy attacks as they developed, rather than dissipate their efforts in airborne standing patrols. If no precise and timely information had been available as to the strength and position of enemy raids, all that the defending fighter squadrons could have done would have been to patrol likely target areas and approach routes on the off-chance of encountering a worthwhile target. A further important characteristic of the RAF system was its flexibility, as neither group nor sector boundaries marked rigid divisions of effort and squadrons could be – and often were – directed outside their normal area of operations to the point where they were most needed. By the opening of the Battle of Britain, all elements of the air defence system has been well exercised and many weaknesses had been recognized and rectified. None the less, there remained various shortcomings inherent in the system and its equipment which simply had to be coped with by controllers and fighter squadron leaders as best they could.

Even with the help of radar early warning, the time available to the defenders in which to react to a developing threat was critically short. This was especially true during the early phases of the Battle, when the Luftwaffe was making only comparatively shallow penetrations of British air space. The well-established Kent radar stations were generally able to give some twenty minutes' advance warning, but the newer stations to the west were often less efficient. Even under the most favourable conditions, some four minutes elapsed between a radar contact being made and its corresponding plot appearing on the operations rooms' plotting-tables. A further thirteen minutes was needed for a Spitfire squadron to scramble and climb to an altitude of 20,000 feet (Hurricane squadrons took three minutes longer). So the time available to the group controller in which to assess the seriousness of the threat and issue the appropriate orders to his sectors was minimal if a timely engagement was to be made.

When the Luftwaffe switched the main weight of its attack from No. 11 Group's airfields to London, this problem was greatly eased, as the deeper penetrations of the air defences, which raids against the capital entailed, increased the time available for interception. Whereas in the earlier phases of the Battle 23 per cent of Fighter Command's sorties had succeeded in engaging the enemy, after 7 September the successful interceptions increased to 40 per cent of sorties flown. In the final phase of the Battle, when the Luftwaffe mounted daylight fighter-bomber raids and fighter sweeps at high altitude over south-east England, the defenders' problems of reacting within the available warning time recurred. Such was the speed of these single-engined fighter formations that only twenty minutes elapsed between the first radar warning and the fighter-bombers releasing their bombs over central London. Moreover, flying at altitudes of about 25,000 feet they were difficult for the Observer Corps to track. As it took a squadron of Spitfires 22 minutes to reach this altitude (and a Hurricane squadron 25 minutes) after take-off, airborne standing patrols had to be instituted to give the RAF fighters a chance to intercept the fighter-bombers before they reached London. Even so their chances of success were not high: thanks to its efficient variable-speed supercharger, the Bf 109E outperformed even the Spitfire at 25,000 feet.

Under these conditions of limited reaction time, a great burden of responsibility fell to the group controller (or to the group AOC if he were available to make the necessary decisions). If he committed the greater part of his forces too early, he could find that he had inadequate resources to counter a later raid. This problem was exacerbated by the ambiguous indications which radar often provided, quite apart from deliberate attempts by the Luftwaffe to complicate the defenders' problems by mounting feint or diversionary raids. Radar was of course still in an early stage of development and many technical problems had still to be solved. In particular, the early equipment, while giving accurate information on range, was less reliable with regard to the target's bearing. Height-finding too was often wildly inaccurate and and the estimation of a raid's size from its radar echo was usually a matter of guesswork. As radar operators gained in experience, so the quality of their information improved, but in general the group controller was forced to make his dispositions without any truly reliable information available as to the nature of the impending attack. It is hardly surprising that he often erred on the side of caution and that fighter squadrons could find themselves engaging vastly superior enemy forces – often at a serious height disadvantage.

The sector controller's job of directing the interception not only required him to bring his squadron into contact with the enemy, but equally importantly to ensure that his fighters were placed in a position of tactical advantage. An ideal position from which the squadron could make its initial attack would be up-sun from the enemy formation and above it, but this was rarely attainable. It was essential for the fighter leader to have confidence in his controller's tactical abilities and for this reason controllers were often selected from officers who themselves had experience as pilots. Once a bombing raid had crossed the coast, an accurate assessment of its strength, composition, height, position and course was available from the sightings reported by the Observer Corps, but cloud and haze could sometimes hamper their work.

Radar returns of friendly aircraft were differentiated from those of the enemy by use of the IFF (identification, friend or foe) device. This was a small transmitter fitted to all British aircraft and produced a distinctive 'blip' on the radar screen. The absence of an IFF response did not necessarily mean that the radar operator could classify the contact as an enemy raid – RAF crews sometimes failed to switch on their IFF transmitters – but, until the radar plot could be positively identified as a friendly aircraft, it had to be treated as a 'bogey' (an unidentified and potentially hostile aircraft). Consequently, during cloudy weather the control rooms were sometimes swamped with reports of unidentified aircraft, all of which had to be tracked and intercepted, or otherwise positively identified.

The sector control rooms monitored the positions of airborne RAF fighter squadrons, not by radar or Observer Corps reports, but by a system of high-frequency radio direction-finding. Each fighter was fitted with a device known as 'Pip-Squeak', which automatically switched on the HF R/T transmitter for a fourteen-second burst every minute. This transmission was picked up by three ground direction-finding stations, enabling the aircraft's position to be fixed quickly and very accurately by triangulation. The system did have one shortcoming. Up to four squadrons could be differentiated by allocating them separate quarter-minute time segments, but if further units needed to be controlled (and sectors sometimes had to deal with up to six), their positions could not be determined using radio direction-finding, but had to be fixed by dead-reckoning navigation, which was a slower and usually less accurate process. During most of the Battle radio communication between ground controllers and the fighter formation leaders (and also between aircraft in the air) was by HF R/T transmission.

It had been recognized well before the war that the fighters' TR9 HF set was far from ideal; it lacked range and the clarity of speech was poor, due to interference and distortion. Indeed, one distinguished Battle of Britain pilot wondered how the RAF's foreign pilots ever made out any HF R/T transmission at all; the sound quality was so poor that he usually had the greatest difficulty in hearing properly himself. The remedy was the introduction of a VHF R/T set for the fighters. The TR1133 and its appropriate ground equipment had been designed, but development problems delayed the new equipment's introduction into service. It had been planned to re-equip all of Fighter Command by May 1940, but in fact it was not until the end of September that even the first four sectors and their squadrons were fully equipped with the VHF sets.

The most surprising aspect of Fighter Command's preparations for war was its neglect of the tactics of air fighting. This can be explained first by the RAF's complete lack of recent combat experience, except for air control operations against dissident tribesmen in the Middle East and army co-operation work in India. The Luftwaffe, by contrast, had put its combat experience gained during the Spanish Civil War to good use in developing highly effective tactics for its fighter aircraft. The RAF's backwardness was also due to the belief that the United Kingdom's air defences would only have to deal with raids by unescorted bombers. Even so, the official view that there could be no fighter-versus-fighter combats between the new monoplanes because the 'g' forces exerted on the pilots would be too great is very hard to understand.

The RAF's tactics for attacking bomber formations were highly formalized and quite inflexible. A series of six 'Fighter Command Attacks' (themselves based on the earlier 'Fighting Area Attacks') were intended to meet all likely eventualities. Squadron commanders were ordered not to practise any other forms of attack, unless authorized to do so by HQ, Fighter Command, but they were encouraged to submit any ideas of their own for official approval. No radical departures from the set-piece Fighter Command Attacks were likely to be introduced so long as expert opinion held that: 'The high speed of modern fighter aircraft makes it impracticable to carry out synchronized attacks with fixed guns from different directions, involving sudden changes of course and wide deflection shooting.' One example of a Fighter Command Attack will be sufficient to illustrate their regimented approach to air fighting. Sections of three fighters in echelon formation were to form up astern of the leading section. They would then follow it in an orderly sequence into a formation attack on the rear of the bomber formation. After firing, the fighters would break away and then re-form to repeat the process. It is doubtful whether these attacks would have proved to be particularly effective against unescorted bombers, but when fighters accompanied the enemy force they were little short of suicidal.

Practical experience in combat soon led the RAF fighter squadrons to abandon the Fighter Command Attacks. As Wing Commander George Unwin, who flew with No. 19 Squadron as an NCO pilot from 1936 to 1941, trenchantly observed, 'the attacks practised in pre-war days were for air displays only'. Even so, as late as November 1940 HQ Fighter Command could still, amazingly, affirm that officially they were still in force.

The standard RAF 'vic' formation of three fighters in arrow-head had been shown to be unsatisfactory by combat experience, but no thorough-going modernization of tactics was possible on the eve of Fighting Command's decisive battle. The lessons of the Battle of France and the air fighting over Dunkirk had not been wholly absorbed and the Luftwaffe's advantage over the RAF, conferred by its superior fighter tactics, was not fully appreciated. The responsibility for deciding on standardized fighter tactics nominally lay with HQ, Fighter Command; but since the officially-approved methods had proved to be inadequate, in practice decisions on fighter tactics were made within the groups. Much of the work of devising practical counter-measures to the Luftwaffe's tactics was extemporized by the squadrons themselves without guidance from higher commands, although, within No. 11 Group, Park had a reputation for maintaining a close personal contact with his squadrons.

On the eve of the Battle, Fighter Command's doctrine concerning the problems of air fighting was enshrined in a tactical memorandum issued to the squadrons in June 1940, as a guide to the recommended methods of attacking escorted bomber formations. It begins with a preamble outlining the strategic situation and emphasizing that the role of the RAF fighter squadrons is the destruction of enemy bombers, with action against German fighters being only a means to that end. Although it claims to have been based on a careful study of recent combat experience, the memorandum makes the unduly dismissive claim that 'the Hurricane and Spitfire are more than a match for either the Me 109 or the Me 110'. Perhaps this was intended simply as a boost to the morale of the fighter squadrons, but it was certainly not borne out by the evaluation reports on captured enemy fighters, prepared by RAF experts.

A Messerschmitt Bf 109E, captured in France, had been tested at the Royal Aircraft Establishment, Farnborough, and the Aeroplane and Armament Experimental Establishment, Boscombe Down, from May to June 1940, and the trials had included mock combats with both Spitfires and Hurricanes. The Bf 109E was assessed as being superior to the Hurricanes in virtually all aspects of performance, except for turning circle and low-altitude manoeuvrability. In comparison with the Spitfire, the German fighter was marginally faster, could outclimb the British fighter at heights below 20,000 feet and could usually elude it in a dive, although on balance the two aircraft were evenly matched. No example of the Messerschmitt Bf 110 twin-engined fighter was available for assessment until July 1940, but RAF assessments then dismissed it as indeed being inferior to both the Hurricane and Spitfire.

The tactical memorandum recommended that fighter squadrons should 'always patrol higher than the anticipated or reported heights of the enemy'. This was a counsel of perfection, which took no account of No. 11 Group controllers' problems in assessing enemy intentions with minimal advance warning, nor of the imperative need to maintain forces in reserve to meet future attacks. The need to compensate the inherent disadvantages of the vic formation was recognized, however, and the tactical memorandum's recommendation formed the basis of most squadrons' defensive tactics during the Battle.

One of the major problems with the vic was that in such a formation every pilot except the leader has to concentrate on keeping his position and so was unable to maintain a good look-out, especially to the rear. The palliative suggested by HQ, Fighter Command was to employ the rearmost section of the formation as look-outs. Colloquially they were known as 'weavers', because they were required to fly a continuous series of turns in order to keep a satisfactory watch to the rear of the formation. Another disadvantage of the vic, which was not satisfactorily addressed in Fighter Command's memorandum, was that in combat it tended quickly to break up into single aircraft, which were far more vulnerable than the Luftwaffe's Rotte, a mutually-supporting pair (leader and wingman) into which the German formations broke down. All that the memorandum could suggest was that 'whenever possible fighters should remain together so that they may afford mutual support', which recognized the problem without offering a practical solution to it. The third serious drawback of the vic formation was the difficulty of manoeuvring in concert and particularly of turning together, which was of course one of the reasons why the RAF fighter formations tended to break up soon after combat was joined.

In contrast, the Luftwaffe's loose formations, built up of pairs of fighters, were manoeuvrable, easily maintained a good look-out and were much less likely to break up. Their well-conceived tactical formations, an outcome of combat experience in Spain, had been well proven during the early battles of the Second World War and they gave the German fighter pilots a significant advantage over the RAF throughout the Battle of Britain. Not all of the lessons drawn from the Condor Legion's experience in Spain proved to be so valuable; the Luftwaffe's bomber force tended to rely on the speed of its aircraft to evade interception, and to neglect armoured protection and defensive firepower.

The tactics of bomber formation attack had much occupied Fighter Command's planners before the war, and the results of their thinking had been codified in the Fighter Command Attacks. That these techniques had taken no account of the need to deal with enemy fighter escorts did not, however, predispose Fighter Command to abandon them entirely in June 1940. They were instead modified to take account of the changed conditions, while retaining the essential features of the old system. Thus the tactical memorandum stated: 'Whenever possible, fighters should attack enemy bomber formations in equal numbers by astern and quarter attacks from the same level . . .' The idea that RAF fighters would engage any but the smallest raiding forces in equal numbers proved to be pure wishful thinking. The Luftwaffe's bombers frequently operated in Geschwader strength of nearly a hundred aircraft, plus fighter escort, while it was rare for more than two RAF squadrons (24 aircraft) to be able to go into the attack at any one time. Even a Gruppe of thirty bombers would outnumber the RAF's fighters.

The memorandum warned against giving the bombers' gunners an easy target and advised that a short burst of fire of two or three seconds might well be decisive, 'but in any case this should not be exceeded without breaking away to ensure that an enemy fighter is not on one's tail'. While the bombers were being attacked by one element of the British formation, another was to 'draw off their escort and if necessary attack them' and 'every effort should be made to achieve surprise'. These are further examples of the Fighter Command memorandum's propensity for pointing out desirable conditions, while giving the fighter formation leaders absolutely no guidance as to how they were to be achieved. A similar attitude was adopted towards the problem of attacking and breaking up large bomber formations. The approved doctrine sought to bring massed firepower to bear simultaneously, by recommending attacks in formation rather than individually, and pointed out that this would also prevent the enemy gunners from concentrating their defensive fire. 'Should the fighters not be numerically strong enough to engage the enemy bombers, aircraft for aircraft, then it will be necessary to nibble from the flanks.'

It seems almost superfluous to point out that it was rare for Fighter Command to be able to engage enemy bombers on a one-for-one basis during the Battle. Consequently, the RAF fighter pilots had a very real problem in deciding how to approach a massed enemy formation. 'Nibbling from the flanks', while often resorted to, did not produce particularly good results and some squadrons adopted the dangerous but often very effective tactic of the head-on attack.

Fighter Command's memorandum anticipated the Luftwaffe tactics of mounting independent fighter sweeps over Britain, and, in line with its policy of concentrating all efforts against the enemy bombers, recommended that whenever possible they should be ignored. This was because Fighter Command believed that the Luftwaffe would send in fighter sweeps well ahead of the bomber formations in order to draw off the defenders, who would then be on the ground refuelling and re-arming when the bombers arrived. Sound though this reasoning was, it ignored the possibility that (as often happened) fighter sweeps would be timed to arrive over south-east England just ahead of the bombers and catch the RAF fighters at a disadvantage, climbing for altitude to engage them. While Fighter Command saw the enemy fighters as a diversion from its main quarry, the German bombers, from the Luftwaffe's viewpoint the bombers increasingly became regarded as the bait that would tempt the RAF fighters into combat. What the RAF's commanders had not fully realized in June 1940 was that the Luftwaffe's main initial objective in the coming battle would be, not British industry and population centres, but the forces of Fighter Command itself.

Thus the RAF entered the Battle of Britain not entirely pre-pared for the severe test that it was to face. It is true that much effective work had been put into the United Kingdom's air defences. In particular, RAF Fighter Command had a command and control system that was well in advance of any other, and adequate supplies of fighter aircraft would be available to make good the losses, but serious shortcomings remained. The RAF's most numerous fighter, the Hawker Hurricane, was inferior in performance to the Messerchmitt Bf 109E. The supply of trained pilots to replace battle casualties was critically deficient. Fighter Command's tactics were poor in comparison with those of the Luftwaffe fighter force, and the RAF's fighter leaders lacked the combat experience of their enemies. In the final analysis, the RAF's commanders had done all that experience and forethought had suggested was necessary to prepare Fighter Command for the coming battle. Thereafter its outcome would depend in large measure on the personal and professional qualities of its fighter leaders and the calibre of the pilots whom they led into battle.

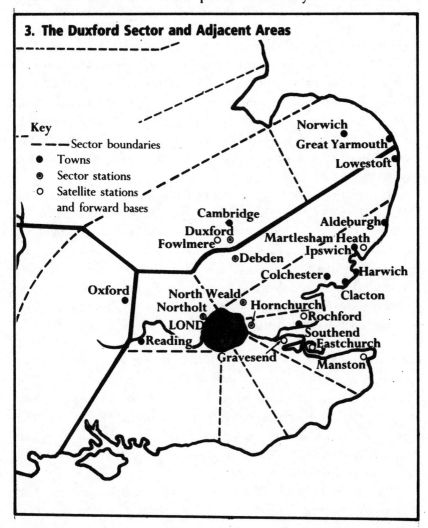

3. The Duxford Sector and Adjacent Areas

Key
– – –Sector boundaries
● Towns
◎ Sector stations
○ Satellite stations
and forward bases

No. 19 SQUADRON

No. 19 Squadron was the first front-line unit in RAF Fighter Command to be equipped with the Supermarine Spitfire, beginning its conversion from Gloster Gauntlet biplane fighters at Duxford in Cambridgeshire during August 1938. By the outbreak of the Second World War it was fully operational with the new aircraft and its pilots were eager for action. Yet Duxford, an inland Sector station in No. 12 Group, was not well placed to take part in Fighter Command's skirmishes of the 'Phoney War' period, which were generally fought over coastal waters. Duxford was, however, a key sector in Fighter Command, since it was the nearest one in No. 12 Group to London and so was ideally placed to reinforce the No. 11 Group squadrons in defence of the capital.

So it was not until the spring of 1940 that the Squadron was able to claim its first victory over the Luftwaffe. The combat occurred during a temporary detachment to the airfield at Horsham St. Faith in Norfolk. The three Spitfires of Blue Section, led by Flight Lieutenant W. G. Clouston, commanding 'B' Flight, intercepted and shot down a Junkers Ju 88 on the afternoon of 11 May. Clouston was a New Zealander who had joined the RAF on a short service commission in 1936 and had been posted to No. 19 Squadron the following year. This combat proved to be a curtain-raiser to the air battles of Dunkirk in which the Spitfire squadrons met the Luftwaffe in strength for the first time. Until then it had been Dowdwing's policy to conserve his precious Spitfires, and the Hurricane squadrons had borne the brunt of the fighting in France and the Low Countries. Now the plight of the British Expeditionary Force was so desperate that Dowding could no longer withhold this last resource.

On the evening of 25 May, No. 19 Squadron flew to RAF Hornchurch, Essex, and the following morning it was in action over the Dunkirk beaches. In the course of ten days of patrolling, the Squadron encountered enemy aircraft on five occasions and claimed more than thirty confirmed and probable victories for the loss of three pilots missing in action and three pilots wounded (two of these being only slightly injured). The Commanding Officer, Squadron Leader G. D. Stephenson, was shot down and made prisoner of war in the Squadron's first combat on the morning of 26 May. His successor, Squadron Leader P. C. Pinkham, arrived at the end of the month, but tactical leadership of the Squadron during most of the Dunkirk patrols fell to the officer commanding 'A' Flight, Flight Lieutenant B. J. Lane. Lane had joined the RAF in 1936 and had flown Gauntlet fighters with No. 66 Squadron and then with No. 213 Squadron. He remained with the latter unit until shortly after the outbreak of war, converting with them on to the Hurricane early in 1939. He joined No. 19 Squadron as a flight commander on 10 September 1939 and at that time he was officially assessed as a fighter pilot of exceptional ability.

On 5 June the pilots of No. 19 Squadron returned to Duxford in confident mood, for although their losses over Dunkirk had been far from negligible, it was felt that they were outweighed by the victories they had gained. In fact this confidence was to some degree misplaced, since the RAF fighter squadrons engaged over Dunkirk had overestimated the German losses, claiming two enemy aircraft destroyed for every one actually shot down. Yet it did mean that Fighter Command's pilots faced the decisive air battles of the summer assured of their ability to beat the Luftwaffe.

So far as No. 19 Squadron was concerned, its self-confidence was further boosted by two successful combats on the night of 18/19 June. Night patrols from Duxford had begun on 8 June, after all pilots had returned from a well-earned 48-hour leave period. From that date until 28 June the Squadron flew a total of twenty such sorties. Early on the morning of 19 June, Flying Officer John Petre sighted a Heinkel He 111 and was able to shoot it down. Petre's Spitfire was hard hit by return fire and he was forced to bale out, badly burned on the face and hands. The second victory of the night, another He 111, was claimed by Flying Officer G. E. Ball. Five days later, Ball was promoted to flight lieutenant and posted to No. 242 Squadron as a flight commander, serving with this unit throughout the Battle of Britain.

On 25 June No. 19 Squadron moved from the Sector station at Duxford to nearby Fowlmere. This was a recently reactivated First World War aerodrome, which was to serve as a satellite airfield. The purpose of satellite airfields was to reduce congestion at the Sector stations; whereas each Sector was able to control four fighter squadrons, HQ, Fighter Command considered that no more than three such units should be based on a single airfield. The satellite airfields were therefore brought into use to accommodate the extra squadron. At this time, in fact, only two squadrons were based in the Duxford Sector; but, as Dowding had foreseen, once the Luftwaffe's assault on London opened, the Sector would be operating at full capacity. Ironically, Fowlmere's original hangars and permanent buildings, which had been constructed on a similar pattern to those of Duxford, had been demolished during the 1920s and so the accommodation on the airfield for both men and machines was primitive in the extreme. No. 19 Squadron's first stay there was a short one, since on 3 July the Defiant-equipped No. 264 Squadron moved in to assume the Sector's night flying commitment, allowing the Spitfire unit to return thankfully to the well-ordered comforts of Duxford.

As the RAF's most experienced Spitfire squadron, it was inevitable that No. 19 Squadron should be regarded in some degree as an operational trials unit for the aeroplane. It had therefore been decided to re-equip the entire Squadron with the first available batch of cannon-armed Spitfires. Three of these aircraft – known as the Spitfire Mk IB to distinguish it from the version armed with eight machine-guns which became the Spitfire Mk IA – were delivered to the Squadron in late June and conversion on to the new type was completed in July. Armed with a pair of wing-mounted 20mm Hispano cannon, the fighter had been rushed into service as an insurance against the possibility that increased armouring of German bombers would make the machine-gun armed fighter impotent against them. In fact, although the Luftwaffe's bombers had been fitted with armour plate to protect their crews, and fuel and oil tanks were self-sealing, the aircraft's engines were unprotected from fire from the rear. Fighter Command considered that, so long as this remained the case, the RAF's eight-gun fighters would be able to shoot them down in attacks from astern. Should the Germans decide to fit armour plate to this vulnerable part of the bombers, the only effective means of attack left to the machine-gun armed fighters would be fire from ahead and abeam. Both of these forms of attack required great skill to carry out accurately, not only on the part of individual squadron pilots, but also by the formation leaders who must position their fighters for the attack. So it was thought to be essential that the fighter squadrons retain the option of attacks from astern. This was why it was so important for Fighter Command to have the cannon-armed Spitfires in service, because their 20mm shells were capable of penetrating the enemy aircraft's armour.

The RAF's Hispano cannon was a licensed-built French design, which had been chosen because of its high rate of fire and comparatively light weight. Its high muzzle velocity and heavy projectile gave it an excellent penetrative ability against armour and it was fundamentally a very fine weapon indeed. The original design had been envisaged as an engine-mounted cannon (fitted between the cylinder banks of a V-engine and firing through a hollow propeller shaft) and serious problems were encountered when adapting it for installation in the Spitfire's wing. One difficulty was that of devising a sufficiently rigid mounting in the wing to absorb the cannon's recoil. Another was that in order to accommodate the bulky 60-round magazine in the Spitfire's thin-section wing, without the need of too large a bulged fairing which would seriously reduce the aircraft's performance by its drag, the cannon had to be mounted on its side. This was to lead to endless troubles with ammunition feed and empty cartridge ejection. And lastly, the cannon's 60-round magazine was an unsatisfactory system, not only because it complicated the problems of installing the weapon, but also because its ammunition supply was inadequate. The Spitfire Mk IB's firing time was only some six seconds, while by comparison the eight-gun Spitfire had sufficient ammunition for eighteen seconds of firing. Ultimately, the unsatisfactory magazine was replaced by a belt-fed system. This was much less bulky and so eased the problem of installation. It also allowed the ammunition capacity for each cannon fitted to the Spitfire to be doubled. Although the benefits had been foreseen and a requirement issued for a belt-fed mechanism as early as 1938, it was not until 1941 that it reached the fighter squadrons.

It is now clear that the Spitfire IB's cannon installation was insufficiently developed by the summer of 1940 to allow it to perform satisfactorily in squadron service. Even at the time, Dowding had his misgivings about the aircraft. In April 1940 he wrote to the Air Ministry to seek an assurance that the troubles which had been experienced with the prototype cannon installation would be eliminated before any cannon-armed Spitfires were issued to No. 19 Squadron. The first cannon Spitfire had been evaluated under operational conditions during the previous winter and its weapons had suffered numerous stoppages. Dowding was told by the Director of Operational Requirements that the gun installation in the thirty Spitfires allotted to No. 19 Squadron was a modified one and that it should be free of the troubles experienced previously. Dowding's doubts about the Spitfire Mk IB were not confined to the problem of stoppages and he saw inherent limitations in the twin-cannon armament. In late July he was urged by Sir Archibald Sinclair, the Secretary of State for Air, to commit No. 19 Squadron to action so that information could be gained about the combat effectiveness of the cannon Spitfire as soon as possible. Dowding's reply made it clear that he was reluctant to deploy the Squadron in the No. 11 Group area, since the cannon Spitfire would then have to take on the Messerschmitt Bf 109E and it was 'extremely badly equipped for that task'. Its two cannon, with their limited ammunition supply, would be no match for the German fighter's armament of twin cannon and two machine-guns (inadequate though the RAF experts thought that to be). He felt that, since the cannon Spitfire had been conceived as a stop-gap bomber destroyer, it was in that role that it should be tried out.

Meanwhile, No. 19 Squadron was grappling with the practical problems of introducing the Spitfire Mk IB into front-line service. The CO, Squadron Leader Pinkham, realized that he would have to evolve special tactics for the fighter as its armament characteristics were so different from that of the standard eight-gun Spitfire. He recognized that the main disadvantages of the cannon Spitfire were the too-frequent gun stoppages and the fact that once one gun had failed it became very difficult to maintain a steady aim with the other because of the asymmetric forces exerted by its recoil. Pinkham shared Dowding's misgiving about the aircraft's ability to deal with enemy fighters; its ammunition would quickly be expended leaving it defenceless. Lastly, by comparison with the eight-gun Spitfire, the cannon's fire lacked 'spread' and much more accurate marksmanship would be necessary. On the credit side, when the cannon worked, their destructive power was terrific; the weapon's high muzzle velocity reduced the amount of 'lead' necessary in deflection shooting; and both range and accuracy were much better than with the Browning machine-guns.

In Pinkham's view, the Spitfire Mk IB's restricted firing time was the key factor in the formulation of realistic combat tactics for the aircraft. Accordingly, he worked out a new method of attack which would allow the cannon to be used to their best advantage. Sections of fighters, flying in echelon, would begin their attack from a position 2,000 feet above and to the side of the target aircraft. They would then dive and pull around dead astern of the enemy, closing in rapidly. Once their sights were on target and steadied, they would fire a short burst, before breaking away downwards and to the side. The speed built up in the dive could be used to climb back to resume the attack from the same position. The great disadvantage of this method was that if the enemy were flying just below the cloud base, as they often did, it would be unworkable. Pinkham's tactical innovations did not end with this new scheme of attack, however, for he took the opportunity provided by the period of retraining needed to introduce the Spitfire Mk IB to exercise his squadron in an entirely new formation. Abandoning the unsatisfactory vic of three aircraft, he substituted sections of two fighters flying in line astern. It was 'at once attractive to watch and easy to manoeuvre', commented the Squadron diarist.

From the outset it was obvious that the problem with cannon stoppages had not been eliminated, despite the assurances to the contrary given to Dowding in April. On 5 July 1940 the squadron carried out air firing training at Sutton Bridge, the experienced pilots shooting at a towed target and the less experienced at ground targets. The results were disappointing, with many stoppages, and only one shell hit the towed target. The main problem was diagnosed as faulty ejection, the empty case not falling cleanly away but rebounding, being caught by the forward movement of the breechblock and jamming the mechanism as the next round was fed in. This was due to the mounting of the cannon on its side, which meant that the shell case was ejected sideways instead of downwards as the weapon's designer had intended. It was thought that if deflector plates were fitted to direct the ejected case downwards, the problem would be solved, and this work was put in hand by the Squadron's armourers. Another cause of stoppages was failure of the magazine to supply a live round to the cannon's firing chamber. When this occurred, the shell's nose was depressed too much and it did not feed in cleanly, but jammed. In the view of the experts at the Ministry of Aircraft Production, the fault lay in poor work by a British contractor, whose redesign of the original French magazine was inadequate.

On 22 July the cannon Spitfires began to operate from an advanced base at Coltishall, in the hope that they would encounter unescorted enemy bombers. Six days later Sub-Lieutenant A. G. Blake, flying with Red Section from Coltishall, sighted a Junkers Ju 88, but it escaped in cloud before he could engage it. Blake was a 23-year-old Fleet Air Arm pilot, one of 58 naval pilots transferred by the Admiralty to Fighter Command to help alleviate its chronic shortage of trained aircrew. He was nicknamed 'the Admiral' by his RAF comrades. This was the squadron's only contact with enemy aircraft during July, despite daily patrols from base and from Coltishall (or occasionally Martlesham Heath) during the latter part of the month. On 24 July the unit had moved back to Fowlmere and it was to operate from this airfield for the remainder of the Battle. There had been some improvements to the amenities since the squadron's earlier stay; whereas then they had had only two Nissen huts, now there were six. Living conditions were still far from ideal and two days after the Squadron's arrival torrential rains turned the camp area into a sea of mud.

No. 19 Squadron's first combat with the Spitfire Mk IB, which was fought on the morning of 2 August, only served to confirm the cannon armament's reputation for unreliability. Flight Lieutenant Clouston was leading Blue Section on patrol off the Norfolk coast in a machine-gun armed Spitfire Mk IA, but Pilot Officers E. Burgoyne and R. A. C. Aeberhardt flew Mk IB aircraft. At 1115 hours the section intercepted a Heinkel He 111 bomber and each pilot had the opportunity of getting in a good burst of fire before the enemy aircraft escaped in clouds. Clouston's machine-gun bullets disabled the He 111's starboard engine and it was thought that he might have killed the mid-upper gunner. The two cannon Spitfires both suffered stoppages and no results were observed from their fire. After all the work that the Squadron's armourers had put into fitting deflector plates, this result was very disappointing. Air firing trials had shown that when the cannon worked and were accurately sighted they were highly effective weapons, so it was considered worth persevering with efforts to eliminate the stoppages.

The problem of the Spitfire Mk IB's inadequate ammunition supply had led to the experimental installation of four machine-guns and two cannon in a Spitfire, but there were misgivings about the effect that the weight of this armament would have on the fighter's performance. The modified aircraft was delivered to No. 19 Squadron on 11 August for flying trials, and Squadron Leader Pinkham reported that its flying qualities were not noticeably different from those of the standard Spitfire. The general opinion in the Squadron was that this installation was a step in the right direction and it was adopted as standard armament for the Spitfire Mk IBs issued to No. 92 Squadron in November 1940. In the meantime, No. 19 Squadron had perforce to make the best use it could of the twin cannon armament.

At this time the German E-boats based on the Channel ports were proving to be very troublesome and the Assistant Chief of the Air Staff ordered urgent action to be taken against them by Bomber, Coastal and Fighter Commands. It was thought that No.

19 Squadron's cannon Spitfires would be effective in strafing these vessels in port and, if they were used, none of the already over-worked squadrons in No. 11 Group need be diverted from their vital air defence duties. Accordingly, Squadron Leader Pinkham led the six Spitfires of 'B' Flight to RAF Eastchurch in Kent on 12 August in preparation for this mission. The Luftwaffe was to get its blow in first, however; on the following morning Eastchurch was heavily bombed by the Dornier Do 17Zs of Kampfgeschwader 2.* Damage to the airfield was extensive: the station operations room received a direct hit, five Bristol Blenheims were destroyed and more than fifty personnel were killed or wounded. Fortunately, No. 19 Squadron's Spitfires were well dispersed and 'B' Flight survived the bombing unscathed. Two days later, the airfield at Martlesham Heath came under attack from Messerchmitt Bf 110s. All the squadron's available Spitfires, thirteen aircraft, were scrambled from Fowlmere to meet this attack, but the orders had come too late and by the time that they reached the Suffolk coast the raiders had long been gone.

On 16 August, the squadron was operating from Coltishall and, after an uneventful afternoon patrol, the two flights left separately to return to Fowlmere. The seven Spitfires of 'A' Flight, led by Flight Lieutenant Lane, took off at 1715 hours and soon afterwards were ordered to investigate an 'X-plot', or unidentified radar contact. After following various courses on the controller's instructions for some fifteen minutes, the flight was then ordered to circle a position thirty miles east of Harwich at 12,000 feet. Soon afterwards they sighted a large force of enemy aircraft, estimated as 150 strong, flying on a southerly course. The bombers were slightly above the Spitfires' altitude, with an escort of Bf 110s stepped up behind and a group of Bf 109s 1,000 feet above and to starboard of the main formation. Operating in sections line astern, 'A' Flight attempted to slip in unobserved beneath the fighter escort to attack the bombers, but they were spotted by the Bf

---

*The German Geschwader, usually made up of three Gruppen, was designated according to its role; for example Kampfgeschwader (KG), Jagdgeschwader (JG), Zerstörergeschwader (ZG) and Stuka-geschwader (StG). The Gruppen were identified by roman numerals (e.g., III./JG 26). Similarly, each Gruppe was made up of three Staffeln, identified by arabic numerals (e.g., 7./KG 76).

110s, who immediately attacked them, and a general dogfight ensued. As the Spitfires became entangled in a milling combat with about thirty Bf 110s, the bomber formation made good its escape, and the Bf 109s, which were probably low on fuel, took no part in the fight.

All but one of the Spitfires engaged suffered cannon stoppages. Flight Lieutenant Lane, whose port gun fired only five rounds, made no claim. Flight Sergeant G. C. Unwin, flying as Red 3 in Lane's section, opened fire on one enemy aircraft at close range and saw it half-roll and dive vertically. This was assessed as probably destroyed. He was then himself attacked by another Bf 110, but managed to out-turn it, and was presented with a perfect target at 100 yards range. His starboard cannon had jammed after firing only nine rounds, but he emptied the shells remaining in his port magazine into this enemy aircraft. It went into a steep dive, its tail coming off, and Unwin followed it through a low cloud layer and saw the splash of its impact into the sea. Red 2, Sergeant H. A. C. Roden, suffered stoppages in both cannon, but was able to fire fifty shells. He made no claim for enemy aircraft destroyed, but his own Spitfire was slightly damaged by machine-gun fire. Flying Officer F. N. Brinsden, leading Yellow Section, saw a Bf 110 diving to attack the leading section. He pulled up into a climb to engage it, but both cannon stopped after only nine rounds had fired. Sergeant B. J. Jennings also had stoppages in both cannon.

By contrast, Sergeant J. A. Potter was lucky enough to be able to fire all his 120 rounds of ammunition without problems. After shooting at several Bf 110s with no result, he fastened on to one and closed to very short range before opening fire. He saw its starboard engine disintegrate and, as the aircraft flicked over to port, a large portion of its cockpit canopy broke away. Pilot Officer W. Cunningham, bringing up the rear of the flight as Yellow 4, fired at two Bf 110s without scoring hits. He then engaged a third, which broke away to the right exposing its underside to Cunningham's fire. The port cannon stopped after firing 36 rounds, but all 60 were fired from the starboard. Cunningham saw his victim dive into the cloud and thought it was out of control.

Flight Lieutenant Lane corroborated this assessment and it was allowed as a definite victory.

As the first large-scale test of the cannon Spitfire on operations, this combat was closely analyzed. Squadron Leader Pinkham put forward the theory that the poor performance of the cannon was due to the effects of 'g' when the aircraft were manoeuvring violently in combat. He pointed out that the armament of five of the aircraft engaged had previously performed satisfactorily under test and, in support of his theory, cited the experience of Flying Officer Brinsden during this combat. The No. 12 Group armament officer, who visited Duxford two days after the combat, endorsed Pinkham's view. Trials were immediately begun by No. 19 Squadron to establish the theory's validity. On 17 August, Flying Officer Brinsden took up the same Spitfire that he had flown in combat on the previous day and pulled the aircraft up into a loop, opening fire when in the recovery dive and continuing to press the firing button, while pulling out of the dive. Both port and starboard cannon stopped after firing only two and eight rounds respectively. On the following day, Brinsden repeated the experiment flying the Spitfire that had fired so well for Sergeant Potter on 16 August. Again both cannon suffered stoppages after only a few rounds had been fired.

At this stage, a representative of the Aeroplane and Armament Experimental Establishment, Boscombe Down, suggested that incorrect tensioning of the magazine springs might be the source of the problem, and two further tests were carried out on Spitfires with correctly tensioned magazines. Flight Sergeant C. Sydney flew the first of these and one of his cannon stopped; the CO himself carried out the second, and both cannon stopped.

By this time Pinkham was convinced that the ejection stoppages were due to the unsatisfactory installation of the cannon on its side and to the small width of the ejection shute. He could see no solution to this problem, unless the gun were mounted in an upright position and the magazine replaced by a belt feed, but his experiments had shown that one of the causes of a magazine stoppage (when the round was not fed cleanly into the firing chamber) was that the magazine was only properly supported under conditions of positive 'g' and so any skidding, slipping or negative 'g' manoeuvre could cause a stoppage.

Pinkham's report on the cannon trials was submitted on 23 August, by which time the squadron had fought another combat with the Spitfire Mk IBs. Green Section, led by Flying Officer L. A. Haines, took off from Fowlmere at 1810 hours on 19 August and 35 minutes later intercepted a single enemy aircraft eight miles east of Aldeburgh. Green 2, Flight Sergeant H. Steere, opened the attack with a 2½-second burst which stopped the enemy aircraft's port engine. Green Leader then followed up, but had to break away when both cannons stopped. Sergeant D. G. S. R. Cox and Flight Sergeant Steere then finished off the German aircraft, Steere's port cannon stopping after it had fired half its ammunition. Flying Officer Haines identified his target as a Bf 110, but as he saw four crew members bale out, this suggests that it was in fact a bomber (quite possibly a Do 17Z of 7./KG2 which had earlier bombed RAF Honington). When flying back to the coast after this engagement, Flight Sergeant Steere noticed a Spitfire from No. 66 Squadron at Coltishall which appeared to be in trouble. He followed it until, about four miles short of land, it began to pour smoke and lose height rapidly, and its pilot baled out. Steere circled his position before flying to the coast to attract the attention of rescuers. Despite his efforts, it was fifty minutes before the pilot, Pilot Officer J. A. P. Studd, was reached by the Aldeburgh lifeboat. He was picked out of the sea unconscious and died shortly afterwards. This tragic incident was an all too typical illustration of the inadequate British air-sea rescue organization during the Battle.

In common with other RAF fighter squadrons, No. 19 Squadron was fortunate in having a nucleus of highly trained and able NCO pilots. David Cox (himself a sergeant pilot, who was to rise to the rank of wing commander) recalls that 'the three senior NCO pilots of the squadron were all strong characters and very experienced pilots – Flight Sergeant Steere, Flight Sergeant Unwin and Sergeant Jennings'. Unwin and Steere were close friends, who had gone through flying training together in 1935–6 and were then both posted to No. 19 Squadron. George Unwin remembers Harry Steere as 'a very good pilot and an ex-Halton apprentice; completely reliable in every way both in the air and on the ground'. He was killed in action later in the war flying Mosquitos with the Pathfinder Force. George Unwin had joined the RAF in 1929 as an apprentice clerk and after leaving No. 19 Squadron in 1941 he became a flying instructor. In January 1944 he returned to operational flying when he was posted to No. 613 Squadron at Lasham in Hampshire. This was a Mosquito Mk VI unit, which specialized in Intruder operations. After the war, George Unwin commanded No. 84 Squadron, which flew Brigands in the Middle and Far East. He retired from the RAF as a wing commander in 1961.

At 1545 hours on 24 August twelve of No. 19 Squadron's Spitfires were scrambled from Fowlmere and were directed to intercept a force of escorted bombers operating north of the Thames estuary. It was the first time since the air battles of Dunkirk that the squadron had gone into combat at full strength. The interception was not completely successful because the raiders had already bombed RAF North Weald and were making their escape over the estuary before No. 19 Squadron could engage them. The enemy formation, about fifty aircraft strong, consisted of Do 17Z bombers with Bf 110s astern flying at 15,000 feet and a Staffel of Bf 109s above them. Flight Lieutenant Lane, leading the squadron, sighted the bombers above him and climbed beneath the Bf 110s with the sun at his back. The twin-engined fighters saw the Spitfires just before they got into range and turned to engage them. A dogfight then developed between the Bf 110s and the six Spitfires of 'A' Flight. Green Section of 'B' Flight meanwhile occupied the attention of the Bf 109s flying above the main German formation.

Flight Lieutenant Lane opened fire on the nearest Bf 110, but then had to break away as tracer from an enemy aircraft behind him passed over his cockpit. This fire seemed to be hitting the Bf 110 which Lane had fired at, but apparently without result. He then got into position below a second Bf 110 and saw his shells hitting its port engine. The enemy aircraft dived and Lane saw it hit the sea. He had fired all 120 rounds of ammunition without a stoppage. Sergeant Jennings, flying as No. 2 in Yellow Section, picked out a loose formation of four Bf 110s and attacked the rearmost aircraft. His opening burst disabled its starboard engine, knocking the propeller off, and Jennings saw the enemy aircraft going down in a steep dive. He then broke away beneath the remaining three Bf 110s and then climbed again to re-engage. Jennings next fired a fairly long burst at another Bf 110 and saw a large portion of its tailplane, including the starboard rudder and tail fin, break off. The Bf 110 swung to port and dived. Jennings tried to follow, but lost sight of his victim. His turn had brought him into position behind two other enemy aircraft and he transferred his attention to them. He opened fire with one cannon, his port weapon having stopped after firing 31 rounds. A Bf 109 then flashed between his sights and the Bf 110 and, thinking that there could be more behind him, Jennings broke away. He could not see any other Bf 109s and so fired the ammunition remaining in his starboard magazine at a Bf 110 without achieving any hits. The results of Jennings's combat were assessed in strict accordance with Fighter Command's instructions on the verification of claims and he was only awarded a probable victory against his first opponent; the second was classed as damaged. All but two of the Spitfires engaged in this fight experienced cannon stoppages.

If No. 19 Squadron's armament problems were far from being solved, the unit's communications were much improved at this time by the fitting of VHF radios to its Spitfires. The first aircraft to be so modified was collected from RAF Wittering, Northamptonshire, on 20 August. Ironically though, this technical advance could not prevent a breakdown in control due to human failure on 26 August. All available Spitfires were scrambled to meet a raid on RAF Debden, Essex, but they did not make contact. This was because the squadron was ordered to patrol above cloud, while the raiders were flying beneath cloud. No. 310 (Czech) Squadron, operating from Duxford, did succeed in intercepting the Debden raid and fought the unit's first combat of the Battle of Britain. The Czech pilots, few of whom could speak English, had arrived at Duxford on 12 July wearing French uniforms with Czech air force insignia. Four of these pilots, Pilot Officer F. Dolezal, Pilot Officer F. Hradil, Sergeant S. Plzak and Sergeant F. Marek, were attached to No. 19 Squadron on 24 August. They were, in the words of the

Squadron Operations Record Book, 'very keen and eager to have a crack'.

No enemy aircraft were seen during squadron patrols over the No. 11 Group airfields of Debden, North Weald and Biggin Hill, between 28 August and 30 August (although the latter airfield was in fact bombed from high level during the Squadron's patrol on 30 August). The squadron had received information on the new German tactics introduced on 24 August and decided to prepare an appropriate countermeasure. In addition to dispatching smaller numbers of bombers with a strengthened fighter escort, the Luftwaffe had also tightened up its bomber formations and improved the co-ordination of the gunners' defensive fire to the rear. These measures made astern attacks much more difficult for the RAF fighters and No. 19 Squadron accordingly began to practise attacks from head-on, but the pilots were unsure whether this was a practical solution to the problem, since the fast closure rates were 'rather frigthening' and left little time for the accurate sighting which was so necessary for the cannon armament.

The Luftwaffe's increasing pressure on No. 11 Group's airfields was inexorably drawing No. 19 Squadron into the heavy fighting in the south. This was in spite of Dowding's well-founded doubts that the cannon Spitfires could fight effectively against enemy fighters even when the armament was working properly. On the morning of 31 August – the day of Fighter Command's heaviest losses during the Battle of Britain – the Luftwaffe penetrated north of the Thames in force, bound for the fighter airfields of Debden, North Weald and Duxford. The raid on Duxford was intercepted and turned back by the Hurricanes of No. 111 Squadron, but Debden was heavily attacked. Eleven Spitfires of No. 19 Squadron were scrambled and ordered to patrol Duxford at 20,000 feet. They were then vectored south-east to cover Debden, and intercepted a strong force of enemy bombers and fighters south of Colchester. These comprised Do 17Z bombers escorted by Bf 110s and Bf 109s in a leading formation about sixty strong, with a second formation of up to 100 enemy aircraft behind. Flight Lieutenant Clouston led the attack on the leading Do 17Z bombers. The squadron – outnumbered and again suffering numerous cannon stoppages – was badly mauled in the combat. Flying Officer J. B. Coward, leading Green Section, was seriously injured and baled out. Flying Officer Brinsden also had to take to his parachute, but landed unhurt. Pilot Officer Aerberhardt attempted to land his damaged Spitfire back at base with inoperative flaps, but the aircraft crashed and he was killed. In return for these losses, Sergeant Cox claimed a Bf 110 probably destroyed and Clouston put in a joint claim with Pilot Officer Burgoyne for a second enemy aircraft.

This operation brought the problems of the cannon Spitfire to a crisis; the fighter had been given a fair trial and had proved to be totally unsuitable for combat. Squadron Leader Pinkham, in a trenchant letter to his immediate superior, Wing Commander A. B. Woodhall (Officer Commanding RAF Duxford), set out the case for the squadron's immediate re-equipment with machine-gun armed Spitfire Mk IAs. In the course of five engagements the squadron had suffered 26 cannon stoppages. Had the squadron been equipped with eight-gun aircraft, it could have inflicted far heavier losses on the enemy. It was, moreover, unfair to expect pilots to take on the large formations that had recently been encountered with unreliable armament. It was the view of Captain E. S. R. Adams, the Ministry of Aircraft Production's leading gun expert, that the weapons would never work without major modifications to their installation. Pinkham concluded by suggesting that his squadron's Spitfire IBs should be exchanged for the Spitfire IAs of an operational training unit. Woodhall forwarded this letter to No. 12 Group, fully endorsing Pinkham's arguments and affirming that No. 19 Squadron's pilots had no confidence in their weapons. The matter was referred to HQ, Fighter Command for a decision and Dowding ordered that the cannon Spitfires be replaced by Spitfire Mk IAs from No. 7 Operational Training Unit at Hawarden.

Before their cannon Spitfires could be withdrawn, however, No. 19 Squadron had to fight one more action with these aircraft. On the morning of 3 September the eight available Spitfires, led by Squadron Leader Pinkham, were ordered to patrol between Duxford and Debden at 20,000 feet. They were flying not in the RAF's usual three-aircraft sections, but in pairs line astern. The

Squadron was vectored on to a large enemy formation of about fifty bombers, escorted by more than 150 fighters, which had just bombed RAF North Weald and was heading eastwards. Squadron Leader Pinkham attempted to carry out a front quarter attack on the bombers, but the squadron was headed off by a group of Bf 110s and broke up into pairs to engage them. This was a notable tactical innovation, for the three-aircraft vic invariably broke down into single aircraft and were consequently more vulnerable to surprise attack. Pairs flying in line astern proved to be 'very wieldy indeed'. Significantly, none of No. 19 Squadron's aircraft was lost during this combat, but the unreliable cannon again robbed them of any worthwhile success.

Flying Officer Haines, flying as Green 1, was able to claim one Bf 110 destroyed, but he was flying a machine-gun armed aircraft, unlike the other seven pilots, and he needed to fire a total of 2,194 rounds to achieve his victory. This was a very telling indictment of the inadequacy of the Spitfire Mk IB's ammunition capacity (120 rounds in total) in the kind of combats in which the RAF was engaged at this time. A second confirmed victory went to Flight Sergeant Unwin, flying as Red Leader, who despite the handicap of a jammed starboard cannon, shot down a Bf 110 which crashed south of Malden. Sub-Lieutenant Blake claimed a probable victory before both of his cannon failed and only Sergeant Roden, who made no claim, had no problems with stoppages. (Pilot Officer A. F. Vokes, flying as Green 2, had no opportunity to fire).

On the following day, No. 611 Squadron flew its Spitfires south from RAF Digby, Lincolnshire to assume No. 19 Squadron's operational readiness commitment while the change-over to machine-gun armed Spitfires took place. The Operational Training Unit's Spitfire Mk IAs had not been maintained to the same high standards as No. 19 Squadron's fighters, but at any rate they now had an armament that worked. The opportunity to try this out came on the morning of 5 September. At 0947 hours the squadron was ordered to take off and patrol Hornchurch at 15,000 feet. Squadron Leader Pinkham was leading, flying as Blue 1 in 'B' Flight with six fighters in two-aircraft sections, while the five Spitfires of 'A' Flight (led by Flying Officer Brinsden) brought up the rear.

They sighted an enemy formation approaching the Thames estuary from the west. It was made up of about forty Do 17Z bombers flying in stepped-up vic formations, with the same number of Bf 109s slightly astern and 5,000 feet above the bombers. No. 19 Squadron had not then reached its assigned patrol height and so had to climb to attack. Shortly before it made contact, another RAF squadron attacked the bombers and the enemy formation turned south into the sun. This put No. 19 Squadron into an extremely poor attacking position, with insufficient height and the disadvantage of attacking into the sun, but the danger to RAF Fighter Command's airfields was so great that to refuse combat was unthinkable.

Pinkham led his three sections into an astern attack on the Do 17Zs, and ordered 'A' Flight to take on the escort fighters. Brinsden put his five Spitfires into line astern and began a climbing turn up to the Bf 109s' altitude, but in turning into the sun, he lost sight of the enemy fighters and 'A' Flight did not regain contact with them. In any case, until Brinsden's Spitfires had gained altitude, they could not threaten the Bf 109s. The German fighters chose to ignore 'A' Flight and instead dived to attack 'B' Flight. Squadron Leader Pinkham was last seen engaging a vic of Do 17Zs. It is believed that he was shot down and killed by the Bf 109s, in their initial attack. Pinkham's No. 2, Pilot Officer Burgoyne, lost contact with his leader when turning into the sun and so attacked alone. He had opened fire on one of the rearmost bombers, when he was attacked from behind by a Bf 109 and forced to break away. His tailplane, elevator and rudder were damaged, but Burgoyne managed to bring his fighter back to a safe landing at base.

'B' Flight's second section (designated Black Section) were also able to reach the bombers before the Bf 109s intervened. Flying Officer Lawson, Black 1, saw his fire on a Do 17Z take effect: the enemy aircraft fell out of formation and dived away. This was allowed as a probable victory. He and Black 2, Pilot Officer Dolezal, were then fired on by Bf 109s and Lawson's Spitfire was damaged. After breaking away from the bombers, the two pilots sighted and attacked Bf 109s, but did not claim to have damaged any of them. Green Section was intercepted by German fighters before they could reach the bombers, but Green 1, Flying Officer Haines, saw a pair of Bf 109s diving on him and was able to turn on to the tail of the second one. After firing most of his ammunition (2,740 rounds) into the enemy fighter, which had dropped to low level in an attempt to escape, Haines saw the German pilot climb to 800 feet and bale out in the vicinity of Ashford. Green 2, Sergeant Plzak, claimed another Bf 109 as probably damaged. Given the initial position of disadvantage from which they had engaged, No. 19 Squadron's pilots had performed very creditably, but one certain victory and two probables were poor return for the loss of Squadron Leader Pinkham, a brilliant tactician and a gallant leader.

The death of Squadron Leader Pinkham shows how misguided was the policy of selecting fighter squadron commanding officers from outside Fighter Command. Pinkham was in many ways an outstanding officer. David Cox remembers him as very correct and courteous and, as a former Central Flying School instructor, an exceptional pilot. 'Unfortunately CFS instructors do not always make good fighter pilots,' Cox writes. 'To be a successful fighter pilot and survive one has to have very sharp reactions and perhaps be ham-fisted with the controls of one's aircraft. The CFS instructor was a man of logic who flew his machine very correctly.' Pinkham was very keen on Squadron training in formation flying and air gunnery, but Cox only had two practice dogfights before going into action in August 1940. 'I was fortunate', he writes, 'that Flying Officer Leonard Haines, who had encountered Me 109s over Dunkirk, took me under his wing and with his guidance taught me how to throw a Spitfire about if attacked by Me 109s. The result was that I destroyed two Me 109s before being shot down and wounded at the end of September.'

The Officer Commanding 'A' Flight, Flight Lieutenant B. J. Lane, was promoted to squadron leader and took command of No. 19 Squadron. The flight commander's vacancy was filled by promoting Pilot Officer Lawson. Lane, a very able and experienced fighter leader, was an excellent choice as Pinkham's replacement. He was to remain in command of the Squadron until June 1941. He then served as a staff officer in Britain and the Middle East, but was killed shortly after his return to operational flying in December 1942. Lawson's promotion as officer commanding 'A' Flight, however, could have created ill-feeling, since 'A' Flight's deputy flight commander, Flying Officer Brinsden, had a strong claim to the job. Brinsden took this disappointment in good part, however, and two months later himself became a flight commander in No. 303 Squadron. One cannot help reflecting that had Fighter Command's senior officers behaved with the same magnanimity, the notorious 'Big Wings' controversy need never have occurred; for, as Park's biographer Vincent Orange has pointed out, the enmity between Park and Leigh-Mallory began when the latter was passed over for the command of No. 11 Group. As a component squadron of the Duxford Wing from its inception, No. 19 Squadron was to be very much involved in this controversy in so far as it concerned fighter tactics.

The Duxford Wing, which initially comprised Squadron Leader Douglas Bader's No. 242 Squadron, No. 310 (Czech) Squadron and No. 19 Squadron, began to operate on the morning of 6 September, but it was not until the afternoon of the following day that the Wing made contact with enemy aircraft. Ordered to patrol North Weald, the Wing sighted a formation of about twenty German bombers at 15,000 feet, with fifty fighters flying above and behind them. No. 19 Squadron, led by Lane, was behind the two Hurricane squadrons and was flying about 5,000 feet below the German aircraft. Only eight aircraft strong, it had abandoned a formation built up of pairs and instead flew with three aircraft of Red Section in the lead, two aircraft of Yellow Section tacked on behind, and a three-aircraft vic of 'B' Flight (Blue Section only) bringing up the rear. As the squadron climbed to engage, a single Bf 110, already under attack from two Hurricanes, dived past. The five Spitfires of 'A' Flight finished it off. The crew baled out and the German fighter crashed in the vicinity of Hornchurch.

It was the only success that day for the squadron operating as a unit, but three pilots broke away to hunt on their own account and between them accounted for a further five enemy aircraft. Flight Sergeant Unwin, Red 3, joined a Hurricane squadron and became involved in a desperate dogfight with Bf 109s, shooting two of them down in flames. He remained in action until all his ammunition had been expended. Pilot Officer W. Cunningham, Yellow 2, also teamed up with a Hurricane formation and followed them in to attack a group of 24 He 111s. His fire set one bomber alight, and he saw it crash about ten miles inland from Deal or Ramsgate. The three Spitfires of Blue Section had been too far behind the squadron formation to reach the enemy aircraft, but Blue 3 (Pilot Officer Dolezal) later got into combat with a group of Bf 110s and claimed one of them as destroyed.

The Luftwaffe had switched the main weight of its attacks from Fighter Command's airfields to London on 7 September, and after a day's lull in operations it again attacked the British capital in force. The Duxford Wing was ordered on patrol over North Weald at 1700 hours and an hour later sighted a large formation of enemy bombers flying north-west at 15,000 feet with escorting fighters flying above them at up to 20,000 feet. Flight Lieutenant Clouston was leading No. 19 Squadron, which was flying in three sections of three Spitfires each at 20,000 feet. Ordering the squadron into line astern formation, Clouston climbed to 23,000 feet to set up an attack against a formation of seven Bf 110s. It had been previously arranged that No. 19 Squadron would engage the fighters, leaving the bombers to the Hurricanes. As Clouston was about to attack the Bf 110s, two Bf 109s cut across in front of him and so he opened fire on them instead, claiming one as destroyed and the second as probably destroyed. His ammunition exhausted, Clouston took no further part in the combat and his No. 3, Pilot Officer Burgoyne, stayed with him. Blue 2, Flight Sergeant Steere, cut across in front of Clouston's Spitfire to open the attack on the Bf 110s. He claimed one as a probable victory and chased a second nearly to the French coast. Flight Lieutenant Lawson, leading Red Section, latched on to the tail of a Bf 110 and stayed with it until it crashed about five miles east of Biggin Hill. He reported that another Spitfire and two Hurricanes were in at the kill. Yellow 1, Flying Officer Brinsden, followed the leading two sections into an attack in line astern on the Bf 110s. No. 19 Squadron's formation then broke up and Brinsden attacked a pair of Bf 109s, but saw no results from his fire. The enemy fighters turned into the sun and he lost sight of them. Shortly afterwards, he joined a Hurricane in attacks on an He 111 and the bomber, with both engines stopped, came to earth to the south of Detling.

Once the squadron formation had broken up, the members of Red and Yellow Sections had a better chance of finding targets. Red 2, Sub-Lieutenant Blake, followed the main bomber formation out to sea, dived on to a straggling He 111 and left the bomber on fire and sinking towards the sea. Blake himself had a lucky escape when a bullet passed through his cockpit canopy, hit the windscreen and finished up in the top petrol tank. Red 3, Pilot Officer Cunningham, fastened on to a stray Bf 109 which passed right in front of him and set it on fire. His own fighter was damaged by a bullet through its port wing's mainspar. Pilot Officer Vokes, Yellow 2, found a Do 17Z straggler, fired all his ammunition, but could only claim it as damaged. Yellow 3, Sergeant Cox, was more fortunate, for after dogfighting with a number of Bf 109s, he got on to the tail of one of them and sent it diving eastwards in flames. His own aircraft was slightly damaged by enemy fire. Unlike the Duxford Wing's first engagement on 7 September, the No. 12 Group squadrons had been ordered up sufficiently early to gain a good attacking position on 9 September; and, despite problems with ground-to-air R/T reception, they had achieved an effective interception. Five enemy aircraft were assessed as definitely destroyed by No. 19 Squadron and a further victory was shared with another unit.

On 11 September Lane led an all-Spitfire wing over London. It was made up of No. 19 Squadron and No. 611 Squadron, operating from Fowlmere, with No. 74 Squadron (like No. 242 Squadron based at Coltishall) using Duxford as a forward base. For the most part, the Spitfires were flying in sections of four aircraft in line astern, but No. 19 Squadron's formation of only eight aircraft was made up of Red Section with four Spitfires and Blue and Green Sections operating as pairs. At about 1615 hours Lane spotted anti-aircraft fire south of Gravesend and this drew his attention to a formation of about fifty enemy aircraft, followed by two other large formations. He was then flying at 23,000 feet and was able to dive in a head-on attack on the leading He 111s 3,000 feet below.

Red Section followed him with the four Spitfires echeloned to port. This initial attack broke up the leading twelve bombers' formation and made follow-up attacks by individual fighters from astern more feasible. Lane spotted three Bf 110s flying near the bombers and opened fire on the rearmost from astern. He last saw it diving with its starboard engine alight. Lane then carried out head-on and beam attacks on the He 111s, finishing his ammunition in an astern attack which set fire to a bomber's starboard engine.

Red 2, Sergeant Jennings, followed his head-on attack with two bursts of fire from astern on an He 111, which went down apparently out of control. He then found a formation of Bf 110s, attacked the rearmost and saw it fall behind with a smoking engine. Jennings fired again from above and behind and saw his victim crash between Sittingbourne and Maidstone. Sergeant Roden also made a solo attack on a formation of Bf 110s which were milling around in a large circle. He dived out of the sun from 1,000 feet above them, and pulled up beneath one of them in an astern position. He gave it a 5-second burst and then had to break away, as other Bf 110s were turning into a firing position behind him. With so many enemy aircraft in the vicinity, Roden could not see what happened to his target; it was last seen in a shallow dive with one engine smoking. Flight Sergeant Unwin, flying as Red 4, opened fire at short range on an He 111 and saw it going down in a steep spiral. He then attacked a Do 17Z from below and astern, finishing off his ammunition, but his Spitfire was hit by return fire from the bomber's ventral gunner and he had to break away. Shortly afterwards, Unwin had to switch off his engine, which was pouring smoke and running roughly, but he brought his aircraft down safely in an extremely skilful forced-landing in the vicinity of Brentwood.

Blue 1, Flight Lieutenant Lawson, followed up Red Section's attack on the bombers, claiming an He 111; his No. 2, Sergeant Cox, was attacked from behind by a Bf 109 and had to break away. After a brief skirmish with Bf 110s, he picked out a straggling Do 17Z and dived on it from out of the sun. He carried out three attacks before his ammunition ran out and he last saw the Do 17Z crossing the coast with one engine disabled. It was assessed as probably destroyed. Green Section, flying at the rear of No. 19 Squadron's formation, was engaged with enemy fighters from the outset. Flying Officer Haines, Green 1, climbed above the bomber formation to attack a covering force of about forty Bf 110s, which immediately went into their customary defensive circle. Picking out one of the enemy aircraft which was flying a little lower than the rest, Haines closed in to 200 yards and opened fire, setting the Bf 110's port engine alight. It broke away from the circle and Haines followed, giving it a long burst which set fire to the remaining engine. During this attack, Haines continually had to evade Bf 109s, which were diving on his Spitfire. His aircraft was hit by several bullets and crashed on landing at base, because both tyres had been punctured.

Pilot Officer Dolezal engaged a Bf 109 which was about to attack a Spitfire. He saw black smoke pouring from the enemy fighter, but was unable to confirm its destruction, as his fighter was then hit by fire from behind. He broke away and returned to base, slightly wounded by a splinter in the right knee, and with his Spitfire severely damaged. No. 611 Squadron had claimed one enemy aircraft shot down and No. 74 Squadron a total of six confirmed victories. Although over-claiming during Wing engagements was certainly very high, there can be no doubt that on 11 September the Duxford Spitfire Wing helped to inflict a serious defeat on the Luftwaffe. Kampfgeschwader 26's losses were especially serious during this engagement, with six He 111s being lost and a further eleven damaged, and the losses of Zerstörergeschwader 26 were also high with five Bf 110s lost and one damaged.

A welcome reinforcement reached No. 19 Squadron on 12 September, with the arrival of eight additional Spitfires and three operational Spitfire pilots. Pilot Officer R. L. Jones, Sergeant H. D. Charnock and Sergeant D. E. Lloyd had been transferred from No. 64 Squadron, which had become a Category 'C' Unit under Dowding's reinforcement scheme introduced on 7 September and was therefore liable to lose most of its experienced pilots to reinforce Category 'A' Units. (Nos. 19, 242 and 310

Squadrons were the only Category 'A' Squadrons in No. 12 Group). During its past three engagements, No. 19 Squadron had been operating at reduced strength, with eight or nine Spitfires instead of twelve. Another handicap was the need to re-fit its Spitfire Mk IAs with VHF radios in place of the older HF units (this had of course already been done for the now-departed Spitfire Mk IBs). During the changeover, Spitfires with both types of radio had to fly in mixed formations and this incompatibility often made communications difficult.

Notwithstanding the infusion of fresh aircraft and pilots, chance intervened to prevent No. 19 Squadron from putting up a full-strength patrol on the morning of 15 September. Flight Lieutenant Clouston, who should have led, took off late because his oxygen bottle had not been refilled; Squadron Leader Lane had trouble starting his engine and so he, Pilot Officer Cunningham and Sub-Lieutenant Blake also took off late. The depleted squadron formation, led by Flight Lieutenant Lawson, joined up with the rest of the Duxford Wing (now five squadrons strong) and inter-cepted the enemy over London at 1210 hours. Flight Lieutenant Lawson carried out a head-on attack on a Do 17Z and then turned to fire on the same aircraft from astern. Meanwhile, Bf 109 escort fighters were diving to engage the Spitfires. Flight Sergeant Unwin opened fire on one of them and saw its pilot bale out and the aircraft crash between Redhill and Westerham. Flight Sergeant Steere fired on two Bf 109s and one of these was assessed as probably destroyed. Flying Officer Haines and Sergeant Cox also fought with the Bf 109s, each claiming one as destroyed. Squadron Leader Lane's section never caught up with the Wing formation, but the three Spitfires engaged an escorted bomber formation in the London area and Pilot Officer Cunningham joined two Hurricanes in shooting down a Bf 110. Clouston, flying alone, engaged three Bf 110s south of London and sent one spinning down into the clouds in flames.

At 1410 hours the same day the squadron was airborne again and, in Squadron Leader Lane's insouciant description, the Wing 'ran into the whole Luftwaffe' over London. In fact the three main attacking waves had already been engaged and broken up by the

No. 11 Group squadrons, but some 200 enemy aircraft in scattered formations were encountered over the capital. The Squadron was flying in three-aircraft sections, with Lane as Red 1 in the lead. The CO began to climb to engage the enemy top cover of Bf 109s, flying at about 30,000 feet, but the enemy fighters were quick to exploit their tactical advantage and dived on the Spitfires. In the dogfight which followed, Sergeant Roden's aircraft was hit and he had to crash-land, slightly injuring himself and writing-off his aircraft. Red and Yellow Sections were broken up by these attacks and the pilots then fought individually. Squadron Leader Lane, after briefly skirmishing with a formation of Bf 110s, sighted a pair of Bf 109s above him. He got on to the tail of one of them and fired several short bursts, causing the enemy fighter to take violent evasive action and head for cloud cover. Lane was able to get his sights on for one further burst, after which the enemy aircraft flicked on to its back and went into cloud in a shallow dive, apparently out of control. It was assessed as probably destroyed. Flight Sergeant Unwin, Red 3, followed one Bf 109 down in a dive, but lost contact when his windscreen froze over. He climbed to 25,000 feet and spotted two more enemy fighters flying over his head. Giving chase, he caught up with them in the vicinity of Lydd and claimed both of them as destroyed. Pilot Officer Cunningham, flying as Yellow 3 in the second section of 'A' Flight, joined forces with a Hurricane to attack a pair of Bf 109s and saw the aircraft he had fired at dive into the clouds on fire.

Meanwhile, 'B' Flight had not followed Lane into his climb because its leader, Fight Lieutenant Clouston, flying as Blue 1, had spotted six Do 17Zs below him just as No. 19 Squadron approached the main fight. He led Blue and Green Sections down on to them, but was unable to inform Lane as his Spitfire was fitted with VHF, whereas the CO's had an HF radio. Clouston singled out one enemy bomber and chased it out to sea, finally leaving the Do 17Z heading for the water in a badly damaged state when his ammunition was exhausted. Flight Sergeant Steere, Blue 2, attacked another Do 17Z and saw its crew bale out before the smoking bomber dropped into the clouds. Sub-Lieutenant Blake, Blue 3, was about to attack the Do 17Zs when he spotted Bf 109s above. He pulled up to engage them, sending one enemy fighter down in flames. He next joined three other RAF fighters in finishing off a stray He 111, but his Spitfire had been hit during the engagement with Bf 109s and was by then smoking badly, so Blake executed a hasty forced-landing at RAF Rochford, Essex. Green 1, Flying Officer Haines, also engaged the Bf 109s sighted by Blake and shot one of them down in flames. He then climbed to 25,000 feet and patrolled the coast near Beachy Head in anticipation of meeting enemy aircraft on their way home. Picking out a straggling Bf 110, he dived into the attack and, following it to the French coast, saw it crash in flames on the beach.

Pilot Officer Vokes, Green 2, came under attack from a Bf 110, which had got on to his tail unseen. The pilot's first warning was the sight of tracers flashing past his starboard wing and one bullet went through the mainspar. He climbed steeply and after a couple of turns was able to reverse the position. The Bf 110 was last seen diving into cloud with its starboard engine streaming smoke and it was assessed as probably destroyed. Sergeant J. A. Potter was posted as missing in action after this engagement. He was later reported as a prisoner of war, having been wounded and forced to ditch just off the French coast.

At 1620 hours on 18 September the five squadrons of the Duxford Wing were ordered to patrol Hornchurch at 20,000 feet. As there was a layer of cloud at this altitude they climbed to 25,000 feet. Seeing AA fire bursting through the clouds, the three Hurricane squadrons and No. 19 Squadron went down to investigate, leaving the Spitfires of No. 611 Squadron on patrol above. Two formations of enemy aircraft, each about thirty strong, were seen over the Thames estuary. No. 19 Squadron followed the Hurricanes in to attack, by which time the German formations had been much broken up. Flight Lieutenant Clouston, leading the squadron as Blue 1, picked out a group of ten Ju 88s flying in two vics of five and attacked the starboard outer aircraft in the second vic. He saw it drop from the formation, its crew baled out, and the bomber crashed to the west of Deal. Flight Sergeant Steere, Blue 2, closed in on an He 111, just as another British fighter was completing a beam attack on the enemy bomber. Steere then fired a 5-

second burst at it, followed the enemy aircraft down through cloud and saw it hit the sea. He then climbed and met a Ju 88 diving. Steere fired a short deflection burst at it and saw it go vertically into the cloud with one engine aflame. He reported that two or three Spitfires above him had evidently fired on the bomber and Flying Officer Haines was awarded a share in the victory.

Flight Sergeant Unwin, Blue 3, engaged a Bf 110 and, as the rear gun was not firing (presumably because the gunner had been killed in an earlier attack), he was able to close in to 50 yards. His fire took immediate effect, the pilot baled out, and the Bf 110 crashed near Eastchurch on the Isle of Sheppey. After initiating the attack on the Ju 88 which was finished off by Steere, Flying Officer Haines was set upon by two Bf 109s. He got into a firing position against one of them and the German fighter half-rolled and dived for cloud emitting black smoke. This was allowed as a probable victory, although Haines reported that the smoke could have been engine exhaust. The two Czech pilots, Pilot Officer Dolezal and Sergeant Plzak, flying as Green 2 and Green 3 respectively, each opened fire on He 111s and reported seeing their victims crash. The three leading pilots in Red Section, Flight Lieutenant Lawson, Pilot Officer Cunningham and Sergeant Lloyd, jointly claimed a Ju 88 destroyed, which Cunningham saw crash at Sandwich. Lawson's Spitfire was hit by return fire and he force-landed at RAF Eastchurch with a holed radiator. Red 4, Pilot Officer Hradil, was the only pilot engaged not to submit a claim.

Of all the Duxford Wing's combats, that of 18 September has become the most notorious. This is because, whereas the Wing's claims amounted to thirty German aircraft 'confirmed destroyed', the Luftwaffe lost only nineteen aircraft to enemy action during the entire day. No. 242 Squadron claimed ten of these victories, No. 302 (Polish) Squadron and No. 19 Squadron seven each and No. 310 (Czech) Squadron six. The main objective of their attack was undoubtedly III Gruppe of Kampfgeschwader 77, which lost nine of its Ju 88s over the Thames estuary that afternoon. No. 19 Squadron's claims for three He 111s and one Me 110 destroyed cannot be reconciled with known Luftwaffe losses and must therefore be regarded as errors in aircraft identification. Even assuming that all KG 77's losses were inflicted by the Duxford Wing alone, its squadrons were still claiming more than three enemy aircraft for every one actually destroyed. It was a telling indictment of the 'big wing's' tactical flexibility that so many pilots should be concentrating their attacks on a small number of enemy aircraft. It seems beyond reasonable doubt that the main reason for excessively inflated claims in this combat was that too many victories were attributed to individuals, rather than being assessed as shared between groups of pilots. The inadvertent multiplication of enemy's losses was naturally more common during large-scale engagements and it was by no means confined to the claims of the Duxford Wing.

The following week was a quiet period for No. 19 Squadron and none of the Duxford Wing's patrols saw any action. On the afternoon of 22 September, however, a single Do 17Z took advantage of cloud cover to make a bombing attack on Fowlmere. One of 'B' Flight's Spitfires was destroyed on the ground, and Red Section, which was on patrol over the nearby Sector station, was unable to catch the raider before it regained the clouds. The squadron's first few Spitfire Mk IIs were delivered on 25 September. The Mark's more powerful engine gave it a rather better performance than the Mk I, and its cartridge starter system speeded up scramble take-offs, but by the time that the squadron had been fully re-equipped with the improved Spitfire, it had little further part to play in the Battle of Britain.

The Duxford Wing fought its last significant action at 1215 hours on 27 September. No. 19 Squadron joined with the Spitfires of No. 616 Squadron to provide top cover for the Hurricanes of No. 242 Squadron and No. 310 Squadron on patrol over Hornchurch. The squadron was to have flown in three sections of four aircraft, but Squadron Leader Lane's take-off was delayed and so the leading section was reduced to three Spitfires. The Wing had reached its assigned patrol height of 25,000 feet when it sighted an enemy formation flying south of the Thames estuary. It comprised some twenty bombers with a close escort of thirty Bf 109s flying at 15,000 feet, with a further twenty Bf 109s at the same level as the RAF's fighters, and nine Bf 109s above them. Flight Lieutenant

Lawson followed the Hurricanes in an attack on the middle formation of Bf 109s with the squadron behind him in line astern. At this point the upper formation of Bf 109s intervened, diving on the Spitfires.

Squadron Leader Lane, who by that time had caught up with the Wing formation and was flying one of the new Spitfire Mk IIs above it, attempted to break up this attack. He was able to fire only two short bursts at fleeting targets during his initial dive, and when he tried to pull up to regain height he found that his Spitfire was no longer answering to the controls. He had felt the aircraft skidding as he started the dive, but was unable to correct this movement by adjusting the rudder's trim tab. The initial problem was caused by a 'bowed' rudder and was exacerbated by the trim control being wrongly adjusted, so that Lane could not correct the skid in the normal manner. Once fully developed, the skid caused the Spitfire's vertical tail surfaces to blanket one of the elevators, rendering it ineffectual, hence his difficulty in pulling out of the dive. As his fighter passed through 10,000 feet, Lane decided to take to his parachute. Before doing so he made one last attempt to recover control and by exerting all his strength managed to pull the aircraft's nose up. By that time he was down to only 3,000 feet and could take no further part in the fight. It was very rare for a faulty aircraft to be passed by the manufacturers' production test pilots and Lane's unhappy experience was fortunately quite untypical.

Meanwhile, Flight Lieutenant Lawson had picked out a Bf 109 and fired several short deflection bursts at it. The fighter dived away towards the French coast and Lawson followed, firing his remaining ammunition into it. The Bf 109 dived into the sea ten miles off Cap Gris Nez. Red 2, Sub-Lieutenant Blake, did not follow Lawson, but pulled out of line to attack the Bf 109s coming down from above. He fired several bursts at one of these and followed it down, seeing it go into the sea. Other German fighters had dived to sea level and were heading for France at top speed. Blake picked out one of these ahead of him and to the right. He turned and gave it a deflection shot which sent the Bf 109 into the sea. Red 3, Pilot Officer Hradil, made no claim. Flight Sergeant

Unwin, leading Yellow Section, had also seen the Bf 109s attacking from above and decided to engage them. He was able to claim one Bf 109 as destroyed, but exhausted his ammunition in the process. His No. 2, Sergeant Jennings, carried on to attack the main enemy formation and saw the Bf 109 that he had fired on begin to smoke. He then had to break away, as four enemy fighters dived on him. Red 3, Sergeant Cox, was not so fortunate, as his Spitfire was shot down and Cox baled out wounded. Sergeant Lloyd, Yellow 4, was unable to gain a satisfactory firing position and so made no claim.

The four Spitfires of Green Section had begun their attack on the main enemy formation when they were attacked from behind. Pilot Officer E. Burgoyne, flying as Green 4, was shot down and killed. Green Leader, Flight Sergeant Steere, had opened fire on an enemy fighter when he saw the Bf 109s coming in from astern, and broke away. His No. 2, Sergeant Plzak, saw this aircraft going down in flames. Plzak then closed in on a Bf 109 from above and behind, gave him three bursts, and saw his victim crash near Sandwich. He then joined up with No. 616 Squadron and became involved with them in a dogfight against fifteen Bf 109s, but he made no further claim. Flying Officer D. T. Parrott, Green 3, broke formation when he saw three Bf 109s passing to starboard, and turned on to their tails. Selecting one of these, he followed it down in a vertical dive to 10,000 feet, firing intermittent bursts. He then pulled out behind and pursued it out to sea. The Bf 109 began to burn and finally plunged into the water.

It had been an especially successful combat for No. 19 Squadron, with seven enemy aircraft credited to it as confirmed destroyed, although at a cost of one pilot killed and a second wounded. The combined claims of the other three squadrons in the Wing amounted to only six confirmed victories. Moreover, these claims had not been inflated beyond the bounds of possibility, since the Luftwaffe lost nineteen Bf 109s in combat on 27 September. As the Battle entered its final phase, it was apparent that the Duxford Wing was unlikely to see much more action, as speed of reaction was essential in meeting the Luftwaffe's high-flying fighter sweeps. Even when No. 19 Squadron had been operating on its own during August, it had often been ordered up too late to make an effective interception. Park, justifiably anxious that the German bombers should not reach their targets unscathed, saw these failures as deliberate obstructionism on Leigh-Mallory's part. Leigh-Mallory countered by claiming that requests for his Groups' assistance were received too late to enable a timely reaction. Whatever the truth – and it is more likely that inexperience rather than bloody-mindedness was the root cause of No. 12 Group's shortcomings – Park had come to the conclusion that he could not rely on the Duxford Sector squadrons for reinforcement. Although many Wing patrols were flown during October, the only contact with the enemy was a one-sided skirmish which resulted in the loss of the able and popular Sub-Lieutenant Blake. The Wing was on patrol over Kent on the afternoon of 29 October, when AA fire alerted the pilots to the presence of enemy aircraft. Some of No. 19 Squadron's pilots saw a small group of Bf 109s above them, but none was engaged. Blake, who was acting as a 'weaver' behind the formation, was thought to have been surprised by them and was shot down and killed.

Early in October 1940 a single Spitfire Mk IB was re-issued to No. 19 Squadron for trials and it was found that at last the problem of recurrent cannon stoppages had been solved. A month later Flight Lieutenant Lawson claimed a Bf 109 destroyed when flying this aircraft during a skirmish over the Thames estuary on the afternoon of 5 November. It was fitting that the squadron that had suffered the tribulations of the cannon Spitfire's development problems should have been given this opportunity of proving that its work had not been in vain. The cannon-armed Spitfire was to become the mainstay of RAF Fighter Command in 1941.

The fighter wing was to become the standard formation during the RAF's offensive fighter operations over France in 1941. But the pioneering work of the Duxford Wing's squadrons in developing such tactics has long been a matter of controversy. It is now generally accepted that the 'Big Wing' was a quite inappropriate formation for Park's No. 11 Group squadrons to adopt in the Battle. The usual criticisms of the Duxford Wing, that it was slow to assemble and unwieldy to control once airborne, are not borne out by the experience of Wing Commander George Unwin. He writes that, 'bearing in mind that the wing of five squadrons took off from two adjacent aerodromes and that it took ten minutes to climb to height and arrive over London, it worked very well'. (He also points out that the Hurricane squadrons' usual casualty rates were reduced when they operated as part of the wing.)

This evidence suggests that the failures of the Duxford Wing to react in time to requests for assistance from No. 11 Group were indeed due to lack of sufficient advanced warning, as Leigh-Mallory contended. The fact that individual squadrons operating from the Duxford Sector had experienced similar problems before the Wing was formed bears out this argument. The entire tactical controversy was distorted by the bitter rivalry of the two group commanders. None of this can tarnish the reputations of the squadrons that operated with the Duxford Wing. No. 19 Squadron had fought bravely and effectively during the Battle of Britain, and its record will stand comparison with that of any squadron of RAF Fighter Command.

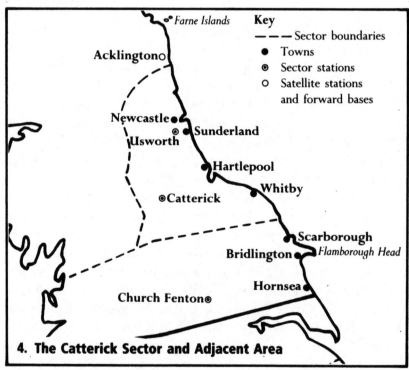

4. The Catterick Sector and Adjacent Area

NO. 41 SQUADRON

At the outbreak of the Second World War No. 41 Squadron was based at RAF Catterick, Yorkshire, and was flying Spitfire Mk Is. Its motto 'Seek and Destroy' was redolent of a long association with single-seat fighter aircraft. In October 1916 it had begun operations over the Western Front with FE 8 'pusher' scouts and had remained in France until after the Armistice, flying the famous SE 5a for the last year of the First World War. Disbanded in 1919, No. 41 Squadron was re-formed in 1923 and took its place in the newly reconstituted British air defence organization. It was based at RAF Northolt, Middlesex, and was successively equipped with Snipes, Siskins and Bulldogs during those years when to be a pilot in an RAF fighter squadron was to belong to the finest flying club in the world. In 1934, the Squadron became a two-seat fighter unit flying Hawker Demons and during the Abyssinian Crisis of the following year it was dispatched to Aden. This interlude of overseas service ended in August 1936, when No. 41 Squadron returned to Britain and settled at Catterick. It also reverted to single-seat fighters, operating Fury Mk IIs until re-equipped with Spitfires in January 1939.

During the period of the 'Phoney War' No. 41 Squadron carried out training flights and convoy patrols from Catterick and, apart from a squadron detachment to RAF Wick in Caithness during October 1939, remained at its peacetime base until the following spring. Contacts with the enemy were infrequent. On 17 December Flight Lieutenant J. T. Webster, commanding 'B' Flight, had an inconclusive encounter with a Heinkel He 115 floatplane off Whitby, but it was not until 3 April 1940 that the Squadron gained its first confirmed victory. Flight Lieutenant E. N. Ryder, 'A' Flight's commander, intercepted an He 111 bomber off the Yorkshire coast and shot it down into the sea. However, fire from the He 111 had disabled Ryder's Spitfire, its engine seized and he was forced to follow his victim down to ditch in the angry grey waters. The Spitfire plunged straight under and Ryder was lucky to escape from his cockpit and fight his way to the surface. He was picked up by a trawler and taken to West Hartlepool. Experiences such as Ryder's were to show that it was better to bale out of a Spitfire over the sea, rather than attempt to bring it down on the water.

On 28 May No. 41 Squadron began to fly patrols over the Dunkirk beaches, operating from RAF Hornchurch in company with the Spitfires of Nos. 19, 222 and 616 Squadrons in Wing strength. This period of intensive combat flying came to an end on 4 June. No. 41 Squadron returned to Catterick, changing places with No. 54 Squadron. These two Spitfire units were to alternate between Hornchurch and Catterick during the coming Battle, since it was Dowding's policy to relieve the hard-pressed No. 11 Group squadrons with fresh ones from the quieter sectors. No. 41 Squadron began July with its full establishment of aircraft: sixteen Spitfires, plus an immediate reserve of two fighters and a Miles Magister for communications duties. Total pilot strength comprised 26 officers and NCO pilots and there were three non-flying officers and 184 groundcrew serving with the unit. Its commanding officer was Squadron Leader H. R. L. 'Robin' Hood, a former flight cadet at the RAF College, Cranwell. He had served as a fighter pilot with No. 23 Squadron at Kenley, flying Gloster Gamecocks, in 1929–30 and then flew Fairey Flycatchers with the Fleet

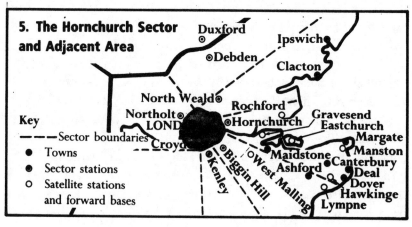

Air Arm, before training as a flying instructor in 1933. He took command of No. 41 Squadron on 19 April 1940, having previously commanded No. 3 General Reconnaissance Unit, which operated Vickers Wellington DWI minesweeping aircraft from RAF Manston.

Patrols from Catterick during July were generally uneventful, but the Spitfires of Blue Section, led by Flying Officer A. D. J. Lovell, did intercept a single Junkers Ju 88 off Scarborough on the morning of 8 July; they were joined by three Hurricanes of No. 249 Squadron from RAF Church Fenton, Yorkshire, in finishing off the enemy aircraft. In No. 11 Group's area of operations, however, July was a month of heavy fighting. The Luftwaffe was concentrating its attacks on coastal shipping and the RAF found these convoys very difficult to defend. This was because radar warning of the raids was usually too short to allow the RAF fighters to meet them by scrambling from their airfields. Consequently the convoys had to be covered by small standing patrols of fighters (usually only in flight or section strength), which had to fend off any German attack as best they could until reinforcements arrived. No. 54 Squadron had been in the thick of this action and had suffered heavy casualties. The losses fell especially heavily on the experienced pilots; of the seventeen who had been with the squadron on the eve of Dunkirk, only five remained by late July. It was therefore necessary to give the unit a respite from the strain of daily operations and the opportunity to assimilate newly posted replacement pilots. So on 26 July No. 41 Squadron moved south to Hornchurch to take No. 54 Squadron's place in the forefront of the Battle.

At 1300 hours on 27 July No. 41 Squadron flew from Hornchurch to Manston, which was being used as a forward base for operations over the Channel. The Luftwaffe had carried out two successful raids on Dover that day, hitting the naval barracks and the destroyers HMS *Codrington*, and forced the Royal Navy to abandon the port as a forward base for its destroyers. RAF Fighter Command determined to increase its level of protection for this strategically important port and its valuable installations. No. 41 Squadron carried out seven patrols that afternoon and evening at full-squadron, flight or section strength, but only one of them made contact with the enemy. Six Spitfires of 'B' Flight were on station over Dover at about 1800 hours, when Green 1 (Flight Lieutenant Webster) saw AA fire over the harbour and picked out single-seat fighters below him. Calling up the remainder of the flight, he dived to attack. Webster followed one fighter out to sea, flying at only fifty feet above the water. When he had closed the range to 200 yards, he opened fire, and reported seeing the enemy aircraft hit the sea. By then he was about eight miles off the French coast and on his way back he was attacked by another enemy fighter. The two aircraft went into a series of tight turns at low level above the water. Webster was able to fire three short bursts at his opponent, but they had no effect, and so he broke off the combat. He was credited with a probable victory over the first fighter, since there was no independent confirmation that it had been destroyed; in fact the Luftwaffe reported no Bf 109s lost that day.

On 28 July No. 41 Squadron operated from Manston during the morning and returned to Hornchurch shortly after midday. At 1400 hours about 100 aircraft were plotted heading for Dover. No. 74 Squadron's Spitfires were immediately sent up to engage the fighter escort, while two squadrons of Hurricanes were dispatched against the bombers. Thirty minutes later, No. 41 Squadron was ordered to patrol Dover at 20,000 feet. On arrival they were immediately attacked by fighters. Two Bf 109s dived down on the leading section of Spitfires. Pilot Officer G. H. Bennions, Yellow 1, who was acting as rearguard, saw one enemy fighter follow Squadron Leader Hood's Spitfire as it broke away to port. Bennions, using emergency boost, closed the range and opened fire on the Bf 109 which turned on its side and went down vertically. Bennions followed, giving two more bursts of fire, and this aircraft was last seen at 5,000 feet diving steeply and trailing smoke. Flight Lieutenant Webster, leading Green Section, also saw the Bf 109s diving and shouted a warning to the commanding officer. He then attacked a fighter which was firing on Blue 2, Flying Officer Lovell. This aircraft pulled up and fell away in a spin. It is thought that its pilot was the German ace, Major Werner Mölders, the Kommodore of Jagdeschwader 51, who was wounded in action at this time. Lovell was also wounded in the thigh, and crash-landed his Spitfire at Manston. Webster claimed a second fighter damaged, having chased it out to sea, firing short bursts from astern at 150 to 50 yards' range. He saw its engine emit thick black smoke, but Webster then had to break off the action as he was threatened by attack from a group of Bf 109s flying 2,000 feet above him. After this combat, No. 41 Squadron's claims of one Bf 109 destroyed (Bennions), one fighter probable and another damaged (Webster), closely match the reported casualties of JG 51. That unit lost one Bf 109 with its pilot missing, a second Bf 109 written off in a crash-landing with its pilot (Mölders) wounded, and a third fighter damaged in action.

The next day the Luftwaffe mounted an early morning raid on Dover by a force of Junkers Ju 87 dive-bombers escorted by Bf 109s, which was estimated to be more than one hundred aircraft strong. No. 41 Squadron was in position to meet them, having taken off from Hornchurch at 0445 hours to deploy to Manston. The order to scramble came through at 0717 and by 0735 the squadron formation, eleven Spitfires strong, had arrived over Dover at 12,000 feet. It was at once set upon by two formations of Bf 109s. Ordering the squadron into line astern, Squadron Leader Hood picked out a Bf 109 and, closing in to extremely close range, gave it a 3-second burst of fire. Pilot Officer O. B. Morrough-Ryan, flying as Red 2 in the section behind Hood's, saw this aircraft catch fire and dive into the sea. The CO then followed another Bf 109 down in a vertical dive, but as it pulled out Hood was in danger of colliding with it and had to break away. He then sighted a Ju 87 making for France at low level and finished off his ammunition on it. The Ju 87 dived into the sea about seven miles off Dover.

Pilot Officer Bennions, as Yellow 1 leading the third section in the squadron formation, ignored the attacking Bf 109s and dived on a group of Ju 87s. He opened fire on one of the dive-bombers, but then had to break off sharply as he saw tracer bullets passing over his port wing and felt the impact of bullets. Turning to port, Bennions saw a Bf 109 diving past and followed him down. The German fighter levelled off at 8,000 feet and began a slow climbing turn to retain altitude. Bennions closed in to 200 yards astern and began firing. He then discovered that his port guns were not working, presumably having been damaged during the Bf 109's opening attack. It needed three bursts from his remaining four guns to achieve any effect and then the Bf 109 pulled up into a near vertical climb with its propeller windmilling. Again Bennions felt the impact of enemy bullets on his Spitfire and had to break off his attack. He half-rolled and dived away. On pulling out he saw oil streaming over the port wing and his oil pressure had fallen to zero. He returned to Manston and, despite the loss of his flaps and a punctured port tyre, brought the aircraft down without further damage, but the Spitfire was a write-off.

Yellow 2, Flying Officer W. J. Scott, followed Bennions into the attack on the Ju 87s and he too was attacked by fighters from behind. Scott brought the crippled Spitfire back to Manston, where he crash-landed, but the aircraft was damaged beyond economic repair. Yellow 3, Sergeant R. A. Carr-Lewty, had broken away from his section to go to the help of a No. 56 Squadron Hurricane, which had a Bf 109 on its tail. Carr-Lewty's fire sent the enemy aircraft spinning down out of control. He then attacked a Ju 87, but without effect.

Flight Lieutenant Webster, Green 1, was flying at the rear of the squadron formation as look-out when the Bf 109s attacked. After transmitting a warning, he closed in on one of the fighters and sent it spinning down in flames. He then saw a formation of Ju 87s about to dive-bomb Dover and attacked the rearmost, but was forced to break away to engage some Bf 109s. Discovering that he had fired all his ammunition, Webster carried out dummy attacks on these fighters, while dropping to sea level and then made for the coast at maximum speed. His aircraft had been damaged in this combat, so Webster decided to return to Hornchurch, where repair facilities were better than at the forward base. He crashed on landing, fortunately without suffering injury. The squadron had suffered two further casualties: Flying Officer D. R. Gamblen had been shot down and killed and Pilot Officer J. N. Mackenzie crash-landed his Spitfire near Deal. For the loss of one pilot killed, three Spitfires destroyed and two damaged, the squadron had claimed five enemy aircraft destroyed (four of these being unconfirmed victories) and one damaged. In view of the disadvantages under which they had engaged, it was hardly a discreditable performance; Fighter Command could much better afford the loss of aircraft than it could that of trained pilots.

The following week was a quiet one for No. 41 Squadron; patrols were flown daily but there was no contact with enemy aircraft. Six Spitfires of 'B' Flight were patrolling over a convoy off Dover on the afternoon of 5 August when they were warned of an approaching raid. Cloud and haze greatly reduced visibility, so when a single He 111 was spotted Flight Lieutenant Webster was detached to engage it and the remaining five Spitfires stayed above the convoy. Webster caught up with the bomber just before it reached cloud cover and carried out a series of attacks as the enemy aircraft dodged in and out of cloud. On finishing off his ammunition, he noticed that one of the He 111's engines had stopped. He then had to break away as a large formation of Bf 109s appeared from above cloud. Three days later, Webster was again in action when the three Spitfires of Green Section were detached from a squadron patrol to investigate a group of six or seven aircraft sighted in the vicinity of Manston. Webster, Green 1, dived from the squadron's patrol height of 25,000 feet to 12,000 feet and identified the aircraft as Bf 109s. His No. 3, Pilot Officer R. W. Wallens, opened the attack on the rearmost enemy fighter. Webster followed him in and reported that the enemy aircraft crashed into the sea. After this shared victory, the two pilots separated. Webster claimed a further three Bf 109s shot down into the sea and Wallens claimed another two, also seen to crash. The third member of the Section, Flying Officer Lovell, flying as Green 2, experienced trouble with his oxygen supply and took no part in this fight. The two pilots' claims for six enemy aircraft destroyed in a single combat were not credited by RAF Intelligence and they were awarded two aircraft destroyed and one damaged in the final assessment. Since the Luftwaffe's total reported casualties for the day included only nine Bf 109s lost in action, the reduced claim was probably much closer to the truth.

After a period of two weeks in RAF Fighter Command's firing line, No. 41 Squadron returned to Catterick on the afternoon of 8 August. It had engaged the Luftwaffe on five occasions during this time, but in order to bring about these combats had flown a total of 234 operational sorties on patrol. The pace of operations in No. 13 Group was altogether less stressful and usually no more than single enemy aircraft were encountered. Just such a combat took place on 11 August. Green Section was ordered on patrol at 1825 hours and Flying Officer Boyle, Green 2, sighted a Ju 88 in the vicinity of Thirsk, flying 2,000 feet above the Spitfires at 18,000 feet. The Ju 88 immediately dived for cloud cover at 10,000 feet and Boyle was able to fire one burst into it before it disappeared. Pilot Officer Wallens, Green 1, followed it into cloud at a range of only 40 yards and was able to maintain contact. He fired one burst and saw his de Wilde incendiary ammunition hit. Its port engine stopped and the Ju 88 lost speed. Shortly afterwards both aircraft came out into a clear patch and Wallens fired again, before losing the enemy aircraft as it re-entered cloud. By that time Green 3, Sergeant E. V. Darling, had gone below the cloud layer and shortly afterwards he saw the Ju 88 above him. He attacked it from the beam, turning in to dead astern, and fired all his ammunition. He last saw the enemy aircraft going down slowly in a shallow dive. It was reported to have crashed near Whitby and three of its crew were taken prisoner.

Sergeant Pilot Frank Usmar (who retired from the RAF as a squadron leader in 1964) recalled the daily routine of operations from Catterick at this time. '[There was a] section of three at forward base, Hartlepool, which was at immediate readiness, a section of three at Catterick at readiness, then sections at fifteen minutes and thirty minutes. When the section at Hartlepool took off on patrol, the section at readiness at Catterick took off for Hartlepool. Then the other sections were brought forward in readiness.' Usmar had been posted to No. 41 Squadron in June after completing his flying training, but he had not gone through an OTU course. He remembered that during the squadron's period at Hornchurch from late July to 8 August it flew mainly convoy patrols. 'I spent a lot of time flying a Magister to and from

Manston, taking spares or picking up pilots. The Flight Commander told me to fly low and keep out of trouble if possible, so I enjoyed the hedge-hopping down to Manston. When I think of it now, it was a bit risky flying in east Kent in a small training plane painted yellow, with 109s strafing Manston at odd times of the day, with no wireless to warn me or even a pea-shooter to defend me.'

On 15 August, the day of the Luftwaffe's greatest effort during the Battle of Britain, No. 13 Group fought its only major action. Radar gave good advanced warning, but a force estimated as 30 plus turned out to number almost 100 aircraft. The Spitfires of No. 72 Squadron were the first to make contact off the Farne Islands. Hurricanes of Nos. 79, 605 and 607 Squadrons followed up their attack, together with No. 41 Squadron's Spitfires. No. 72 Squadron's attack had split the enemy force into two groups and No. 41 Squadron engaged the southernmost one off the coast of Durham. Thirteen Spitfires were led by Pilot Officer Bennions, who had taken over from Flight Lieutenant Ryder when the latter's R/T became unserviceable. The bombers, He 111s of Kampfgeschwader 26, were flying at 13,000 feet and were escorted by Bf 110s of I Gruppe Zerstörergeschwader 76 flying 500 yards astern. Bennions ordered the six Spitfires of 'B' Flight to attack the escort, while he ordered Yellow and Red Sections into line astern and carried out a beam attack on the bombers. He had hoped that this attack would break up the bombers' formation, but when he saw that it remained intact he led his section against the escorting fighters.

Bennions reasoned that these would have to be dispersed before he could attack the bombers, otherwise the Spitfires would be caught between the He 111s' rear fire and forward fire from the Bf 110s. Picking out the rearmost Bf 110s, Bennions sent one down with its port engine smoking. He was unable to see what happened to it, since low cloud and haze made visibility near the ground very poor, and could only claim the Bf 110 as damaged. An attack on a second Bf 110 produced better results. Bennions saw smoke and fuel or coolant fluid streaming from its port engine and it glided down towards Barnard Castle. As a Bf 110 crashed in this vicinity, Bennions' victory was confirmed. Flight Lieutenant Ryder, flying as

Yellow 2, fired all his ammunition into a Bf 110 and saw a violent explosion in its fuselage. Pilot Officer Mackenzie, leading Red Section, also reported seeing this explosion, but Ryder was only awarded a probable victory.

After the initial attack, Red Section broke away from Yellow and climbed above the enemy formation. It then split up and carried out individual attacks. Pilot Officer Mackenzie claimed a probable victory and Red 3, Pilot Officer Lock, sent a Bf 110 diving into cloud with both engines disabled. His Spitfire was hit in the port wing by return fire – the Squadron's only casualty in this engagement. Flying Officer Lovell, leading 'B' Flight as Blue 1, went straight in to attack the Bf 110s. Picking out the rearmost machine, Lovell gave him a 6-second burst and saw the enemy aircraft explode in flames. He went on to attack a second, which was assessed as probably destroyed. Pilot Officer E. A. Shipman, Green 1, ordered his section into echelon port and followed Blue Section into its attack on the enemy fighters. Shipman had picked out three Bf 110s as a suitable target, when the enemy aircraft turned into Green Section's attack. He carried out a head-on attack on the leading Bf 110, but saw no result from his fire. He next engaged a second German escort fighter, finishing his ammunition on it. The enemy aircraft disappeared in cloud with one engine disabled.

Green 2, Pilot Officer Wallens, had evaded the Bf 110s' head-on attack by executing a half-roll and coming down on the tail of one of the enemy aircraft. He then broke away and dived on another Bf 110 in a deflection attack from the quarter. He saw his fire take effect and his victim dived into cloud trailing thick smoke. Green 3, Sergeant F. Usmar, began his attack on a Bf 110 which was attempting to turn onto Wallens' tail, giving it a short burst of fire. He then found himself in position for a head-on attack against an He 111. He fired a short burst and then pulled up to starboard. The enemy bomber exploded and Usmar's Spitfire was thrown forty feet upwards in the blast, his fire having apparently detonated its bomb load. The explosions seen by Lovell and Ryder after they had fired on Bf 110s were caused by ignited petrol fumes in the aircraft ventral fuel tanks. These jettisonable long-range tanks, known to the Germans as Dackelbauch (dachshund's belly), were a poor design which had caused I./ZG 76 many problems.

The Luftwaffe's raids on north-east England on 15 August had been convincingly repulsed (a second attack on the RAF's Yorkshire airfields by Kampfgeschwader 30's Ju 88s had also been badly mauled). It had been the German hope that Luftflotte 5, operating from bases in Scandinavia, would strike an unprotected flank, while the greater part of the Luftwaffe occupied Fighter Command's attention over southern England. That they had failed was primarily due to Dowding's enlightened policy of rotating his squadrons between heavily threatened and quieter sectors; consequently there were sufficient fighter squadrons based in the north to deal with any force that Luftflotte 5 could send against them. Moreover, since the Germans were operating well beyond the range of their single-engined escort fighters, it was exactly the threat that Fighter Command had long prepared to meet. KG 26 lost eight He 111 bombers and I./ZG 76 seven Bf 110s, plus a further aircraft which crashed on its return to Denmark, and two Bf 110s damaged and with wounded aircrew.

No. 41 Squadron's claims were for one He 111 and three Bf 110s confirmed destroyed, four aircraft probably destroyed and five damaged. They lost no pilots in this action and only one fighter was slightly damaged. Quite clearly Fighter Command had taken the measure of the Luftwaffe's long-range bombing forces. In future only isolated raiders were to penetrate No. 13 Group's defences in daylight and even these would not escape unscathed. On 21 August Pilot Officer Shipman, leading Green Section, caught an He 111 off Flamborough Head and sent it diving into the sea.

Early in September, No. 41 Squadron returned to the very different air war that was being fought by No. 11 Group. No. 54 Squadron was long overdue for replacement, but had remained at Hornchurch so that one experienced squadron could operate alongside two newly arrived units until they got into their stride. At last, on 3 September No. 41 Squadron relieved the hard-pressed squadron. Its pilots looked as though they had not slept for a week, Flying Office Lovell later recalled. This was hardly surprising, because since No. 41 Squadron had last operated from Hornchurch in early August the Battle had entered a new and critical phase. The Luftwaffe's attacks had been redirected from convoys and coastal targets to Fighter Command's airfields, and the pressures on the fighter squadrons had become wellnigh intolerable. Hornchurch itself had been bombed on 31 August and No. 54 Squadron was caught on the point of take-off. Three Spitfires were wrecked by bomb blast and their pilots (including the seemingly indestructible Flight Lieutenant A. L. Deere) were lucky to escape with their lives. Only a timely interception on 2 September had prevented the airfield from being heavily bombed a second time.

No. 41 Squadron had also to contend again with the Luftwaffe's highly effective Messerschmitt Bf 109E single-engined fighter which would be its main antagonist during the final phases of the Battle. Yet the Spitfire had no appreciable margin of superiority over the German fighter and tactical advantage and pilot skill would decide the outcome. The equality of the contest was given ominous point by the overall casualties of 3 September – 16 aircraft lost by both sides.

On the morning of 5 September the tactical advantage lay with No. 41 Squadron. Twelve Spitfires took off from Hornchurch at 0915 hours and, by the time that the enemy had crossed the coast at 0940, the squadron was at 27,000 feet over Canterbury. Two bomber formations, each of some twenty Do 17Zs flying at 16,000 feet, were protected by about fifty Bf 109s on the flanks and to the rear, stepped up to 22,000 feet. Squadron Leader Hood led Green and Blue Sections down to engage the bombers, ordering Flight Lieutenant Ryder, leading 'A' Flight, to protect them from the Bf 109s. The CO dived to attack the rear section of the bombers, breaking up a small formation of Bf 109s on his way down. He fired a long burst at one Do 17Z, but then had to turn away sharply as Bf 109s attacked him from behind. As his engine was running roughly, Hood broke off the engagement and returned to Hornchurch. His No. 2, Flying Officer Wallens, followed in line astern until Hood swung in behind the Do 17Zs. Wallens then pulled out to one side to give himself a clear field of fire in attacking the bombers. He saw four or six Bf 109s coming in to attack, broke away to port and dived to 12,000 feet. Having shaken off his pursuers, Wallens climbed to 18,000 feet and chased after the main enemy formation. Shortly after crossing the coast, he caught up with a single Bf 109 and opened fire from 250 yards astern. The enemy fighter began to smoke and dived steeply for mid-Channel. Green 3, Flying Officer Boyle, broke formation to pursue the Bf 109s which Hood had scattered in his initial dive. He fastened on to one and gave it a 4- or 5-second burst; it caught fire, rolled on to its back and spun down. It was assessed as confirmed destroyed.

Flight Lieutenant Webster, Blue 1, followed Green Section into its dive, flying line astern. He fired on one of the Bf 109s encountered in the dive, seeing hits on its engine. Webster then tried to reach the bombers, but on three attempts was forced to break away by Bf 109s coming in behind him. He then fired at a fighter which burst into flames. After this attack he pulled up steeply and saw a Spitfire being chased by three Bf 109s. Webster forced one of these to break away, but then lost sight of the Spitfire. He then followed another fighter down to ground level, opened fire and saw it crash in the vicinity of Maidstone. Meanwhile, Ryder had led Red and Yellow Sections in line astern against a formation of Bf 109s, one of which he claimed as probably destroyed. His No. 2, Pilot Officer Bennions, saw two enemy fighters diving from the right and, calling out a warning, turned into their attack. He turned again to get on their tail, but half way around noticed a third Bf 109 closing in behind him. Bennions went into a steep right-hand climbing turn. The enemy fighter turned to follow him, but stalled and fell out of the turn. Bennions turned down on to its tail, followed the Bf 109 in a climbing turn and chased him at full throttle in a south-easterly direction. Closing to 100 yards, he fired two short bursts, saw coolant fluid stream from the Bf 109's radiator, but then had to break off to avoid collision. The fighter went down in a series of steep gliding turns, but Bennions did not see it crash and so could only claim a probable. Sergeant Carr-Lewty, Yellow 2, also claimed a probable victory. On his return flight, short of fuel, he could not locate the airfield in the haze and force-landed, damaging his Spitfire.

At 1500 hours the same day, the squadron engaged a second major Luftwaffe raid. A formation of bombers, reported to include both He 111s and Ju 88s, was sighted over the Thames estuary at 15,000 feet. Squadron Leader Hood ordered the squadron into line astern and then echelon port, leading them into a head-on attack on the bombers. As the attack developed, the Bf 109 escort pounced on the Spitfires and the brunt of their onslaught fell on 'B' Flight. Four of its six fighters were lost. Squadron Leader Hood and Flight Lieutenant Webster were killed; Pilot Officer Wallens baled out wounded, but was able to claim one of the Bf 109s destroyed; Flying Officer Lovell also took to his parachute and landed unhurt. 'A' Flight, following behind, were more fortunate. Flight Lieutenant Ryder, Red 1, saw a Bf 109 attacking the rear Spitfire of 'B' Flight. He fired five bursts into it, followed it down to 8,000 feet, and saw the German fighter explode in flames.

As the squadron formation broke up and individual fights developed, Pilot Officer Lock, Red 2, engaged an He 111. He followed the bomber down and saw it crash into the estuary. Climbing back to 8,000 feet, he saw another He 111 straggling from the main formation. Lock attacked this aircraft and set its starboard engine on fire. Its undercarriage dropped, indicating that the hydraulic system had been hit, and the He 111 started to go down. So intent was Lock on watching his victim, that he did not see a Bf 109 coming in to the attack. The German fighter's opening burst slightly wounded him in the leg, but on breaking away the Bf 109 presented Lock with an easy target and his fire caused it to explode. He watched the He 111 go down into the sea, before joining up with Red 3, Pilot Officer Morrough-Ryan, to return to base. That pilot, who had witnessed both of Lock's He 111s go down, himself claimed a Bf 109 destroyed. Yellow 1, Pilot Officer Bennions, claimed a 'probable' Ju 88 and a Ju 88 damaged, and Sergeant R. C. Ford a Bf 109 probably destroyed.

Group Captain Norman Ryder believes that Squadron Leader Hood and Flight Lieutenant Lovell died when their Spitfires collided. It was a serious loss to the squadron, for Hood, although inexperienced on Spitfires, was a popular commanding oficer. Flight Lieutenant Terry Webster, on the other hand, was a very experienced Spitfire pilot. Norman Ryder writes 'It was a happy fact that most of the pilots of No. 41 Squadron had flown Spits for nine months before the war started: we knew our stuff.' He himself had first flown a Spitfire in 1938 and by the time the Battle of Britain started 'probably had well over 300 hours on the wonderful aircraft'. It was to Flight Lieutenant Ryder that *de facto* leadership of the Squadron passed. Frank Usmar recalls: 'We were hoping that Norman Ryder, who took over the lead, would be promoted to squadron leader and Bennions to flight lieutenant to be flight commander.' Officialdom in its wisdom failed to confirm these appointments, however, although both officers had already shown great ability as fighter leaders. Flight Lieutenant Webster's place as leader of 'B' Flight was taken by Flight Lieutenant Tony Lovell. Norman Ryder remembers him as 'a devout Catholic, not a boozer like the rest of us, quite content with his own world, an extremely nice fellow without any malice. I think he was one of the unsung fighter boys.' Lovell ended the war with more than eighteen victories to his credit, but was killed in a flying accident shortly afterwards.

Despite the losses of the previous day, the squadron was able to send up twelve Spitfires to patrol base on the morning of 6 September. The patrol was uneventful, but Pilot Officer Lock reported that he passed out at 20,000 feet (presumably due to lack of oxygen) and did not regain consciousness until he was down to 8,000 feet. This accident gave him the opportunity to go hunting on his own account and he engaged a Ju 88 over the Channel and saw it crash twenty miles inland from the enemy coast. It was a gallant action, but a flagrant contravention of Park's instruction that single aircraft and small formations should not be pursued over the Channel – let alone into occupied territory. That afternoon Flight Lieutenant Ryder led eight Spitfires to the forward base at Rochford, Essex. At 1735 hours they were ordered on patrol and twenty minutes later ran into large numbers of Bf 109s over the Thames estuary. Ryder put the six Spitfires of Red and Yellow Sections into line astern and dived to attack small formations of fighters flying several thousand feet below. He ordered the two Spitfires of Green Section, flown by Pilot Officer Bennions and

Sergeant Usmar, to remain above as rearguard, since there were considerable numbers of Bf 109s flying higher than the Squadron.

Ryder picked out a Bf 109 and followed it through various evasive manoeuvres, firing several short bursts. His target finally exploded and fell into the sea off Southend pier. Flying Officer Mackenzie attacked one Bf 109, which went down in smoke and was assessed as probably destroyed. He then saw another Bf 109 passing to starboard and followed it down to low altitude firing in short bursts until his ammunition ran out. This fighter crash-landed in a cornfield to the north of Canterbury. Flying Officer Lovell chased a Bf 109 out to sea, opened fire and saw white smoke trail from its engine and the left undercarriage leg come down. It dived towards the sea, but then pulled up, and so Lovell closed in again and fired a 7-second burst. The German fighter exploded and spun into the sea. Sergeant Darling and Flying Officer Scott each claimed a Bf 109 probably destroyed. Meanwhile, Bennions was flying a series of S-turns above the main combat and saw two groups of Bf 109s coming down to engage Red and Yellow Sections. He turned in behind one of these and fired on the rearmost aircraft which burst into flames and plunged down. Bennions then turned to the other formation and again shot the rearmost Bf 109 down in flames. He saw the pilot bale out.

On the afternoon of 7 September the Luftwaffe launched the first heavy raid on London and the Battle entered a new phase. The No. 11 Group squadrons, expecting further airfield attacks, were caught unprepared and were late to intercept. No. 41 Squadron were ordered up at 1655 hours and received a series of contradictory instructions before finally meeting a formation of about thirty Do 17Zs escorted by forty Bf 109s. With two Spitfires acting as rearguard, Flight Lieutenant Ryder led his remaining six fighters down in line astern on to the bombers. They could only make a single firing pass before the Bf 109s came down on them and the combat broke up into individual dogfights. Ryder saw his fire hitting a Do 17Z before he broke away and engaged the Bf 109s. The third fighter he fired at belched black smoke and was claimed as probably destroyed. Ryder them climbed to above 20,000 feet and carried out a series of diving attacks on the bomber formations. Flying Officer Scott, leading Yellow Section, engaged a Bf 109 and set its engine on fire. The German fighter glided down as though preparing to force-land. Scott flew alongside and saw the pilot signal surrender, but the Bf 109 continued towards the coast and Scott had exhausted his ammunition, so could not finish him off. He last saw the German fighter flying at about 200 feet in the vicinity of Dover.

Sergeant J. McAdam, Yellow 2, had trouble with a rough-running engine and was left behind during the squadron's initial attack. Looking for a straggler, he spotted a single Bf 109 and attacked. The enemy fighter went down in a vertical dive, trailing white smoke, and was probably destroyed. McAdam then climbed over central London and dived to attack a formation of Do 17Zs, one of which was destroyed and a second probably destroyed. His Spitfire had been damaged in this combat and McAdam tried to return to Hornchurch, but the aircraft caught fire and he had to force-land, writing off the Spitfire but fortunately without injuring himself. Two more of the squadron's Spitfires were forced down and damaged in this fight, but their pilots (Sergeant Ford and Pilot Officer Morrough-Ryan) were unhurt.

Pilot Officer W. J. Scott was killed on the morning of 8 September during a squadron patrol of the Dover area. His Spitfire was seen to go down in flames and it was thought that he was a victim of surprise attack by Bf 109s. At this stage of the Battle, Fighter Command's pilot casualties had become so serious that Dowding was unable to continue his policy of relieving exhausted squadrons by fresh units from the quieter sectors. By now there were insufficient fully trained and rested units available to allow this. Instead the hard-pressed squadrons in No. 11 Group and the adjoining sectors (designated Category 'A' Squadrons) would have to fight on indefinitely. Individual casualties would be replaced, but only under the most exceptional circumstances would a squadron be taken out of action. It was a daunting prospect even for so comparatively fresh a unit as No. 41 Squadron, for in the five days since they had joined No. 11 Group, they had lost six Spitfires with three pilots killed, including the CO and a flight commander, and one pilot wounded. Squadron Leader R. C. F. Lister was posted to

No. 41 Squadron as CO on 8 September, but he lacked experience of fighter operations and it was quite wrong that he should have been pitchforked straight into action as a tactical fighter leader. The flight commander's position was not filled until the end of the month, when Flying Officer Lovell was promoted to fill the vacancy.

Norman Ryder has written a penetrating assessment of the demands and strains of combat flying during this latter part of the Battle. 'As a leader of the Squadron, I felt it was my duty to get the boys into the scrap on the best terms I could squeeze out of the situation; not to charge off personally and let things sort themselves out as fate dictated. Perhaps the most debilitating aspect was not the air combat, but the "combat waiting". This really sorted out the weaker spirits. We were up in the dark and groping around our aircraft before dawn. Then into Mae Wests and the long day commenced. A fighter pilot's role is quite unique. Once the hood was closed, he was alone with his thoughts and fears. If he turned away from trouble and took on the lonely smoking target, he alone knew about it and all of us can be hard on ourselves. Another thought for him to carry during the long wait on the ground. Knowing that if he failed again, then all self-respect would be gone and the Squadron had a weak link.

'I made it a rule when in charge of the Squadron that the newest or weakest pilot flew as wingman to myself, or Tony Lovell if in 'B' Flight. We could both do our jobs and look after the new boy. Your eyes definitely became "skinned" in time and you could see things you had no hope of doing during the early stages. Some would come home with bullet holes in their aircraft, yet professed to having seen or felt nothing. Perhaps the worst handicap was having to fight with only one side of the cockpit hood clear of ice, the other opaque and useless. This was due to the torque sweeping over the hood in a corkscrew fashion. It did not always occur, but often enough at 30,000 feet plus. I had the Hornchurch Wing above 30,000 feet, a number of times and the Squadron up to 36,000 feet – quite high with no body heating and probably four pairs of gloves. Frostbite was not that uncommon.'

No. 41 Squadron's twelve Spitfires engaged a large formation of enemy aircraft on the afternoon of 9 September. The squadron was ordered up at 1644 hours to patrol Maidstone and south of London and all the fighters had landed safely by 1825 hours. It was a highly successful combat, the squadron's claims totalling one He 111 and seven Bf 109s destroyed, plus a further He 111 and Bf 109 damaged. Yet astonishingly, apart from an entry in the Squadron's Operations Record Book, no further reports of this action appear to have survived in official records. Flight Lieutenant Ryder's logbook shows that he accounted for one Bf 109 destroyed and another damaged and it was undoubtedly he that led the mission. Similarly, Pilot Officer Bennions' logbook records that he destroyed one Bf 109 in the action. Bennions writes: 'Throughout the latter half of the Battle, I simply did not have the time or the inclination to fill in my logbook. The office staff did that for you from the flight authorization book – which again was not always completed – there simply was not sufficient time for such niceties.'

Frank Usmar, whose recollections have been helped by the discovery of letters he had written to his mother, notes: 'It was a fine afternoon. We intercepted them over Brighton going out to sea. I did what my flight commander had said don't do [Flight Lieutenant Terry Webster had warned Usmar never to follow a Bf 109 down, because its partner would always be in the sun and would come after him]. Two Bf 109s were in front of me. One started to go down. The other started to turn right, climbing into the sun. With quick glances at the one climbing, I got the one going down in my sight. I let go a long burst, trying hard to see if I had time before the other one came down. Blue-black smoke appeared. I then saw the other just coming out of the sun on me and, if he was firing, he went back claiming me, because I flicked the Spit over and pulled back, diving to sea level from 20,000 feet vertically. Brighton sea front faced up to me. I held it down to roof tops and back to Hornchurch. I claimed it was probable, but Gissy [Flying Officer Lord Gisborough] the Intelligence Officer said the blue smoke could have been when he opened his throttle.'

At 1515 hours on 11 September, eleven Spitfires were ordered to patrol over Maidstone. After take-off, Sergeant I. E. Howitt was detached from the squadron formation to carry out a spotter patrol over the coast. It was not until 1615 hours, however, that the ten remaining Spitfires made contact with the enemy and by that time many pilots were concerned about their dwindling fuel. They intercepted a formation of some seventy to eighty aircraft, consisting of Ju 88 bombers and a close escort of Bf 110s, flying at 20,000 feet. No. 41 Squadron's Spitfires, 5,000 feet above them, went into echelon starboard formation. They then peeled off to port, one by one, and dived on the bombers from out of the sun. Flight Lieutenant Ryder opened the attack by diving through the centre of the bomber formation, hoping that it would split into two groups. He fired on several Ju 88s, but could only claim one as damaged. Pilot Officer G. A. Langley saw his opening burst strike a Ju 88, but his Spitfire was then attacked from behind. Finding that his aircraft was no longer under control, Langley had no option but to bale out. Pilot Officer Lock, seeing that the squadron's initial attack had broken up the German formation, picked out a Ju 88 and carried out a series of firing passes against it. He saw the enemy aircraft crash in a field seventeen miles south of Maidstone. On climbing back to rejoin the fight, Lock was attacked by a Bf 110. He outmanoeuvred the twin-engined German fighter and sent it down to crash about ten miles south-east of his earlier victim. By this time he was out of ammunition and very low on fuel so he landed at RAF West Malling, Kent.

Flying Officer Mackenzie's initial dive on the Ju 88 formation had been too fast and too steep for him to take proper aim, but he was able to make good use of his excess speed in zooming back to 30,000 feet and from this vantage-point he sighted a straggling He 111 bomber making for the coast. He dived on it and opened fire in a single, long burst from astern. He then dropped to low level to evade what he believed was an enemy fighter, but which was in fact Pilot Officer Lock's Spitfire. Lock was able to watch the He 111 Mackenzie had attacked glide down to earth. Mackenzie too came down at West Malling; only seven gallons of fuel remained in his Spitfire's tanks. Pilot Officer Bennions engaged the Bf 110s flying behind the bombers, but was forced to break off the fight when his own aircraft was damaged by enemy fire. Bennions himself was slightly but very painfully wounded in the heel by a splinter, and the Spitfire's pneumatic system was hit so that the guns, flaps and brakes were inoperable, but he carried out a successful landing back at base.

After leaving the squadron formation, Sergeant Howitt was directed to the Deal–Dover area. His job was to report on the position and composition of any enemy formations approaching the coast. It had been found that such fighter reconnaissance missions provided the sector controllers with extremely valuable information to supplement their other sources of air raid Intelligence. Later in the Battle two special flights were formed specifically for these hazardous spotter duties. While climbing through 17,000 feet to the west of Maidstone, Howitt saw a formation of about twelve Bf 109s 2,000 feet beneath him. He reported the sighting and turned away into the sun to continue his climb. He finally took up position over Dungeness at a height of 32,000 feet and soon afterwards reported a formation of bombers and escort fighters crossing the coast south of Folkestone. A similar formation was following behind and Howitt radioed this information to control. His Spitfire was then attacked from behind by an enemy fighter and hit by cannon fire. He took violent evasive action and shook off his assailant. Then he noticed two more German formations coming in and reported them to his control. He was ordered to rejoin his squadron, but his oil cooler had been punctured by cannon fire and shortly afterwards the engine seized. Howitt carried out a successful forced-landing without causing any further damage to his fighter.

On 14 September it was the turn of Pilot Officer Lock to fly a solo spotter patrol, but it was not in this audacious pilot's nature to be content with the role of a passive observer. He was flying at about 32,000 feet over the south coast when he saw a formation of twelve Bf 109s some 7,000 feet beneath him in the vicinity of Dover. He was closing in to attack the rearmost section of the German formation, when he saw a second group of Bf 109s preparing to dive on him in individual head-on attacks. Lock opened fire on the first Bf 109 and saw it flash past only a few feet above his Spitfire. Turning to get on its tail, he saw that the German fighter was already in flames. He then met a second head-on attack and claimed this Bf 109 as destroyed, before half-rolling and diving into cloud cover to escape the remaining German fighters. The squadron also encountered Bf 109s during an afternoon patrol, but made no claims. Squadron Leader Lister, who baled out of his Spitfire wounded, was lost. Lister's replacement was Squadron Leader D. O. Finlay, an Olympic athlete and pre-war fighter pilot, who in the previous month had escaped from a desk job to return to flying. Posted to command No. 54 Squadron on 26 August, Finlay had been shot down and wounded in combat on the following day. After this false start, he found his form with No. 41 Squadron and was to remain in command until the following summer.

On 15 September (now celebrated as Battle of Britain day) the Luftwaffe carried out two major raids on London and RAF Fighter Command met both of them in strength. Ten Spitfires of No. 41 Squadron were ordered up at 1140 hours and they intercepted an escorted bomber formation over Kent, but before they could reach the bombers they were attacked from above by Bf 109s. Pilot Officer Bennions managed to get on the tail of one of them, but it half-rolled and dived away. Bennions followed and caught up with it to the west of Ashford. He fired three short bursts and the aircraft burst into flames, its pilot baled out and Bennions saw the aircraft hit the ground. Flying Officer Lovell also chased one of the Bf 109s, set it on fire and saw the pilot bale out. The only other claim was made by Sergeant Darling. After the squadron formation had been broken up and he had evaded the Bf 109s, he climbed to 20,000 feet and patrolled the coast near Dover. He sighted a formation of Do 17Zs heading back for France and engaged a straggler. Darling had set its port engine on fire, when he had to break away to evade an attack from a Bf 109.

During the afternoon engagement, the Bf 109s were not so successful in protecting their charges. At 1410 hours the Squadron was ordered to take off and patrol base at 25,000 feet. They were in position when an escorted formation of thirty Do 17Zs was sighted 6,000 feet below. Flight Lieutenant Ryder, leading the squadron, ordered the Spitfires into line astern and dived through the close fighter escort to attack a Do 17Z which broke formation and headed for cloud cover below. To Ryder's surprise, he was not engaged by enemy fighters and so was able to follow the bomber down through cloud. He was then joined by Flying Officer Boyle and three Hurricanes in finishing off the Do 17Z, which came down on the Isle of Sheppey. Flying Officer Mackenzie also attacked a Do 17Z and saw it dive into cloud with its port engine smoking. After his initial attack on the bomber formation, Pilot Officer Lock saw an isolated group of three Do 17Zs flying just above the clouds, with three Bf 109s escorting them. Teaming up with a Hurricane, he engaged the fighters and shot one down in flames. Then he switched his attention to the bombers, carrying out stern and quarter attacks on one and setting its starboard engine on fire. He saw it crash into the sea.

Not all the Spitfires were able to follow Ryder down to attack the Do 17Zs. Flying Officer Boyle, flying in the rear of the squadron formation and acting as look-out, saw three Bf 109s come out of the sun just after the bombers were sighted. He turned towards them and closed in on one head-on, opening fire at 500 yards. He last saw it spinning down in flames. He then dived on the main bomber formation, before joining Ryder to finish off the Do 17Z. Pilot Officer H. C. Baker also saw the Bf 109s preparing to attack the Squadron, but on climbing to meet them he inadvertently spun and fell away. On recovering, he found himself well positioned for a head-on attack on a formation of He 111s. This he carried out, firing at several aircraft on his way through the bombers and damaging at least one. He then joined a pair of Hurricanes in attacking a straggling He 111 and this aircraft came down in the estuary mudflats.

Sergeant Darling also engaged the He 111 formation and saw the bomber that he had fired on drop away. He then followed up the attack on this He 111, exhausting his remaining ammunition. He last saw it losing height with its main wheels down and both engines apparently stopped. It was assessed as probably destroyed. After firing on an He 111, but seeing no result, Flying Officer Lovell attacked a Bf 109 from behind and saw it pour white smoke, turn on its back and disappear into the clouds. He claimed it as probably destroyed. The squadron's total claims for this combat amounted to two fighters and three bombers destroyed, three aircraft probably destroyed and two damaged. All the Spitfires landed safely at base.

The combat fought over Manston two days later was less one-sided and was to set the pattern for the squadron's operations of the latter half of September. For on 17 September claims for three Bf 109s destroyed and one damaged were balanced by damage to four of the squadron's Spitfires, with one of the fighters being a write-off. Pilot Officer Bennions was leading eleven Spitfires on patrol, when two formations of Bf 109s were sighted above them. The squadron began to climb to engage, but were set upon by small groups of Bf 109s. In trying to evade these attacks Bennions got into a spin and on climbing back met four Bf 109s at 15,000 feet. He engaged the rearmost and saw it dive down into the ground between Canterbury and Herne Bay. Pilot Officer Boyle got within range of one of the higher formations of fighters. As he opened fire, he saw them wheel away and head back towards France. Two of the Bf 109s then collided and spun down. Sergeant J. K. Norwell pounced on three of the Bf 109s diving for home and saw his fire hit one of them. From the squadron's point of view, skirmishing with high-flying Bf 109s was far less satisfying than intercepting the bomber formations. Yet it was Park's policy to use the Spitfire squadrons based at Biggin Hill and Hornchurch to engage the German fighter escorts and thus give other squadrons the chance to reach the bombers.

The AOC, No. 11 Group had also decided that he would pair up fighter squadrons whenever this was practicable. These were not formally constituted Wings, since often there was insufficient time to position even individual squadrons for interception, but the measure did help somewhat to redress the usual imbalance of forces between the RAF and Luftwaffe. No. 41 Squadron was usually teamed with No. 603 Squadron, another of the Hornchurch Sector's Spitfire squadrons. On the morning of 18 September No. 41 Squadron was ordered to patrol Maidstone at 20,000 feet, where it joined up with No. 603 Squadron. They were then told to climb to 25,000 feet and at 1010 hours Pilot Officer Bennions, leading the squadron, sighted large numbers of Bf 109s 5,000 to 7,000 feet above them. The enemy fighters dived to engage and in the ensuing dogfight Bennions and Lock each claimed a Bf 109 probably destroyed. Sergeant Frank Usmar had better fortune. 'We had been at 30,000 feet,' he writes, 'having intercepted some enemy aircraft and as usual when you get into a fight, one minute aircraft are all around you and the next open sky and you are wondering what has happened to them all. I dived down through a thin layer of cloud. As I came out of the cloud, about 500–400 yards in front of me sat two 109s. I was going too fast from the dive and was overtaking. Throttle right back and the horn blowing in my ears trying hard to lose speed, I had the one on the right in my sights and I let drive a long burst. The aircraft spiralled down to the right, with black smoke coming from the side. I was now so close to the other one that I could not use the sights. I flew straight at it with the guns blazing, preparing to chew his wing off. He fell away to the left and I turned very tightly right. I felt sure I was in a trap and his mates were on my tail, but there was nothing. I saw two aircraft going down very steeply towards the marshes.'

At 1250 hours Bennions was again leading the squadron, when it was attacked from above by large numbers of fighters. The formation then split up and individual pilots had some success against scattered groups of Bf 109s. Bennions climbed to 32,000 feet and attacked the rearmost of five fighters, seeing it explode in front of him. He was then fired on from behind and his Spitfire was damaged. He turned on his attacker, firing two short bursts, and saw hits before the Bf 109 half-rolled and dived away smoking. Four more Bf 109s closed in from behind and Bennions turned to attack the No. 4 aircraft, following it down in a dive towards Dover and finishing off his ammunition. Bennions was credited with one Bf 109 confirmed destroyed, one probably destroyed and one damaged. Pilot Officer Lock also gained a confirmed victory and a probable, and Sergeant Darling saw the Bf 109 that he had attacked go down into the sea. Darling was in action again at 1715 hours, acting as squadron rearguard. Sighting a formation of bombers behind, he broke away to attack them and claimed one Ju 88 damaged. Meanwhile, the other Spitfires had become engaged with Bf 109s, Sergeant R. A. Beardsley claiming two damaged and Pilot Officer E. S. Aldous one damaged. The latter two pilots were among a number of welcome reinforcements transferred from No. 610 Squadron after it had become a Category 'C' Squadron.

On 20 September Pilot Officer Bennions had to force-land his damaged Spitfire at Lympne, Kent, after a brush with Bf 109s. However, the squadron's only claims for the day were made by Pilot Officer Lock. Flying alone on a reconnaissance patrol, he shot down a Bf 109 and a Henschel Hs 126 army co-operation aircraft into the Channel. Three days later, No. 41 Squadron's Spitfires had a slight height advantage when they attacked twelve Bf 109s at 33,000 feet over Dover. Pilot Officer Bennions sent one Bf 109 down to ditch in the sea and four other enemy fighters were claimed as probably destroyed or damaged. A further Bf 109 destroyed and one damaged was added to the squadron's score later in the day, when three Spitfires escorted an Anson on a reconnaissance mission across the Channel. On 24 September, though, they lost two Spitfires for no damage to the enemy. Sergeant MacAdam baled out and was wounded, while Sergeant Darling crash-landed without injuring himself. He was less fortunate on the morning of 27 September, when both Darling and Sergeant Usmar were wounded in combat with Bf 109s. Sergeant Norwell was able to claim one of these as destroyed.

That afternoon eleven of No. 41 Squadron's Spitfires, flying in company with No. 603 Squadron, were attacked by Bf 109s over Kent. Flight Lieutenant Ryder had to bale out of his crippled fighter and the only squadron claim, by Sergeant C. S. Bamberger, was for a Bf 109 damaged. The squadron's toll of casualties increased on the morning of 28 September, when Bf 109s were engaged over Charing in Kent. Flying Officer J. G. Boyle was killed and Pilot Officer H. H. Chalder mortally wounded; while Pilot Officer Aldous was slightly wounded and sent on a week's sick leave. At 1230 hours, the squadron, only seven aircraft strong, was sent up to patrol base. It was then directed to intercept an enemy raid over Kent and was attacked by Bf 109s. Two Spitfires were damaged, fortunately without injury to their pilots, and in return

Pilot Officer Bennions probably destroyed two of the German fighters.

Two of No. 41 Squadron's pilots have written vivid accounts of flying the Spitfire – 'this gem of an aircraft' in Norman Ryder's words – against its German counterpart, the Bf 109. Sergeant Bob Beardsley, who was to complete three tours of operations on Spitfires, and who retired from the RAF as a squadron leader, recalled that 'firstly the Spitfire was a very rugged and reliable aircraft. No matter how bad the damage, I always got them down in one piece and never had any engine trouble. Secondly, it was very sensitive and responsive. One really needed to fly it all the time, but it had no vices and one really felt the "man and machine" being one unit. Operating over England German air force fighters were not inclined to mix it, because of their fuel limitation for combat, but their main advantage was height advantage obtained on the climb out from their bases in France. We were then invariably climbing underneath them to gain height to attack; often at low speeds and frequently into the sun, as they came from between the south-east and south-west . . . Whilst one must give the benefit of shooting down most enemy aircraft to the Hurricane pilots, it should also be remembered that they were detailed to attack bomber formations, whereas the faster Spitfire supplied cover against attack by the escorting fighters. I seldom remember being able to attack a nice juicy bomber.'

Norman Ryder thought that 'the 109 was a good fast aircraft: good acceleration in the early part of the dive, not so good as far as manoeuvrability was concerned. Their first tactic, if taken by surprise, was to flip over and go hell for leather diving for the coast and home. If caught at the lower level on their way out, say 7,000 feet, there was nothing they could do. If they tried any manoeuvre the Spit cut the corner and got there quicker. This was not to say it was easy – far from it – and even on good days there was often the coastal cloud. However, with surprise on their side, they were dangerous and had good weaponry. Who saw who first was the name of the game. It wasn't for some time that we realized that the Spit could catch them in the dive – after the initial advantage had gone. A heavy, flush-riveted Rolls after a stud-riveted Ford.'

After a period of tough fighting against heavy odds, September ended with a more successful day's combat for No. 41 Squadron. At 1306 hours on 30 September twelve Spitfires took off from the forward base at Rochford to patrol the estuary at 30,000 feet. They intercepted a formation of about thirty Do 17Zs and dived to attack in line astern. Flying Officer Lovell closed in to short range behind one of the bombers and saw his fire riddle its fuselage. He was then attacked from behind and his Spitfire was damaged. On returning to base he discovered that the undercarriage was jammed and so he had to make a wheels-up landing. Pilot Officer M. P. Brown, one of four Spitfire pilots transferred from No. 611 Squadron the previous day, also damaged a Do 17Z.

Sergeant Beardsley was able to claim one probably destroyed. He had attacked this Do 17Z from the beam and then from astern, leaving it gliding down towards the French coast at 1,000 feet with one engine smoking. He then climbed to 2,000 feet and engaged a Bf 109, firing his remaining ammunition into it. The German fighter went into a steep dive, pouring smoke, and was assessed as probably destroyed. Beardsley then had to evade attacks from six Bf 109s and his Spitfire was badly damaged by their fire. His engine caught fire and flames and glycol fumes reached the cockpit, but Beardsley stuck with his Spitfire and nursed the ailing fighter to the Folkestone area before the engine finally stopped. He was then able to bring off an extremely skilful forced-landing at RAF Hawkinge. Meanwhile, Pilot Officer Baker, who had been detached from the squadron for spotter duties, was flying at 25,000 feet over Dungeness. He sighted and reported a bomber formation flying 10,000 feet below him. He then saw about sixty Bf 109s at 28,000 feet and had to take hasty evasive action as a number of them broke away to attack him. After shaking off his pursuers, Baker continued the patrol and eventually saw a lone Bf 109, which had evidently already been damaged in combat, making for France. He attacked it and saw it plunge into the sea ten miles off Dungeness. A further Bf 109 probably destroyed was added to the squadron's score during a later engagement that day.

During the fortnight beginning on 17 September, No. 41 Squadron had fought fifteen engagements, most of them combats with Bf 109 fighters. They had claimed twelve enemy aircraft destroyed, ten probably destroyed and twelve damaged. However, their own losses had been far from negligible, with two pilots killed, four wounded, eight Spitfires destroyed and nine damaged. When the Battle entered its final phase at the beginning of October, with the Luftwaffe sending over high-level fighter sweeps interspersed with fighter-bomber missions, there seemed little prospect for No. 41 Squadron of a respite from the strain of daily battles with large numbers of German fighters.

On 1 October the Squadron lost one of its most gallant and skilful pilots, when Pilot Officer George Bennions was shot down and seriously wounded. During the first action of the day, at about 1415 hours, the squadron sighted a number of Bf 109s below them and dived to attack. Squadron Leader Finlay, flying as Blue 2 to gain experience, and Pilot Officer D. A. Adams both attacked the same enemy aircraft, which was assessed as damaged. Then at 1550 hours, nine Spitfires were ordered to patrol the Maidstone area. They sighted about 25 enemy aircraft flying 500 feet below them at 30,000 feet and went down to attack. The German fighters dived away into clouds. Flying Officer Lovell (whose promotion to Flight Lieutenant was to be announced that day) fired all his ammunition into a Bf 109, but could only claim it as damaged.

Returning to base, low on oxygen, the squadron sighted a formation of Hurricanes about to be overwhelmed by large numbers of Bf 109s. Since he still had about half of his oxygen remaining, Pilot Officer Bennions decided to break away from the Squadron and attack the Bf 109s. He picked out a fighter flying to the rear of the German formation, fired two bursts into it and saw it catch fire and its pilot jettison the cockpit canopy prior to baling out. At that moment, his Spitfire was struck by cannon fire and Bennions was hit in the head. In his own words: 'everything faded out completely'. He retained sufficient strength to bale out of his crippled fighter and lost consciousness several times on the way down to earth. He descended at Henfield, Sussex, where a local farmer, who had watched as about forty German fighters pounced on Bennions' Spitfire, hurried to the scene to give what help he could. Bennions' skull had been pierced by a cannon shell and his left eye destroyed, yet not only was he to recover from these terrible wounds, but eventually he returned to flying. C. J. Shepherd, the farmer who had witnessed Bennions' last fight, was moved to write to Squadron Leader Finlay, giving him the details. He ended his letter with the heartfelt tribute: 'I, being an ex RAF man, am proud to think that we have such brave lads in the RAF.'

There was no contact with the enemy on 2 October, but Sergeant Norwell was slightly injured when his Spitfire collided with a parked aircraft during a scramble take-off. By contrast, 5 October was a day of hectic activity, with three of the squadron's four patrols meeting enemy aircraft. In the first combat the squadron was flying at 30,000 feet and was able to surprise a small group of Bf 109s, 4,000 feet below them, claiming two enemy aircraft destroyed and three damaged. Flight Lieutenant Lovell's Spitfire was slightly damaged, but otherwise the squadron escaped without loss. Later that day the squadron again engaged enemy fighters from above, after being forced to split up in scattered cloud. Pilot Officer Lock and Flying Officer Mackenzie each gained a confirmed victory and Lock a further probable.

Lock was again successful during the third fight of the day. Acting as rearguard in the squadron formation, he sighted twelve Bf 109s closing in from behind and below. He turned to engage and claimed one of them as a probable victory. Two days later, eleven Spitfires set upon a solitary Do 17 and shot it down; but return fire from the bomber hit Pilot Officer Adams' Spitfire, forcing him to bale out, and Flying Officer Mackenzie's Spitfire was also damaged. Later the same day the squadron was on patrol over Biggin Hill when it surprised a small group of German fighters and Pilot Officer J. R. Walker shot one of them down.

The squadron again engaged with a slight advantage of height on 9 October, when they met a small formation of Bf 109s over Maidstone. As they attacked, a second formation of German fighters fell on them from behind. Pilot Officer Lock, acting as rearguard and flying 2,000 feet above the Squadron, was able to break up this attack, shooting one Bf 109 down. The Spitfires of No. 222 Squadron then came into the fight and the combat broke up into a series of individual dogfights. No. 41 Squadron's only loss was one Spitfire damaged; the CO's aircraft was hit during the combat and he was forced to make a wheels-up landing. In return they claimed two Bf 109s destroyed, one probably destroyed and two damaged. The arithmetic of claims and losses was to be much less favourable during the following week. On 11 October the squadron was ordered to patrol base at 30,000 feet and encountered about fifty Bf 109s flying above them. In the ensuing combat, the Spitfires flown by Sergeant L. R. Carter and Flying Officer D. H. O'Neill collided, the latter pilot being killed, and Pilot Officer J. G. Lecky died in combat with the Bf 109s. Only Pilot Officer Lock was able to inflict any damage on the enemy, claiming one Bf 109 destroyed. Next day Sergeant McAdam's Spitfire suffered an engine failure during take-off and the pilot was lucky to be able to crash-land without injuring himself. Then on 15 October Sergeant P. D. Lloyd was shot down and killed in a surprise attack by Bf 109s.

At 1540 hours on 17 October No. 41 Squadron was ordered to a patrol line in the Maidstone area at 15,000 feet. This was a newly instituted procedure, which was intended to position squadrons on standing patrol ready to intercept high-flying fighter sweeps. By flying at 15,000 feet they would conserve oxygen supplies, until ordered to climb to 30,000 feet when an approaching force was detected. On this occasion sun and haze made a co-ordinated squadron attack impossible, and the Spitfires split up to engage scattered enemy formations. Pilot Officer Aldridge and Pilot Officer E. P. Wells each claimed a Bf 109 destroyed. The same patrol procedure was employed on 20 October, when No. 41 Squadron flew in company with No. 603 Squadron. The two Spitfire units had been on station for an hour and were preparing to return to base, when they were ordered to climb and engage a force of between fifty and sixty Bf 109s flying at 25,000 feet. Reaching a height of 30,000 feet, No. 41 Squadron was able to dive on the rearmost enemy fighters, and claimed three Bf 109s destroyed, one probable and one damaged for no loss to themselves.

The squadron's ability to fight at high altitude was improved on 24 October, when they exchanged fourteen of their Spitfire Mk

Is for a similar number of No. 611 Squadron's Spitfire Mk IIs. The latter unit, based at Digby, Lincolnshire, was by then a Category 'C' Squadron. No. 41 Squadron fought two actions with its new aircraft on the following day. At 0900 hours twelve Spitfires took off to patrol between Hornchurch and Rochford and joined up with No. 603 Squadron at 23,000 feet, before climbing to high altitude. They then intercepted a group of about thirty Bf 109s, diving on them from out of the sun. Sergeant McAdam claimed one fighter destroyed and the rest of the squadron accounted for four probables and three damaged. Pilot Officer Aldridge's Spitfire was damaged by fragments from his victim, but otherwise the squadron suffered no casualties.

The day's second combat was fought at 1600 hours over Dungeness, when two Spitfires were damaged in return for one Bf 109 destroyed and four damaged. Sergeant Beardsley damaged one Bf 109 and sent a second diving vertically into the clouds in flames. He then came under attack, his Spitfire's engine was damaged, and he force-landed at Hawkinge for the second time in a month. Flying Officer Mackenzie, after damaging a Bf 109, had to force-land in a field east of Redhill due to shortage of fuel and he damaged his Spitfire in the process. Pilot Officer Wells, who flew the same Spitfire in both morning and afternoon engagements, each time suffered problems with the guns' pneumatic firing system but this did not prevent him from claiming a Bf 109 damaged in the afternoon combat.

On 27 October two Bf 109s were destroyed for no loss to the squadron, and on 30 October it fought two actions. In the morning, flying with No. 222 Squadron, it engaged and broke up a formation of more than thirty Bf 109s over Kent. Flight Lieutenant Ryder, Flying Officer Mackenzie and Pilot Officer Aldridge each claimed a Bf 109 destroyed and a further three Bf 109s were damaged. At 1615 hours the squadron was again engaged, but lost two Spitfires and could make no claims against the enemy. Sergeant L. A. Garvey was killed and Pilot Officer G. G. F. Draper baled out slightly wounded. By official reckoning, this was the squadron's last combat in the Battle of Britain, but in fact the Luftwaffe's fighter sweeps continued until early December 1940, and No. 41 Squadron fought its last combat of the campaign on 27 November.

The squadron's first casualty of November was not due to enemy action but to an accident. Pilot Officer N. M. Brown, flying in bad visibility on 1 November, struck a balloon cable and his aircraft was wrecked, but he escaped uninjured. On the following day, Pilot Officer Wells shot down a Bf 109 in flames, after he had broken away from the squadron formation to investigate an unidentified aircraft. After a week's lull, the squadron was again in action on 9 November. Pilot Officer Lock had to force-land his damaged Spitfire at Manston, but the squadron made no claims.

On 11 November Pilot Officer Wells fought two solo actions. This 24-year-old New Zealander was fast developing into an aggressive and skilful fighter pilot in the mould of Bennions and Lock. At 1035 hours Wells took off with an 11-Spitfire patrol, but had to land with an overheated engine. He took off again and went out over the Channel, flying just beneath the cloud base at 9,000 feet. About five miles to the North of Cap Gris Nez he spotted a Henschel Hs 126 circling above the water and dived to attack it. He made four firing passes, scoring many hits and killing the rear gunner, but then his ammunition ran out and so Wells could only claim a probable victory. In the afternoon Wells fought one of the RAF's few encounters with Mussolini's Corpo Aereo Italiano, which had been dispatched to Belgium in late October to take part in the Battle. No. 41 Squadron was flying a convoy patrol east of Orfordness on the Suffolk coast, when Wells broke away to investigate a patch of burning oil on the sea. He then sighted several groups of Fiat CR 42 biplane fighters, which came down to attack him. He evaded their fire and climbed at full throttle to get above them. Then he made a series of diving attacks on the Italian fighters, but on each occasion his target half-rolled rapidly away and all he could claim was one aircraft damaged. 'What struck me most', he later reported, 'was their extreme manoeuvrability.'

The whole squadron was in action on 17 November, when twelve Spitfires intercepted about seventy Bf 109s over the estuary. At 30,000 feet the Spitfires were 5,000 feet above the German formation, and went into line astern to attack. They claimed a total of five Bf 109s destroyed and one damaged, but lost Pilot Officer Lock, who crash-landed badly wounded at Alderton in Suffolk after shooting down two of the German fighters. Lock returned to operational flying in the following summer, but was posted missing from a sortie over France on 3 August 1941. His final score of 26 enemy aircraft destroyed was the highest of any of No. 41 Squadron's Battle of Britain veterans. Pilot Officer Aldridge also crash-landed after the combat on 17 November, but was unhurt. A further victory was gained for the squadron on the morning of 23 November, when five Bf 109s were sighted over Tonbridge, Kent, and Squadron Leader Finlay shot one of them down. The squadron's last combat of the year was fought in the same area at about 1530 hours on 27 November. Squadron Leader Finlay led twelve Spitfires from out of the sun on to a loose formation of Bf 109s. Attacking in pairs, the squadron achieved complete surprise and claimed eight enemy fighters destroyed and one damaged. Since moving to Hornchurch on 3 September, the Luftwaffe's Bf 109s had been the squadron's main adversary and so it was appropriate that it should end the Battle with so complete a victory over its old antagonist.

No. 41 Squadron, with claims for more than ninety enemy aircraft destroyed, was one of the high scoring fighter squadrons of the Battle of Britain. It had taken part in much hard fighting, including the convoy and coastal patrols of the first phase of the Battle, during which Fighter Command lost most of the advantages of its carefully planned command and control system and so often had to accept combat at a disadvantage. During the Luftwaffe's attacks on the No. 11 Group airfields, the squadron had been in a quiet sector, only returning to Hornchurch at the end of that phase of the Battle. Yet, during that time it had taken part in the defeat of Luftflotte 5's raid of 15 August, which had shown beyond doubt that without its single-seat fighter escorts, the Luftwaffe was no match for Fighter Command's defences. The squadron then operated from Hornchurch throughout the Battle's two final phases, when its primary role had been the early interception of the German single-seat fighters – the Bf 109s – first flying as bomber escorts and then on their own account during the Battle's last phase. It had been an unremitting contest against a fighter that was the Spitfire's equal on most counts and, in the significant factor of altitude performance, its superior. Under such conditions, much depended on the skill of individual pilots. In this respect, No. 41 Squadron had been particularly fortunate, for although (with the possible exception of Eric Lock) its pilots were never given the recognition accorded to the more widely publicised RAF aces, their achievements during the Battle of Britain mark them as fighter pilots of exceptional ability and courage.

NO. 56 SQUADRON

No. 56 Squadron had been one of the most famous fighter units of the First World War. It was the first squadron to fly the SE 5 scout and its pilots had included Ball, McCudden, Rhys-Davids and Bowman. On the outbreak of the Second World War it was flying Hawker Hurricanes from North Weald in Essex, its permanent peacetime station for most of the inter-war years. The squadron's baptism of fire came soon afterwards, in the bizarre and tragic skirmish known as the 'Battle of Barking Creek'. At 0645 hours on 6 September 1939 an enemy raid was detected approaching the Thames estuary, and fighters were scrambled to meet it. In fact, due to a technical fault in one of the early-warning radars, the alarm was a false one and there was no incursion by the Luftwaffe, but a flight of No. 74 Squadron's Spitfires mistook No. 56 Squadron's Hurricanes for German fighters and attacked, shooting down two of them. One of the pilots was killed. There followed the usual Phoney War routine of convoy patrols, occasionally enlivened by encounters with single enemy aircraft. Then on 10 May, with the launching of the German assault in the west, the squadron was committed to action over the Continent. It flew daily patrols from airfields in Britain and during four hectic days in mid-May the six Hurricanes of 'B' Flight operated from Vitry-en-Artois in France.

The strain of combat flying, with its inevitable casualties, had taken its toll of the squadron, but it was allowed only a brief respite at RAF Digby, Lincolnshire, in No. 12 Group, before returning to North Weald to resume patrols over France and then prepare for the coming Battle of Britain. At this critical moment in the squadron's history, its able and experienced CO, Squadron Leader E. V. Knowles (a strict disciplinarian, known to his pilots as 'The Führer'), was posted away to a job at the Air Ministry. Knowles was later to carry out valuable pioneering work on clandestine air operations in support of the Special Operations Executive, before his untimely death in an air crash. His successor, Squadron Leader G. A. L. Manton, lacked experience of wartime fighter operations, as did so many of the officers appointed to the command of fighter squadrons at this time. This problem was belatedly recognized later in the Battle, and such officers were often attached as supernumeraries to the more experienced squadrons for short periods so that they could gain at least some up-to-date knowledge before taking over their new commands. It was not until after the Battle, however, that the principle of drawing on the pool of Fighter Command's battle-tested flight commanders to fill the squadron commander vacancies became generally established. Fortunately for No. 56 Squadron, Manton was prepared to defer to the judgement of his flight commanders until he himself gained the necessary experience and it is to the credit of the officers concerned that the arrangement worked· without friction.

'A' Flight's commander, Flight Lieutenant J. H. Coghlan, had already claimed five German aircraft confirmed or probably destroyed during the fighting over France. With his short, stocky figure and close-cropped bullet head, he looked more like one of the dreaded enemy than a fellow countryman, or so thought one of his pilots, Pilot Officer Geoffrey Page. Flight Lieutenant E. J. Gracie, the officer commanding 'B' Flight, was by contrast quite unmilitary in appearance, his rotund figure and waddling gait earning him the nickname 'Jumbo'. He had joined No. 56 Squadron in late June 1940, on posting from No. 79 Squadron, and was soon to prove himself – appearances notwithstanding – to be a fighter leader of considerable ability. In 1942 he took part in the air defence of Malta as a squadron commander and later as wing leader. Gracie was killed in action in February 1944. Another officer who was to influence the fortunes of No. 56 Squadron during the Battle was RAF North Weald's station commander, Wing Commander F. V. Beamish. A pugnacious yet warm-hearted Irishman, Beamish not only kept a fatherly eye on the squadrons operating from North Weald, but himself often flew in combat with them. Although No. 56 Squadron was not to suffer the leadership problems that dogged some fighter units, it did begin the Battle at a disadvantage in the vitally important matter of pilot strength. Its establishment was for 26 pilots, but on 1 July 1940 the posted strength was no more than 22, comprising thirteen officers and nine NCO pilots.

'North Weald was a comfortable, fully-equipped, pre-war station,' recalled Innes Westmacott. 'When at readiness, we had a substantial wooden dispersal hut to sit in on the far side of the airfield, which also housed the squadron commander's and adjutant's offices. The flight offices were in a similar hut nearby. When we were due to be at readiness early in the morning, we slept in the hut on camp-beds. I think we all used to get into pyjamas, despite the fact that if we were on dawn readiness, we had to emerge from our beds with extreme reluctance at about 3.30 am. There were a number of blast pens for the aircraft, with air raid shelters beneath their foundations. There was also an advanced satellite airfield at Rochford near Southend, from which we regularly operated. There we had a tent at dispersal. The

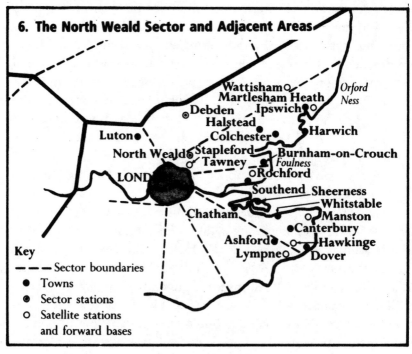

6. The North Weald Sector and Adjacent Areas

Key
— — — Sector boundaries
●   Towns
◉   Sector stations
○   Satellite stations
      and forward bases

aircraft stood in the open reasonably dispersed. There were two squadrons of Hurricanes based at North Weald (Nos. 56 and 151). Usually one of the them would operate from North Weald and the other from Rochford, alternately; but as facilities for providing meals at Rochford were limited, the changeover was whenever possible arranged so that meals could be taken at North Weald.'

July began quietly for the squadron and during the first week of the month only one combat was recorded. Flight Lieutenant Coghlan led Red Section to intercept an X-plot raid on 3 July. One of the Hurricanes became separated from the other two in cloud, but Coghlan and Pilot Officer M. H. Mounsdon engaged a Do 17 ten miles west of Orfordness. After Coghlan's second attack, the enemy aircraft's port engine was in flames, but it then evaded the British fighters in cloud. A searchlight crew later reported that an aircraft had crashed into the sea off Burnham and this is believed to have been Coghlan's victim.

A week later, on 10 July, the whole squadron was in action in defence of a Channel convoy steaming off Dover. A flight of No. 32 Squadron's Hurricanes was on patrol over the merchant ships, when the first indications of an impending raid were picked up by radar at about 1330 hours. No. 56 Squadron, operating from the forward base at Manston, were scrambled to reinforce them and intercepted a force of fifty plus aircraft just as the attack on the convoy was beginning. The Hurricanes attempted to intervene, but were unable to penetrate the German fighter screen, which consisted of Bf 110s circling at 10,000 feet and Bf 109s, 4,000 feet above them. Flight Lieutenant Coghlan engaged the Bf 110s, but was himself attacked from behind by Bf 109s. After a short dogfight, he was able to fire a good burst into a twin-engined fighter, seeing his bullets hit the centre fuselage and wings. An engine burst into flames and the Bf 110 broke away downwards. Coghlan then saw tracer fire passing over his wing and, pulling up and throttling back, he forced his attackers to overshoot. This manoeuvre placed him above and behind a pair of Bf 109s on which he dived, seeing his fire hit both of them in the vicinity of the engine. He was then attacked head-on by a third Bf 109 and so could not press home his advantage. The Bf 110 was assessed as probably destroyed and the Bf 109s as damaged. After this combat Coghlan reported that by lowering ten to fifteen degrees of flap, he could better outmanoeuvre the enemy fighters, with no appreciable loss of speed.

Flight Lieutenant Gracie, on finding that he could not dive through the fighter escort to reach the bombers, instead led his section against the circle of Bf 110s. Opening fire on one of these from about 200 yards range, he saw parts of the tail break away and a crew member bale out, before it spun down out of control. Gracie's Hurricane was then hit and its engine damaged. He managed to bring it back to the vicinity of Manston before the engine seized and he crash-landed on the airfield. The only other pilot to claim was Sergeant C. Whitehead, flying as Blue 3 in Gracie' section. He fired all of his ammunition into a Bf 110 and it was seen to go down in flames.

The need to protect offshore shipping made it necessary for No. 56 Squadron to use a number of airfields near the coast as forward bases. On 12 July at first light it flew to Manston to carry out convoy patrols, returning to North Weald later in the morning. In the afternoon, nine aircraft patrolled from Rochford and then 'B' flight, after carrying out an east coast patrol from North Weald, landed back at Martlesham Heath. On the following day, again operating from Rochford, ten of the squadron's Hurricanes carried out a sweep over the Channel towards Calais. Flying Officer R. E. P. Brooker, who had taken over the lead when Flight Lieutenant Coghlan's R/T failed, sighted twelve Ju 87 Stukas crossing the French coast escorted by four Bf 109s. Ordering the squadron into sections line astern, he led them down on to the rear quarter of the dive-bomber formation from out of the sun. Brooker picked out the leading Ju 87 and opened fire in a continuous burst, closing from 300 yards to close range. Coghlan and Sergeant R. D. Baker saw this aircraft crash into the sea. As Brooker finished his attack, a bullet came through his Hurricane's cockpit canopy, wounding him slightly with splinters in the hand and legs. When the attack began, Flight Lieutenant Coghlan saw the Ju 87s jettison their bombs and commence a dive to sea level to evade the Hurricanes. The dive-bomber at which he was firing flew straight into the sea, as did Sergeant J. R. Cowsill's target. They were then attacked by the Bf 109 escort and Cowsill was shot down and killed. Sergeant J. J. Whitfield also failed to return from this combat. After outmanoeuvring his attacker, Coghlan saw a Bf 109 on the tail of a Hurricane and fired a long burst into it. He saw it fall into the sea.

Sergeant Baker fired a short burst at a Ju 87, which turned steeply to evade him. Baker then stall-turned, putting his Hurricane in a good attacking position behind and above the Ju 87. After a second short burst, white smoke poured from the engine of the enemy aircraft and it spiralled down out of control. Baker had not been troubled by the fighter escort and, finding no further targets, he flew back to the Kent coast. Over the Canterbury area, his Hurricane's engine began to run roughly and he had to make a crash-landing in a corn field. Pilot Officer Page fired on two Ju 87s without apparent result and, seeing a Hurricane under attack from a Bf 109, broke away to engage the enemy fighter. As his tracer ammunition flew all around the Bf 109, it half-rolled and dived for the sea, but Page could not see what happened to it because he was attacked by a second enemy fighter. However, Coghlan reported seeing the Bf 109 crash and on the strength of his evidence Page was awarded a confirmed victory.

Sergeant G. Smythe fired all his ammunition into a Ju 87, which dived steeply for the water. He then lost sight of it, but believed it to have crashed. Squadron Leader Manton and Sergeant P. Hillwood also claimed dive-bombers destroyed. The squadron's claims were therefore for seven Ju 87s destroyed (two of them confirmed victories) and two Bf 109s destroyed (one confirmed). Luftwaffe reported casualties were in fact only two Ju 87Bs, from II Gruppe, Stukageschwader 1, while the fighter escort, Bf 109Es of Jagdgeschwader 51's 4. Staffel, apparently escaped unscathed.

On 14 July ten of the squadron's Hurricanes patrolled from Manston, landing back at Rochford and then returning to North Weald. They saw no action. The following day appeared to be even less propitious, with low cloud and heavy rain over southern Britain, but the Luftwaffe dispatched fifteen Do 17Z bombers of Kampfgeschwader 2 to attack Convoy 'Pilot' steaming off

Harwich. Forewarned by radar, Hurricanes of No. 56 and No. 151 Squadrons were sent up from North Weald to cover the convoy. Blue Section of No. 56 Squadron, led by Flight Lieutenant Gracie, made contact as the Do 17Zs were bombing. Visibility was about only two miles and so the Hurricanes had little opportunity to follow up their initial attack on the bombers. Gracie and Flight Sergeant F. W. Higginson each claimed a probable victory, but no German losses were reported from this combat. The third member of Blue Section was Pilot Officer M. H. Constable-Maxwell, whose elder brother had served with distinction in No. 56 Squadron during the First World War. Wounded during a sortie over France on 8 June, Constable-Maxwell had only returned to the squadron on 9 July. Wing Commander Constable-Maxwell recalls that his main impressions as a junior pilot on No 56 Squadron were the lack of thought given to fighter tactics and the reluctance of the various squadrons to exchange information. He was given very little chance to practice gunnery, which was of course one of the basic skills of the fighter pilot. He remembers that his brother, Gerald, was appalled that so many of the lessons of the First World War had been forgotten and thought that too much emphasis was placed on close formation flying, which was of no use in combat.

Gracie was again in action early on the morning of 20 July, when Blue Section were vectored on to a Ju 88 off Burnham, the controller's instructions resulting in a perfect interception. On sighting the Hurricanes, the enemy aircraft dived for cloud, but before it could reach their cover Gracie opened the attack. He fired all his ammunition in a single long burst, while closing in from 400 to 200 yards. Blue 2, Pilot Officer Page, then followed up, seeing his fire hit before the Ju 88 disappeared into cloud. Flying Officer P. S. Weaver (Blue 3) then picked it up below cloud and chased it in a north-easterly direction. As he did not appear to be gaining, he gave it a 2-second burst from 600 yards – well outside effective range. The Ju 88 then carried out a series of gentle turns from side to side, an unnecessary manoeuvre since it then slowed up allowing the Hurricane to catch it. When Weaver had closed the range to 250 yards, he opened fire again and used up all his ammunition. The German mid-upper gunner was still in action at this time, having hit both Weaver's and Page's Hurricanes but inflicting only slight damage. Weaver therefore broke away and lost contact with the Ju 88. Shortly afterwards, control notified the section that it had come down in the sea. In fact, the Ju 88, a reconnaissance aircraft from 4.(F)/122, had crashed at St Osyth and the four crew were taken prisoner. Weaver, whose nickname on the squadron was 'Squeak', had only recently returned to operational flying after a period of duty as a controller in the North Weald sector operations room.

Operating from Rochford on 25 July, No. 56 Squadron was sent to the assistance of the destroyers HMS *Boreas* and *Brilliant* off Dover. These two warships were engaging German E-boats in the Straits when they came under attack from dive-bombers. Squadron Leader Manton led his nine Hurricanes down to engage the Ju 87s, but they were too late to prevent the bombing. Pilot Officer Mounsdon saw the Stuka at which he was firing catch fire and crash into the sea, but he was unable to get confirmation of this victory. Pilot Officer Page singled out another Ju 87 and fired off all his ammunition in two long bursts. The enemy aircraft was making gentle turns from side to side, in order to give the rear gunner a field of fire astern unobstructed by the tail fin. Page noticed return fire passing to one side of his Hurricane. He then saw flames spurt from the Ju 87's engine, but as he was closing in fast he had to pull up and over the enemy aircraft to avoid a collision. Mounsden and Pilot Officer F. B. Sutton saw this Ju 87 go into the sea in flames. Sutton, after firing on one Stuka and then losing it as it broke away, gave chase to a second. He fired a long burst, which silenced the rear gunner, and the Ju 87 then carried out a series of steep turns in an attempt to lose him. This gave Sutton the chance of deflection shots from short range and the second of these caused the Stuka to turn on to its side and crash into the sea. This was witnessed by Flight Sergeant C. J. Cooney.

Flight Lieutenant Gracie fired on a Ju 87 flying at low level and was able to use the splash marks of his fire hitting the water to correct his aim. The enemy aircraft was hit and went into the sea. Yellow Section, flying in the middle of the squadron formation, had remained above to occupy the attention of the German fighter escort. Flying Officer Brooker, by skidding his Hurricane and then throttling back, managed to turn the tables on a Bf 109 which was on his tail. He gave it a 5-second burst, seeing his de Wilde incendiary bullets hit and the enemy aircraft dive away streaming white smoke, but could only claim it as damaged. For the next ten minutes he was engaged by pairs of Bf 109s diving on him from above. In each case he tried to meet their attacks head-on and escaped unscathed. On landing back at Rochford, his ammunition exhausted, he had only ten gallons of fuel remaining. The squadron had claimed four Ju 87s destroyed (two of these confirmed), plus a Bf 109 damaged, and their only casualty was Squadron Leader Manton, who was slightly wounded and his Hurricane damaged.

At dawn on 29 July the squadron flew to Rochford and during an early morning patrol over the Kent coast, they were warned of the approach of a raid fifty plus strong. R/T reception was very bad, however, and it was not until Blue 1, Flying Officer Weaver, spotted a dogfight over the sea to the east of Dover that the squadron could make contact with the enemy. During the combat that followed, Weaver was the only pilot able to make a claim. Seeing a Bf 109 on the tail of a Hurricane, he closed in to engage the enemy fighter, but he was too late to prevent it opening fire and the RAF fighter was hit and streamed white smoke. This may have been the aircraft of Flight Sergeant C. J. Cooney, who was shot down and killed in this combat. When Weaver was within 400 yards of the Bf 109, he fired a short burst and this caused it to turn away from the Hurricane. He then closed in to short range, firing intermittent bursts as the enemy fighter – twisting from side to side in an attempt to evade him – crossed his sights. He saw coolant fluid stream back from the Bf 109 and shortly afterwards it burst into flames. Weaver then had to break away to out-manoeuvre an enemy aircraft on his tail, but Sergeant Hillwood and Sergeant Smythe both confirmed that the Bf 109 was in flames. Pilot Officer Mounsdon's Hurricane was hit by enemy fire, but he was able to land the damaged fighter and was himself unhurt.

During early August, there followed a lull in Fighter Command's operations during which No. 56 Squadron saw no action at all. On 8 August Flight Lieutenant Coghlan was posted to

RAF Ringway, near Manchester, where work was beginning on the creation of Britain's airborne forces. Flying Officer Weaver was then promoted to the rank of acting flight lieutenant to fill the flight commander vacancy. During a convoy patrol on 11 August the squadron lost Sergeant R. D. Baker. He had become separated from the formation and was attacked and shot down, apparently by a Spitfire. His fellow pilots saw Baker bale out, and Weaver circled the pilot to mark his position in the water, but he was dead when the rescuers reached him an hour later. On a later patrol that day, the squadron sighted and chased a formation of Do 17Zs, but were unable to overtake them. Wing Commander Beamish, the North Weald station commander, was flying with them on that occasion.

Fighter Command's coastal airfields, including Manston, Hawkinge, and Lympne, were heavily attacked on the afternoon of 12 August. At about 1830 hours No. 56 Squadron's twelve Hurricanes were sent up from Rochford and they intercepted a force of 27 Do 17Zs, escorted by about forty Bf 109s, heading for Manston. The three leading sections of Hurricanes deployed in echelon right formation and dived from out of the sun on to the rear quarter of the bomber formation. Yellow Section, at the rear, attempted to divert the attention of the Bf 109s, which were flying above the Do 17Zs at between 18,000 and 30,000 feet. Pilot Officer A. G. Page, flying as No. 3 in Blue Section, followed Flight Lieutenant Gracie in to attack the bombers. His Hurricane was hit by their concentrated return fire, fuel in the tank ahead of the cockpit ignited and Page struggled to bale out from a blazing inferno. He succeeded in getting clear and parachuted to the sea, where he was picked up by a coaster.

Page had suffered very serious burns to his hands and face and spent the next two years in hospital recovering. In 1943 he returned to operational flying and finished the war as a wing commander with fifteen victories to his credit. His experience showed one of the Hurricane's most serious weaknesses as an operational fighter. For whereas the aircraft's two main fuel tanks in the wings had been covered with self-sealing material, the reserve fuel tank in the fuselage was unprotected at this time. As a result, many Hurricane pilots suffered serious injury from burns which could have been avoided if a relatively simple modification (later incorporated into the aircraft) had been made.

Innes Westmacott recalled that 'we were all highly conscious of the menace of fire, but some persisted in taking the line that "it can't happen to me" and refused to do anything about it. They were the ones who received the worst injuries when it did happen. I always covered as much of my flesh as possible. I wore goggles, gauntlets, gloves and boots. Moreover, as the Hurricane Mk I had no means of jettisoning the cockpit cover in an emergency, I always locked it in the open position just before going into action and put up with the resulting draught. I did not fancy having a bullet through one of the rails on which it ran, which could so easily jam it in the closed position and thus prevent me from baling out if necessary. Moreover, if the cover was already open, less time was needed to abandon the aircraft if necessary. I personally knew of a number of cases where pilots had been forced to make a crash-landing because they could not slide back the hood, and it needed little imagination to realize what would have happened to them if the aircraft had caught fire. My precautions paid off handsomely when the time came for me, for I left the aeroplane very quickly and my burns were nothing like as serious as they might have been.'

Flight Sergeant Higginson, Green 1, led his section in behind Gracie's and, picking out a Do 17Z on the extreme left of the German formation, Higginson fired a series of short bursts aimed at the bomber's engines. He broke away at 150 yards range, as return fire hit his Hurricane, damaging the cockpit area and wings. He reported that the Do 17Z's port engine was smoking and his No. 3, Pilot Officer Sutton, confirmed this. Sutton's Hurricane too was hit by return fire and he had to force-land at Manston, narrowly missing the bomb craters from an earlier raid. Flight Lieutenant Weaver attacked a Do 17Z from directly astern, firing his opening burst from 400 yards in order to avoid the intense return fire. Seeing no effect from this, he closed the range to 200 yards and fired off the rest of his ammunition. The enemy aircraft began to smoke and Pilot Officer C. C. O. Joubert and Flying Officer I. B.

Westmacott, flying in Weaver's Section, saw it go out of control and explode in the air.

Initially, all that Yellow Section could do to deal with the enemy fighters was to fire across their noses at long range, as they dived to attack the leading Hurricanes. Sergeant G. Smythe, Yellow 2, then climbed to attack one of the Bf 109s and saw his de Wilde incendiary ammunition hitting its wings. The German pilot jettisoned his cockpit canopy and the Bf 109 plunged down pouring blue smoke. Sergeant Hillwood saw it hit the sea. Smythe, a man of an inventive turn of mind, had modified his Hurricane's ammunition tanks to increase their capacity by 400 rounds. The combat had been a fierce one, for in addition to the loss of Pilot Officer Page, no fewer than seven Hurricanes had been damaged by enemy fire.

On the afternoon of 13 August, the Luftwaffe's *Adler Tag* (Eagle Day), No. 56 Squadron was scrambled from Rochford and ordered to patrol over Manston at 10,000 feet. On reaching 5,000 feet, however, they were told that enemy aircraft were approaching Rochford. They climbed through a layer of 10/10th cloud and found themselves beneath a formation of bombers, escorted by about thirty Bf 110s. Flight Lieutenant Gracie, leading the squadron, turned to the right, intending to climb for height into the sun. On looking round, though, he saw four Bf 110s diving in line astern on to his tail. Pulling round to the left, Gracie found himself in the middle of the enemy fighters, which were circling around him. He fired a burst at one, which appeared to be hit and broke away. He then took a snap shot at a stray bomber which passed across his sights, before finishing off his ammunition in a full deflection burst against a second Bf 110. He was then attacked from behind and dived for the cover of the clouds. Sergeant Hillwood, Blue 3, picked out one of the attacking Bf 110s and followed it down to the cloud layer into which it disappeared with one engine streaming white smoke. Climbing back up, Hillwood took a deflection shot at a Bf 110 and was then attacked from head-on by a third twin-engined fighter. 'His cannon shots more or less blew me out of the sky,' Hillwood reported. He abandoned his crippled Hurricane at 12,000 feet, but delayed opening his parachute until he had entered cloud at 6,000 feet. Landing in the sea 2½ miles off Sheerness, Hillwood saw no immediate prospect of rescue and so swam to the shore. He was in the water for about two hours, but found himself none the worse for the experience.

Blue 2, Pilot Officer Sutton, broke away from his section before it was attacked by Bf 110s and climbed in the sun to the level of the main formation of escort fighters. By that time, they had formed their usual defensive circle, but Sutton was able to pick out a straggler. The enemy aircraft dived beneath him and passed behind, but Sutton turned and followed it down to the cloud tops, firing most of his ammunition. The Bf 110 appeared to be out of control and Pilot Officer Mounsdon was able to confirm Sutton's claim. During this engagement, Sutton found that even when he used emergency boost the Hurricane was constantly outclimbed by the Bf 110. Green Section, led by Flying Officer P. F. M. Davies, instead of climbing to engage the Bf 110s, pursued the bombers, but before they could engage, they were attacked by Bf 109s and Davies baled out of his Hurricane with serious burns. Flight Lieutenant Weaver, leading 'A' Flight behind Gracie, climbed to attack the Bf 110s' main formation. Seeing a Bf 110 getting on to the tail of his No. 3, Pilot Officer Joubert, he pulled his Hurricane up into a steep climb and opened fire on Joubert's attacker. Just before his aircraft stalled and fell away, Weaver saw the Hurricane dive away streaming glycol. Joubert was forced to bale out and landed at Faversham in Kent, slightly wounded by cannon splinters in the leg. Weaver then attacked two more Bf 110s and the second went vertically downwards into cloud with both engines on fire. This victory was confirmed by Pilot Officer B. J. Wicks.

Red 2, Pilot Officer Mounsdon, climbed in the sun to 15,000 feet and then dived into the circle of Bf 110s. He only had time for a short burst at one from the quarter, before he was attacked from behind and had to break away. Climbing above the Bf 110s again, he saw that they had broken out of the circle and were heading for France in line astern. He closed in on the rearmost and finished his ammunition against it. The Bf 110 dived vertically into the clouds with its starboard engine smoking. Mounsdon then had to evade two enemy fighters on his tail and so lost sight of his target. Flying

Officer Westmacott also sent a Bf 110 diving into the clouds and it was assessed as damaged. Flying Officer Brooker's Hurricane was damaged in this combat and he wrecked it in a forced-landing at Hawkinge. In return for four Hurricanes lost and one pilot seriously wounded, No. 56 Squadron claimed three Bf 110s destroyed and a further six damaged.

Although 15 August was a day of heavy fighting for Fighter Command, No. 56 Squadron made no contact with the enemy. At 0515 hours on the following day the squadron once again flew to Rochford. Shortly after noon a section patrol was 'bounced' by Bf 109s and Pilot Officer L. W. Graham, slightly injured, was forced to bale out of his Hurricane. However, the main action of the day was not fought until after the squadron had returned to North Weald. At 1651 hours it was ordered up to patrol Chatham at 15,000 feet and then, shortly after take-off, was vectored on to a raid approaching the Thames estuary.

Flight Lieutenant Gracie was to have led the squadron, but his R/T failed and so Flight Lieutenant Weaver took over the lead. Emerging from a cloud layer at 6,000 feet, the squadron sighted a formation of 37 Do 17Z bombers flying above them at 15,000 feet, with an escort of a similar number of Bf 109s higher still. Weaver led Red and Yellow Sections up to attack the bombers, ordering Blue and Green Sections to protect them from the fighters. Forming echelon right, Red Section levelled out 600 yards behind the rearmost Do 17Zs and the three Hurricanes attacked together. Weaver saw his fire hitting a bomber, which jettisoned its bomb load but maintained formation. On breaking away, he was attacked by a Bf 109 and dived through cloud to evade it. He then sighted a straggling Do 17Z, which had already been attacked by Sergeant Whitehead, and his fire set the port wing alight. The enemy aircraft crashed into the sea and both Whitehead and Pilot Officer B. J. Wicks were able to confirm its destruction. Sergeant P. E. M. Robinson, flying as Red 3, saw the bomber he was firing at break away from the German formation. He then lost sight of it, but this may well have been the straggler finished off by his section leader. Flying Officer Brooker, Yellow 1, also fired on a bomber in the rearmost section of three. He saw his bullets hitting its port engine and reported that this vic had then broken up.

As Brooker began his attack on the bombers, enemy fighters dived steeply on to the Hurricanes' tails. His No. 3, Pilot Officer Wicks, turned into their attack and followed one Bf 109 down, but it was going too fast for him to catch and he switched his attack to a straggling Do 17Z. This bomber was already being engaged by a Hurricane, but as the RAF fighter broke away Wicks went into the attack. He saw his fire hit and the Do 17Z went vertically into the clouds, being assessed as probably destroyed. Flight Lieutenant Gracie, who despite his defective R/T had heard Weaver's instructions to engage the enemy fighters, led Blue Section up to 14,000 feet. He then took a snap shot at a Bf 109, which was breaking away from its attack on the leading Hurricanes. Another Bf 109 had got on to a Hurricane's tail and Gracie closed in to extremely short range behind this enemy fighter, opening fire at 200 yards. Its engine belched white smoke, the propeller windmilled and the Bf 109 dived inverted into the clouds. Gracie tried to follow, but his throttle had stuck in the open position. He therefore had great difficulty in recovering from his dive and lost sight of his victim. Pilot Officer Sutton picked out a pair of enemy fighters and sent the first diving into the clouds trailing smoke. He turned his attention to the second and saw his fire hit, but then had to break away to evade further Bf 109s.

Sergeant Smythe followed one of the Bf 109s on its breakaway from attacking the leading sections. Closing to within 200 yards, he saw white smoke pour from the enemy fighter and it dived into the clouds. Smythe then finished off his ammunition on a stray bomber, which appeared to have been damaged in an earlier attack. Green Section, led by Flight Sergeant Higginson, was unable to keep up with Gracie's section and so turned away from the German fighters to engage straggling bombers. Higginson followed a Do 17Z down through the clouds, his fire setting the bomber alight. He then saw it crash on the shore near Whitstable. His Hurricane must have been hit by return fire, for its engine then burst into flames and Higginson had to crash-land south of Whitstable. His aircraft, which was completely burned out, was the squadron's only casualty, in return for claims of two bombers confirmed destroyed, one probable and three damaged, with a further three enemy fighters assessed as probably destroyed.

No. 56 Squadron fought two actions on 18 August, the day of greatest combined looses for both the RAF and the Luftwaffe. At 1250 hours the squadron was ordered to take-off and patrol Canterbury. Flying at about 20,000 feet in the vicinity of Ashford 55 minutes later, they met five Bf 110s approaching from the south at a slightly lower altitude. The squadron was ordered into line astern and went into the attack. As soon as the enemy fighters realized their danger, they attempted to form a defensive circle, but this was easily broken up by the Hurricanes. All five enemy aircraft were claimed as destroyed, the successful pilots seeing the victims crash in all instances. Pilot Officer P. D. M. Down, Pilot Officer Mounsdon, Sergeant Robinson and Flight Lieutenant Weaver were each credited with a Bf 110 confirmed destroyed, while Flying Officer Westmacott and Sergeant Whitehead shared the fifth. Reported German casualties for Zerstörergeschwader 26 on this day identify at least three of the squadron's victims in this combat.

At 1707 hours the squadron was scrambled from Rochford with orders to patrol Manston. They were then vectored on to a large escorted bomber formation flying north of the estuary, making contact at about 1730 hours. This comprised some fifty He 111s of Kampfgeschwader 53, with a close escort of about 25 Bf 109s provided by Zerstörergeschwader 26, and they were bound for No. 56 Squadron's home base at North Weald. The Hurricanes had to chase the enemy formation from astern before they could engage. Squadron Leader Manton, flying as Red 1 in the leading section, decided that as his three Hurricanes were at a greater height they should engage the Bf 110s to clear the way for the following sections to reach the bombers. The CO fired at one Bf 110 without apparent effect and then had to break away to evade an attack on his Hurricane. Climbing back to the fight, he noticed about ten Bf 110s in a circle and attacked them from out of the sun. The circle broke up and Manton selected one Bf 110 and fired his remaining ammunition into it. He last saw it diving away with smoke pouring from both engines. Pilot Officer Moundsdon, flying as Red 2, fired on three different Bf 110s, but on each occasion had to break away when his own fighter was attacked. He did see his fire hitting the third enemy aircraft, however, and one of its engines began to smoke.

Flight Lieutenant Weaver led Yellow Section beneath the escort fighters to attack the rearmost section of He 111s. He saw his bomber begin to burn and break away from the German formation. He then had to take violent evasive action to shake off a Bf 110 from his tail and then skirmished with several of the escort fighters until his ammunition ran out. However, Pilot Officer Moundsdon had seen Weaver's He 111 going down in flames and so he was awarded a confirmed victory. Sergeant Robinson, flying as Yellow 3, fired a 15-second burst into an He 111. The bomber began to smoke, but on breaking away Robinson lost sight of it and could only claim it as damaged. Flight Lieutenant Gracie, in attempting to lead Blue Section in to attack the bombers, was headed off by Bf 110s. He climbed to attack a higher group of bombers, but saw no effect from his fire. Blue Section was then set upon by large numbers of Bf 110s. Gracie sent one of these down in flames and his No. 2, Flying Officer Westmacott, damaged another. After finishing off his ammunition, Westmacott was attacked by three Bf 110s and had to carry out violent evasive manoeuvres to escape them.

The last three Hurricanes in the squadron formation, Green Section led by Flight Sergeant Higginson, began to climb towards the German fighters, but Higginson then saw an opportunity to attack the bombers and closed in on the rear of the He 111 formation. He was only given the chance of one burst of fire, before having to break away to evade fighter attack. He then saw the bomber, apparently on fire, break formation and dive; it crashed near Burnham. Sergeant Whitehead and Pilot Officer Down confirmed this claim. Higginson's Hurricane had been hit by enemy fire, but did not appear to be badly damaged. However, after he had landed, the starboard elevator control cable – which was all but shot through – parted completely. Effective though the efforts of the defending fighters had been, it was the build-up of cloud cover that ultimately forced the German bombers to turn away from their target, and North Weald – at least on this occasion – escaped unscathed.

After the intense activity of 18 August, poor weather intervened to give the defenders some respite during the next five days, although the Luftwaffe (as was its usual practice) took advantage of rain and cloud cover to mount scattered raids by single bombers or small formations. At 1615 hours on 21 August Flight Lieutenant Weaver and Flying Officer Brooker were carrying out an R/T test with the forward base at Martlesham Heath, when they were warned of an enemy aircraft in the vicinity. Weaver caught sight of the raider flying to the north of Ipswich and shortly afterwards the AA guns at RAF Wattisham opened fire on it. The Do 17Z then disappeared in cloud, but Flying Officer Brooker was able to regain contact with it. He closed in astern, opening fire at 200 yards' range and concentrating his aim on the starboard engine. Fire from the bomber's mid-upper gunner then hit the Hurricane's radiator and glycol fumes reached the cockpit, temporarily blinding Brooker. The engine began to run roughly and then seized. Brooker, his view forward obscured by oil on the windscreen, attempted a wheels-up landing, but he misjudged the approach and crashed into a hedgerow. The Hurricane was destroyed, but Brooker fortunately escaped with only slight injuries. His victim, a Do 17Z of 8 Staffel, Kampfgeschwader 2, crashed at Gippeswyk Park, Ipswich, and its crew were taken prisoner.

The Luftwaffe resumed its assault on 24 August, with reduced numbers of bombers operating under the protection of strengthened fighter escorts. That afternoon No. 56 Squadron at Rochford was late getting into the air, as no order to take-off was received. On hearing the air raid sirens in nearby Southend and the sound of enemy aircraft passing overhead, the Hurricanes scrambled. By then, though, they had no time to engage effectively as a squadron and their only successes were gained in isolated combats. Pilot Officer Wicks sighted a lone Bf 109 in the vicinity of Rochford and was able to get on its tail unobserved. He fired a 3-second burst at 300 yards' range and the enemy fighter took violent evasive action, but Wicks managed to stay behind it. He fired a second burst from 100 yards, closed in to thirty yards and nearly collided with the Bf 109 in the process. As he broke away, he saw the German pilot bale out and his aircraft crash. Not only was this corroborated by Sergeant Whitehead, but Pilot Officer E. D. Syson, the squadron's Intelligence Officer at Rochford airfield also saw the enemy pilot's parachute coming down.

Flight Lieutenant Weaver, Yellow 1, and his No. 2, Pilot Officer Mounsdon, became separated from the squadron soon after take-off. They attempted to reach a high-flying enemy formation, but without success, and then sighted two bomber formations 3,000 feet below them at 12,000 feet. Using the sun to mask his approach, Weaver overtook one of these and launched an attack on an He 111 flying on the left of the formation. Opening fire at 250 yards he closed in to thirty yards before breaking away. The German bomber fell out of formation, two of its crew took to their parachutes, and Pilot Officer Mounsdon saw it crash in the sea. Mounsdon then followed up Weaver's attack on the He 111s, seeing white smoke come from the engine of the bomber at which he had fired. Flight Lieutenant Weaver then finished off his ammunition against this aircraft from long range, but with no apparent effect. Both pilots commented on the intensity of the bombers' defensive fire and Weaver's Hurricane was damaged, a bullet passing through the wing spars, oil and petrol tanks.

Pilot Officer Marston, who had dropped behind the squadron formation when his engine overheated, had reached 10,000 feet when he saw a single Bf 109 passing 2,000 feet beneath him in the opposite direction. Marston turned and dived on to its tail without being seen, fired two bursts while closing from 250 yards to 50 yards, and saw the Bf 109 catch fire and crash about six miles south of Sheerness. Marston then had to return to Rochford, as his oil temperature was high. Late in the evening the squadron flew back to North Weald to find that the airfield had been bombed while they were away. Considerable damage had been done, but fortunately none of it seriously impaired the station's operational efficiency.

During its two engagements on 26 August No. 56 Squadron was unable to intercept the German bombers, but became entangled with the fighter escorts. At 1215 hours, when on patrol near Manston, the squadron sighted twelve Do 17Zs escorted by about thirty Bf 109s, but could not catch up with the bombers before the Bf 109s intervened. Pilot Officer Mounsdon saw a group of German fighters positioning themselves for a stern attack and turned towards them. He then noticed another Bf 109 flying below him and pounced on it. After two bursts of fire, the Bf 109 dived vertically into the sea off Whitstable. Pilot Officer Marston also managed to get on the tail of a Bf 109. He saw hits on the wing radiator and engine, and the German pilot prepared to bale out. The Bf 109 then dived steeply into cloud and Marston followed it down, but did not see it crash because his attention was diverted by a second Bf 109 which was diving on the tail of a Boulton Paul Defiant turret fighter. Marston quickly positioned himself behind the enemy fighter, just as the Defiant made a wheels-up crash-landing. He fired a short burst and the Bf 109 crashed within 100 yards of its victim.

No. 264 Squadron lost three Defiants that day, including that of Sergeant E. R. Thorne and Sergeant F. J. Barker whose aircraft Marston saw crash-land. This crew, apparently unaware of the Hurricane's attack, themselves claimed to have shot down the Bf 109 as they went down. At the end of the month Defiants were withdrawn from daylight operations, since their losses in combat had been prohibitive. The Bf 109s shot down two of No. 56 Squadron's Hurricanes, but both pilots survived. Pilot Officer Wicks baled out near Canterbury, while Sergeant Smythe (who a week earlier had been awarded the DFM) wrecked his fighter in a forced-landing near Foulness.

At 1525 hours in the vicinity of Colchester the squadron intercepted an escorted bomber formation which formed part of a large raid directed against the Sector stations of Hornchurch, North Weald and Debden. Although No. 56 squadron was headed off from the bombers by their Bf 110 escorts, the defenders were generally successful in turning back the bombers and only a small force penetrated to attack Debden. As Zerstörergeschwader 26's Bf 110s came down to attack the squadron, Flying Officer Westmacott broke away and climbed in the sun to 20,000 feet. He was then just above the German fighters and was able to engage them as they withdrew. He got on to the tail of the rearmost Bf 110 and fired a 4-second burst. It pulled up in a steep climbing turn to the right, but Westmacott was able to follow. He fired again and the Bf 110's port engine began to smoke. It went down in a near vertical dive and Westmacott fired a third time, hitting the starboard engine. The German fighter did not pull out, but crashed in the vicinity of Marks Tey.

Flight Sergeant Higginson also climbed with the sun behind him to reach the Bf 110s at 20,000 feet. Levelling off 2,000 feet below them, he put his section into line astern and then pulled up to attack a Bf 110 from astern and below. Its port engine was disabled and Higginson's Hurricane was smeared with oil from the Bf 110. After breaking away from his first attack, Higginson saw the disabled Bf 110 retreating over the coast, but he was too far away to resume the attack. Pilot Officer Sutton, after following Higginson in to attack the Bf 110s, broke away since he found that they consistently outclimbed him. He then dived after what he thought was a Bf 109, but lost it in cloud. Finding himself astern of another Bf 110, he attacked it and saw it crash near Tendring, east of Colchester. Flying Officer Westmacott confirmed this victory.

On 27 August the Luftwaffe mounted only small-scale raids and reconnaissance missions. Shortly after noon, Flight Lieutenant Gracie and Flying Officer Westmacott, flying in a two-aircraft section, intercepted a Do 17 in the vicinity of Dover. As he went into the attack, Gracie noticed three Hurricanes breaking away from the enemy aircraft, but apparently without having damaged it. He then closed in to 150 yards' range, firing all his ammunition in a continuous burst and seeing many hits. Flying Officer Westmacott then took over the attack and saw three of the crew bale out. The German aircraft went into the sea eight miles short of the French coast.

At 1228 hours on 28 August No. 56 Squadron was scrambled from North Weald and ordered to patrol Rochford at 15,000 feet. This forward base had already been attacked by a morning raid and was again threatened. Squadron Leader Manton, leading thirteen Hurricanes, intercepted a formation of thirty Do 17Zs (from

Kampfgeschwader 2) with a similar number of escorting fighters flying above and behind, which were approaching over the estuary. Splitting his formation, Manton led Red and Green Sections against the Bf 109s, while Yellow and Blue Sections attacked the bombers. The CO got on to the tail of one fighter and, opening fire from 200 yards, saw his de Wilde ammunition exploding on its fuselage. The Bf 109 dived away steeply and was credited to Manton as a probable victory. He made further attacks on two German fighters without seeing any result and then radioed details of the enemy raid to North Weald control. Under a new procedure, introduced on 26 August, formation leaders were required to provide this information to supplement reports from the Observer Corps.

Flight Sergeant Higginson, Green 1, put his Section into line astern and watched the German fighters cross over the top of the bombers and dive on to Yellow and Blue Sections. He then pounced on them and picking out the leading Bf 109, sent it spinning down into the sea. Green 2, Sergeant Hillwood, attacked the second German fighter and sent it down smoking. Pilot Officer Constable-Maxwell, Green 3, saw further Bf 109s coming in behind them and so turned to engage. Following one fighter in a climbing turn, he fired two bursts into it and saw it go down pouring white smoke. He reported that he could hold the Bf 109 in the climb and, by making a tighter radius turn, gain on it. Shortly afterwards, Constable-Maxwell's engine began to run roughly and he had to make a forced-landing near Herne Bay, wrecking his Hurricane but fortunately escaping without serious injury to himself.

Flight Lieutenant Weaver, Yellow 1, opened the attack on the Do 17Z formation, firing at the rearmost bomber from close range. His Hurricane was hit by return fire and Weaver had to break off the action and force-land near Eastchurch. Sergeant Robinson, Yellow 3, followed up Weaver's attack, seeing his fire hit the Do 17Z. Robinson's Hurricane was also damaged by the German gunners and, seeing Bf 109s behind him, he decided to break away. Although ground observers at Eastchurch told Flight Lieutenant Weaver that this bomber had gone down, niether he nor Robinson were confident that they had destroyed it and so only claimed it as damaged. The third member of Yellow Section, Pilot Officer Down, was unable to reach the bombers before he was attacked by Bf 109s. He fired on two of these and saw the second go down into the sea off Herne Bay. Flight Lieutenant Gracie ordered Blue Section into echelon port formation and followed Yellow Section in to attack the bombers. Gracie selected the leader of the rearmost bomber section and saw it break away after his first burst of fire. He then pursued it down to sea level, making five or six attacks on it in all, and saw it go into the water about three miles north-east of Margate. His claim was confirmed by Pilot Officer Wicks and Pilot Officer Marston.

Sergeant Whitehead, Blue 3, celebrating the award of a DFM the previous week, attacked a Do 17Z and set its port engine alight, claiming it as probably destroyed. His own fighter was slightly damaged by return fire. In return for one Hurricane destroyed and three damaged (two of these only slightly), No. 56 Squadron had claimed three German aircraft destroyed, four probably destroyed and one damaged. More significantly, Rochford had escaped serious damage and continued to be used as a forward base.

Later that afternoon, the Luftwaffe carried out large-scale fighter sweeps over Kent and the Thames estuary. At about 1700 hours, No. 56 Squadron sighted twenty Bf 109s at 20,000 feet in the vicinity of Dover. Flying slightly below them at 18,000 feet, the squadron climbed to engage. Before the Hurricanes could reach their height, the Bf 109s broke off in pairs and dived to attack them and a series of individual dogfights ensued. Flight Lieutenant Weaver carried out a beam attack on a Bf 109 and saw its pilot bale out. Sergeant Smythe got on to the tails of a pair of fighters, but could not close the gap and they pulled away from him. He fired several bursts from long range and then was himself attacked from the rear. One shell passed through the top of his cockpit canopy, penetrated the armoured windscreen and finally pierced the fuselage fuel tank. Smythe was drenched in petrol and nearly overcome by the fumes, but fortunately there was no fire. He managed to bale out and landed near Hawkinge airfield. There he was told that ground observers had seen the pilot bale out from the

Bf 109 he had attacked. Pilot Officer F. B. Sutton was less fortunate. Surprised by an attack from astern, his fuselage tank exploded and Sutton was badly burned before he could parachute from his blazing fighter.

Twelve Hurricanes of No. 56 Squadron scrambled from North Weald at 1625 hours on 30 August and, together with No. 151 Squadron, intercepted an enemy raid heading for the airield. In fact the German bombers passed right over North Weald without attacking. The raid, comprising He 111s (from Kampfgeschwader 53) and Bf 110 escort fighters, went on to bomb Luton, apparently in error as their briefed target was Radlett. As Flight Lieutenant Gracie led the Hurricanes up to engage east of North Weald, the rapidly climbing fighters spread out and so they had to attack individually rather than in squadron formation. Gracie carried out a beam attack on the He 111 formation and saw two bombers break away. He chased one of these, finishing off his ammunition on it, and finally saw it crash three miles east of Halstead. The other He 111 turned back for home with one engine disabled. Gracie then had to crash-land his Hurricane, when the engine – damaged by return fire – ground to a halt. His aircraft burned out and Gracie, who made light of his ordeal, was believed to be unhurt. It was only two days later that it was discovered that he had broken his neck in the crash. Flying Officer Brooker also had to crash-land his Hurricane, but escaped unhurt. Several of the squadron pilots shared in the destruction of a second He 111 and the gallant Wing Commander Beamish, flying with No. 56 Squadron, attacked several enemy aircraft and claimed a Bf 110 probably destroyed.

Pilot Officer Westmacott was attacked by three or four Bf 110s before he could reach the bombers. He turned sharply to the right and got on to the tail of one of them. His fire hit the port engine, but Westmacott then had to break away to evade another attack by Bf 110s. On regaining height, he met a stray Bf 110 in the vicinity of Brentwood. He fired two long bursts into it and saw it go down in flames. Pilot Officer N. Hart of No. 242 Squadron was able to confirm this aircraft as destroyed. Pilot Officer Wicks fired on an He 111 in the rear section of the enemy formation, apparently without effect. He then broke away and was about to deliver a second attack on the He 111s, when two Bf 110s came in at him head-on. Wicks evaded their attack and then saw a Bf 110 diving past him with a Hurricane on its tail. As the British fighter broke away, Wicks continued the attack. After a 2-second burst 'everything seemed to fall off the enemy aircraft' and he saw the pilot bale out. The other Hurricane followed the Bf 110 down and, after it had crashed, Wicks noticed a third Hurricane circling the wreckage. Wicks was credited with the Bf 110 destroyed, but almost certainly this should properly have been regarded as a shared victory.

It was in this way that claims, made in perfect good faith, could be duplicated or triplicated. However, what was most important was that the German raid had been met in strength by Fighter Command and in the process they had destroyed six of Kampfgeschwader 53's He 111s, damaged a further two and knocked down at least three of the escorting Bf 110s.

On the morning of 31 August No. 56 Squadron was again scrambled to defend North Weald and the airfield really was one of the Luftwaffe's targets for that day, although the brunt of their attack was borne by Debden. They took off at 0820 hours and twenty minutes later intercepted a formation of about fifteen Do 17Zs, accompanied by nearly 100 Bf 110 and Bf 109 escort fighters, in the vicinity of Colchester. In attempting to engage the bombers, the Hurricanes became entangled with the fighters and suffered heavy losses. Flight Lieutenant P. S. Weaver, whose award of the DFC was announced that day, was shot down and killed. Pilot Officer Mounsdon and Flying Officer Westmacott were shot down and injured, while Sergeant Whitehead was forced to bale out but escaped unhurt. Only Flight Sergeant Higginson was able to inflict any damage on the enemy in return. Flying as usual as Green 1, he led his section into a beam attack on the bombers and then turned to attack the fighter escort. He picked out a Bf 109 and opened fire. It climbed steeply, pouring white smoke, and then dived straight into the ground between Colchester and Chelmsford. Higginson saw the pilot bale out, and his victory was later confirmed by the local military authorities.

Weaver's death was a great loss to the squadron and it created a serious gap among its tactical leaders. For Gracie had by then been admitted to hospital with a broken neck, thus removing both experienced flight commanders. Moreover, on the day that Weaver was lost Squadron Leader Manton was posted away to command RAF Station, Hawkinge and was succeeded by Squadron Leader H. M. Pinfold. Flying Officer Brooker was promoted to the rank of acting flight lieutenant to fill one of the flight commander positions; the other remained vacant until 10 September, when Flight Lieutenant R. S. J. Edwards was posted in from HQ No. 11 Group. Under these circumstances, it was essential to give the squadron a breathing-space, so that its new commanders had an opportunity to settle in and replacement pilots could be trained up to operational standards. Accordingly, it was arranged that the squadron should change places with No. 249 Squadron, a Hurricane unit based at Boscombe Down, Wiltshire, in No. 10 Group. On 1 September No. 56 Squadron flew to its new airfield and handed over its Hurricanes to No. 249 Squadron, taking over their aircraft in return. Initially, the changeover only involved the squadron's pilots. The groundcrews stayed on at North Weald to service No. 249 Squadron's aircraft until 24 September, when they rejoined the pilots at Boscombe Down.

For much of its first fortnight in No. 10 Group, No. 56 Squadron carried out intensive training, but its new station was

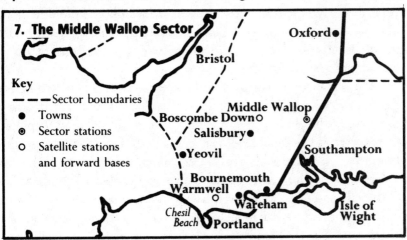

7. The Middle Wallop Sector

Key

— — — Sector boundaries
● Towns
◉ Sector stations
○ Satellite stations and forward bases

Oxford
Bristol
Middle Wallop
Boscombe Down
Salisbury
Yeovil
Southampton
Bournemouth
Warmwell
Wareham
Chesil Beach
Portland
Isle of Wight

by no means far removed from the air fighting. As a satellite airfield of the Middle Wallop Sector, not only was it responsible for the air defence of important targets in western England, but it was also liable to be called on to reinforce the No. 11 Group area. When, on 8 September, Dowding introduced his scheme of classifying units according to their operational commitments, No. 56 Squadron became a Category 'A' Squadron. This meant that it was to be maintained at full pilot strength and was regarded as a front-line fighting unit, rather than as a squadron responsible for training replacement pilots. Yet before it could resume its full operational commitments, the squadron had to assimilate a batch of untrained new pilots. Two Polish officers, Pilot Officer M. Chelmecki and Pilot Officer Z. Nosowicz, were posted in on 31 August and during the following week six pilots who had trained on Fairey Battle light bombers reported to the Squadron.

'Generally speaking, the new pilots we received during the Battle were fairly well trained', remarked Innes Westmacott, 'and all had done between 150 and 200 hours' flying, which included 20–30 hours on Hurricanes. We did our best to give them a certain amount of training flying before they went into action, although it was difficult to find time for this and when they flew operationally they were always put in a section with an experienced leader, at any rate to start with. They learned very quickly – they had to! Here I would point out that there is no substitute for combat experience. An experienced pilot with a lot of hours in his logbook did not necessarily make a good combat pilot straight away. He might become one, but so did many a young man who had only just completed his training.'

The squadron retained a core of experienced veterans of the Battle of France and the summer air combats around whom a new unit could be built. Among the officer pilots only Brooker, Constable-Maxwell and Wicks remained, but they were ably reinforced by the stalwart NCO pilots, Higginson, Hillwood, Smythe and Whitehead. It was the irrepressible Flight Sergeant 'Taffy' Higginson, a rugby-playing Welshman complete with extravagant handle-bar moustaches, who re-opened the squadron's score-card on 14 September. Ordered on patrol over Bournemouth at 1544 hours, Higginson met a Do 17Z flying at 10,000 feet above cloud. He immediately gave chase. firing a 2-second burst at 400 yards' range as the enemy aircraft disappeared into cloud. He then picked it up again and fired another short burst before losing it a second time. When it next reappeared, Higginson was able to get in an 8-second burst, closing the range from 400 to 150 yards. Both of the Do 17Z's engines began to smoke and it crashed into the sea and sank forty miles from land. Pilot Officer Constable-Maxwell, who was flying as Higginson's No. 2, was patrolling below cloud and so missed the action.

Constable-Maxwell was to have more success on 27 September, when the Luftwaffe raided the Parnall aircraft factory at Yate near Bristol. The attack was carried out by ten Bf 110 fighter-bombers of Erprobungsgruppe 210, escorted by forty Bf 110s of Zerstörergeschwader 26. As the raid approached the coast, No. 56 Squadron was scrambled at 1105 hours with orders to patrol Middle Wallop at 25,000 feet. It was then vectored towards the Isle of Wight, but missed the enemy aircraft crossing the coast. Redirected back towards Bristol, it could only engage the raiders as they withdrew. Constable-Maxwell had taken off with the squadron formation, but finding that his oxygen had failed, returned to base to have the defect remedied. He went off again at 1125 hours, but was unable to contact the squadron and so engaged the returning raiders independently about thirty miles west of base. Sighting a group of some 25 Bf 110s, he attacked an aircraft flying at the rear of the formation. His fire hit the Bf 110's port engine and the enemy aircraft lost height. Another Hurricane (believed to be that of Flight Lieutenant A. H. Rook of No. 504 Squadron) joined in the attack and the Bf 110 tried to force-land, but crashed in the attempt. Shortly afterwards, the other Hurricanes of No. 56 Squadron engaged the enemy and harried them over the coast and out to sea. Pilot Officer Marston claimed one Bf 110 destroyed and a second damaged.

Flight Sergeant Higginson attacked a Bf 110 and saw its port engine beginning to smoke. He followed it through a series of evasive climbs and dives, firing off the rest of his ammunition. Higginson then broke away and was attacked by a Bf 109 (fighters from Jagdgeschwader 2 and Jagdgeschwader 53 having been dispatched to meet the returning Bf 110s). Pilot Officer D. C. Mackenzie, one of the former Battle pilots who joined the squadron on 5 September, attacked a straggling Bf 110. He sent it down towards the sea with one engine disabled, but did not see it crash and so could only claim it as damaged. In all, five RAF squadrons engaged in this raid, claiming nineteen victories. The Luftwaffe's actual losses were ten Bf 110s destroyed.

On 29 September No. 56 Squadron began to use Warmwell in Dorset, a Middle Wallop satellite airfield, as a forward base. Its first day operating from there was uneventful. The squadron left for Warmwell at 0910 hours and at 1400 hours two Hurricanes were sent up after an X-plot raid but made no interception. The squadron then returned to Boscombe Down at 1840 hours. The following day began in much the same way, with the squadron leaving Boscombe Down for Warmwell at 0915 hours. Then at 1045 hours it was scrambled and ordered to patrol Warmwell at 22,000 feet, but when the enemy aircraft were sighted the Hurricanes were at 16,000 feet and still climbing. The raid, about seventy aircraft strong, was made up of Bf 110s flying at 20,000 feet with an escort of Bf 109s above them. Pilot Officer Higginson (commissioned on 24 September), who was leading the squadron, climbed for a head-on attack against the Bf 110s. He opened fire on the leading aircraft then became involved in a dogfight with the Bf 109s. Sergeant Smythe reported seeing Higginson's Bf 110 break away and head back for France with an engine smoking. It was assessed as damaged. This was the squadron's only claim, but two of its Hurricanes were shot down by fighters. Flying Officer Marston escaped without injury, but Sergeant Ray was wounded. Although this was an unsatisfactory combat for No. 56 Squadron, more RAF fighters soon entered the fray and the German formation was forced to turn tail and return to France. The Bf 109s were in any case operating at the limits of their endurance.

That afternoon the squadron was again scrambled and intercepted a bomber formation with Bf 110 escort ten miles south of Portland at 1630 hours. Although the Hurricane pilots reported the bombers as 'Do 215s' (itself a common misidentification for the

Do 17Z) they were almost certainly the He 111s of Kampfgesch-wader 55 which had been briefed to attack the Westland aircraft factory at Yeovil. The squadron was flying at 16,000 feet up-sun of the enemy formation when they sighted it. The German bombers, about thirty aircraft in vics of three, were 3,000 feet higher, with the Bf 110s circling behind and 5,000 feet above. Squadron Leader Pinfold ordered his squadron into sections line astern and climbed to the bombers' altitude to deliver the opening attack. Pilot Officer Constable-Maxwell considered that the CO was in a good position for a head-on attack, but because of his inexperience misjudged the turn-in. As it was, the Hurricanes came in from the rear quarter of the German formation. Because of the advantage of the sun, their approach had passed unnoticed. Squadron Leader Pinfold opened fire on a bomber, giving it a 5-second burst while closing from 400 to 125 yards' range. His own aircraft was then hit by return fire and the cockpit filled with glycol fumes. Pinfold broke away and returned to Warmwell where he successfully force-landed. Pilot Officer Higginson saw the bomber that he had attacked going down with both engines smoking and it was assessed as probably destroyed.

Sergeant Robinson followed his CO in to attack, seeing tracer bullets from the German gunners pass around his Hurricane. The bomber that he fired on maintained formation, although Robinson thought that he had disabled one of its engines. He then broke away and found a straggler under attack from another Hurricane. He finished his ammunition off against this target, but the enemy aircraft escaped into cloud. Pilot Officer Higginson, leading Yellow Section, turned away from the bombers to engage the Bf 110s. Climbing vertically to the circling escort fighters, he fired on one from beneath and saw it break away upwards. A Spitfire then attacked it, causing it to dive and Higginson was able to get on its tail. He fired most of his remaining ammunition into it and saw it dive vertically into cloud above the sea. Higginson's victory was shared with the Spitfire pilot, Pilot Officer W. D. Williams of No. 152 Squadron.

Flight Lieutenant Brooker leading the squadron's third section, closed in on the rear of the enemy bomber formation. He saw the aircraft that he had attacked break away to the left and dive. He followed it, continuing to fire, but was overtaking too fast and had to pull away to avoid a collision. As he could not then see what happened to it, he could only claim the enemy aircraft as damaged. Brooker's Hurricane was slightly damaged by a bullet through the starboard wing fuel tank. Pilot Officer Wicks also returned to Warmwell with a damaged aircraft and three Hurricanes had been shot down. Pilot Officer Constable-Maxwell's engine was hit by return fire from the bombers and he had to crash-land on Chesil Bank. Flight Lieutenant Edwards and Sergeant P. H. Fox had to take to their parachutes, the latter being slightly wounded. Cloud cover over Yeovil diverted the German bombers from their target and four of them were shot down by the defenders.

The Luftwaffe returned to Yeovil on 7 October and at 1530 hours ten of No. 56 Squadron's Hurricanes were scrambled from Warmwell. Flight Lieutenant Brooker led the squadron up to 19,000 feet, flying into the sun, before turning towards the course of the bombers to intercept. The enemy aircraft, comprising Ju 88s of Kampfgeschwader 51 and Bf 110s of Zerstörergeschwader 26, were met six miles south-east of Yeovil. The squadron attacked from above and out of the sun, each pilot selecting his target from the widely spread formation of Bf 110 escort fighters. Flight Lieutenant Brooker dived steeply on one Bf 110, giving it a burst of fire at full deflection, but saw no hits. He then climbed into the sun to 20,000 feet and saw five Bf 110s crossing the coast at Chesil Beach. He got on to the tail of one of these and fired his remaining ammunition into it, seeing its port engine blow up. Pilot Officer Nosowicz opened his attack on a Bf 110 from the front quarter, then turned in astern of it. He saw it turn away and dive towards the sea, smoking. Picking out another Bf 110, Nosowicz fired and silenced the rear gunner, but was forced to break away when he himself was attacked. His first victim was assessed as probably destroyed, the second as damaged.

Yellow Section, led by Flying Officer Wicks, dived vertically on to the Bf 110s. Sergeant Hillwood, Yellow 3, fired a short burst at one aircraft on the way down, but was unable to pull out of his dive in time to continue the attack from astern. Instead he selected another Bf 110 and fired a 7-second burst into it, closing from 250 yards to very short range, but could only claim this aircraft as damaged. Sergeant Whitehead saw his opening burst hit a Bf 110 and the engine began to smoke, but he had to pull out of his dive because he was closing in too fast and was not able to re-engage. One Hurricane was shot down and its pilot, Sergeant D. H. Nichols, baled out, but was injured in a heavy landing. No. 56 Squadron claimed two Bf 110s probably destroyed and three damaged. However, as overall German losses to the defending No. 10 Group fighter squadrons had been one Ju 88 and seven Bf 110s destroyed, the squadron's performance was rather better than its claims would suggest.

Apart from two minor skirmishes, this was No. 56 Squadron's last combat of the year. On 10 October the squadron was sent up from Warmwell against an X-plot raid, but was attacked and broken up by Bf 109s over Wareham. Sergeant J. Hlavac, a Czech pilot, who, with fellow countryman Pilot Officer J. Himr, had been posted in from No. 79 Squadron only two days before, was shot down and killed. Further reinforcements from No. 79 Squadron and No. 607 Squadron, both Category 'C' units, reached the squadron in mid-October. Even more welcome was the return of two of the pilots wounded during the summer fighting: Flight Lieutenant Gracie arrived back on 17 October, followed by Flying Officer Westmacott on 4 November. The squadron made its last successful interception on 6 November and sighted enemy fighters over the Isle of Wight. Pilot Officer T. F. Guest (a former No. 79 Squadron pilot) picked out a straggling Bf 109 and sent it down into the sea.

On 17 December No. 56 Squadron left No. 10 Group to return to North Weald in preparation for the air battles of 1941. During 1940 its resilience in combat had been altogether remarkable, since after participating in the Battle of France it had spent the whole of July and August fighting with No. 11 Group. Then after only two weeks' respite in which to make good its losses, it had become operational with No. 10 Group in defence of the West Country. The squadron had therefore fought, virtually without a break, throughout the entire Battle of Britain.

NO. 74 SQUADRON

No. 74 Squadron – the Tiger Squadron – had a tremendous reputation in Fighter Command even before the Battle of Britain, but, surprisingly, it was not one of the long-established peacetime fighter squadrons, like No. 19 Squadron or No. 56 Squadron. Its active service during the First World War had been brief, but spectacular. Formed as a Training Depot Squadron in July 1917, it began to prepare for service in France as a scout or fighter squadron six months later. In March 1918 it flew out to St Omer and fought its first combat over the Western Front in the following month. By the time of the Armistice, it had been credited with a total of 240 aerial victories and among its notable pilots were Major Keith 'Grid' Caldwell, the commanding officer; the legendary Edward 'Mick' Mannock, 'A' Flight commander, and his protégé and successor as 'A' Flight commander, Captain J. I. T. 'Taffy' Jones. The squadron was disbanded in mid-1919 and did not re-appear until the Abyssinian Crisis of 1935, when it flew Hawker Demon two-seat fighters from Hal Far, Malta. After its return to Britain, No. 74 Squadron re-equipped with Gloster Gauntlet single-seat fighters and in February 1939 began its conversion to the Spitfire at RAF Hornchurch, Essex.

In September 1939 No. 74 Squadron took part in the fiasco known as the 'Battle of Barking Creek', shooting down two of No. 56 Squadron's Hurricanes in error. Action against the Luftwaffe had to wait until 20 November, when Yellow Section intercepted a Heinkel He 111 bomber and shot it down into the sea. During this Phoney War period the squadron alternated between Hornchurch and the forward base at Rochford, but it was not until May 1940 and the German assault in the West that it saw any further combat. Then in the week between 21 and 27 May it was heavily engaged on daily patrols over France, claiming sixteen German aircraft confirmed destroyed, ten probably destroyed and three damaged. The squadron lost one pilot killed and three as prisoners of war during this period, one of the missing being 'B' Flight commander, Flight Lieutenant W. F. Treacy. His place was taken by Flying Officer W. E. G. Measures, while 'A' Flight remained in the capable hands of Flight Lieutenant A. G. 'Sailor' Malan. The CO, Squadron Leader F. L. White, himself only narrowly escaped falling into German hands. He had been forced to land at Calais/ Marck airfield with a faulty engine and was picked by a Miles Master trainer flown by Squadron Leader J. A. Leathart, CO of No. 54 Squadron, shortly before the Germans overran the area. Two of No. 54 Squadron's Spitfires which were escorting the Master became heavily engaged with Bf 109s over Calais, but all three aircraft returned safely to Hornchurch.

On 27 May No. 74 Squadron was withdrawn to RAF Leconfield, Yorkshire, for a brief rest period, but on 6 June returned to Rochford. It had been hoped to re-equip the squadron with the RAF's first Spitfire Mk IIs during this interval, but in the event they did not materialize. One more notable combat was fought by the squadron before the opening of the Battle of Britain in July. On the night of 18/19 June, Flight Lieutenant Malan obtained permission to take off from Rochford and attempt to intercept enemy raiders flying over nearby Southend. With the assistance of searchlights, he succeeded in making contact with two He 111s and shot both of them down. It was a tremendous feat of arms at a time when aids to night fighting were virtually non-existent, but it was already clear that Malan was a pilot and fighter leader of exceptional ability. A South African and former merchant navy officer, Malan at thirty years of age was considerably older than the average RAF fighter pilot of the time. Yet, his reflexes and physical co-ordination were as good as any 20-year old's and, in the opinion of one squadron pilot, his prowess as an aerobatic pilot in the Spitfire was equal to that of Supermarine's own test pilots. Malan combined flying skill with good marksmanship and the aggressiveness which is an essential part of any fighter pilot's make-up, but he also had a natural flair for leadership and a maturity which set him apart from many of his fellows. The war artist, Captain Cuthbert Orde, who met most of the outstanding pilots of RAF Fighter Command, wrote: 'I have seldom been more impressed by anyone . . . A very strong face, a very quiet manner and an air of authority made it obvious that here was a leader of great determination and ability.'

The squadron's first loss in July 1940 was due to the elements, rather than to enemy action. Sergeant White, a newly joined pilot was on patrol over the south coast when his Spitfire was struck by lightning and he crashed to his death near Margate. Three days later Blue Section intercepted two He 111s over Dover. Flight Lieutenant Measures, leading the section, turned on to the tail of one of them and opened fire. He then closed in as the enemy aircraft disappeared into cloud and was able to maintain contact with it until the He 111 re-emerged into clear air. He then dropped back to 200 yards' range and re-opened the attack, seeing his de Wilde incendiary ammunition hit the German bomber's fuselage and engine and one burst demolish the mid-upper gunner's position. The He 111 dropped down to only 100 feet above the Channel, heading back for France. Measures followed it, his ammunition by then exhausted, and saw it finally crash-land on the coast near St-Inglevert. Meanwhile, Blue 2, Pilot Officer the Hon. D. H. T. Dowding (son of the AOC, Fighter Command), gave chase to the second enemy bomber through patchy clouds. As the He 111 jettisoned its bomb load, Dowding pulled up underneath it at close range and fired a 10-second burst. After numerous hits, the starboard engine blew up in a cloud of smoke and the He 111's undercarriage dropped and the aircraft fell away to the right, disappearing into cloud. It was assessed as probably destroyed.

Blue Section was again in action on the morning of 8 July. Operating from the forward base at Manston, the three Spitfires were scrambled at 1053 hours with orders to intercept a raid in the immediate vicinity. After climbing through a layer of low cloud, Flight Lieutenant Measures sighted an He 111 about 2,000 feet above the Spitfires at 5,000 feet. He led the section in a fast climb and opened the attack with a short deflection burst from slightly below the German bomber. He and Dowding, Blue 2, then finished off their ammunition in a series of astern attacks, silencing the return fire and setting the port engine on fire. Blue 3, Sergeant W.

M. Skinner, followed them in and sent the He 111 diving into cloud on fire and with its undercarriage down.

That afternoon Sergeant E. A. Mould, leading Red Section on patrol over the Dover area, sighted four Bf 109s on his starboard beam. Ordering his section into line astern, Mould turned and climbed beneath the tail of the rearmost enemy fighter. His opening burst caused the Bf 109 to half-roll and dive to ground level. In attempting to follow, Mould pulled too much 'g' and blacked out, losing sight of his adversary, but his No. 2, Pilot Officer P. C. F. Stevenson, managed to stay on its tail. Mould then sighted another Bf 109 flying at low level and went down to attack it. The German fighter tried to lose the Spitfire by contour-chasing along the valleys behind Dover and Folkestone. Mould could only get his sights on for occasional short bursts of fire, but one of these found its mark. The Bf 109 began to trail vapour and then made a belly-landing near Elham. Pilot Officer Stevenson had meanwhile chased his Bf 109 at low level over Folkestone, firing several long bursts into it. The German fighter became enveloped in thick, oily smoke, but then Stevenson had to break away on seeing a fighter behind him. This turned out to be a Hurricane. On returning to Manston, Stevenson crashed his Spitfire on landing. Both he and Sergeant Mould were awarded confirmed victories.

At 1037 hours on 10 July the six Spitfires of 'A' Flight were ordered to take off and patrol base. Pilot Officer J. C. Freeborn, leading the Flight as Red 1, was then told to patrol over a convoy which had come under attack two miles east of Deal. Flying at 12,000 feet Freeborn noticed enemy aircraft 2,000 feet below him. Increasing his height advantage, he put his flight into line astern formation and attacked the enemy, some thirty Bf 109s accompanying a single Do 17Z, from above and behind. Freeborn got to within fifty yards of a Bf 109 and fired a 4-second burst into it. He reported that it 'just dropped out of the sky'. He was then attacked by numerous enemy fighters, his Spitfire was damaged and he had to force-land at Manston. His No. 2, Sergeant Mould, who had taken one Bf 109 off Freeborn's tail, was also overwhelmed and had to force-land his damaged Spitfire. Both aircraft were repairable. Pilot Officer Stevenson opened his attack on a Bf 109 doing a steep left-hand turn. He saw his fire hit the wing, probably damaging the radiator, but he had to climb away to evade the German's wingman. Stevenson fired on a second Bf 109, which evaded him by half-rolling and diving away. A third enemy fighter dived past and Stevenson went down vertically after it, giving a 6-second burst of fire and seeing smoke pour from its engine. Being fired on from behind, he broke away and last saw the Bf 109 going down vertically at 4,000 feet. It was allowed as a probable victory.

Pilot Officer D. C. Cobden, leading Yellow Section down on to the Bf 109s, noticed another group of enemy fighters to the left and slightly above him and so climbed with his three Spitfires to attack these. The Bf 109s immediately split up, but Cobden got on to the tail of one of them and followed it down, firing at close range. When he broke off, the enemy fighter was going down towards the sea pouring smoke. Yellow 2, Pilot Officer B. V. Draper, went for a Bf 109 that had positioned itself on Cobden's tail. Taking careful aim so as to avoid hitting his leader, he fired four 1-second bursts into it from 300 yards' range. He saw hits on the engine and cockpit area and the Bf 109 went into a vertical dive trailing smoke. Draper was unable to follow, as another enemy fighter was approaching him from below. He dived to attack it, but had to break away as his dive had gone past the vertical and he wished to avoid bunting (performing an outside half-loop with unpleasant effect on the pilot through negative-g and the certainty of the Merlin engine cutting out through the same cause). By the time that he had regained height again, the Bf 109s were withdrawing and he could only fire a short burst at a straggler from long range. Pilot Officer P. C. B. St. John, Yellow 3, opened his attack on a Bf 109 from the rear quarter, but had time for only a short burst, as he then had to climb away to evade an enemy aircraft on his tail. He managed to turn the tables on this attacker and fired all his remaining ammunition into it, but could only claim the Bf 109 as damaged.

At 1330 hours the same day eight Spitfires were sent up from Manston to reinforce the air cover for a convoy steaming past Dover. Fifteen minutes later, Flight Lieutenant Measures sighted an enemy formation about 100 aircraft strong, made up of Do 17Z bombers flying at 4,000 feet, with Bf 110 and Bf 109 escorts stacked above them to 12,000 feet. Measures climbed his Spitfires to 13,000 feet by which time the circling German escort fighters had formed a 'cylinder' above the bombers. He then led the RAF fighters down in a fast dive through the various layers of enemy aircraft. Measures fired a long burst into a Bf 110 and saw its port engine belch smoke, then continued down and attacked a Do 17Z. He reported seeing a Bf 109 collide with one of the bombers, but in fact the fighter was one of No. 111 Squadron's Hurricanes. By this time Measures had finished his ammunition and was set upon by Bf 109s which had followed him down. He managed to evade these attacks, from pairs of enemy fighters diving from each beam and from behind, and regained the coast. Two Hurricanes then appeared and chased off the Bf 109s. Pilot Officer Stevenson, flying as Measures' No. 2, attacked a Bf 110 in the middle layer of the enemy formation and saw his fire hit the rear gunner's position. He then fired the rest of his ammunition into a second Bf 110, before diving away at high speed for the English coast, passing across the noses of a group of Bf 110s *en route*. He reported that throughout the combat enemy aircraft opened fire at too great a range and his Spitfire was not hit. Flying Officer J. C. Mungo-Park selected a vic of three Do 17Zs, which had broken away from the main formation, and saw his fire disable the starboard engine of one of them.

Pilot Officer Cobden, leading Yellow Section, followed Measures' Blue Section down. He picked out a straggling Do 17Z and disabled its starboard engine. He then delivered a second attack on the bomber, but as he was breaking away was set upon by a group of Bf 109s and his Spitfire was riddled with their fire. Cobden engaged emergency boost and broke away from his attackers in a steep climbing turn. He then brought his crippled aircraft into a wheels-up landing on Lympne airfield. Yellow 2, Pilot Officer Draper, and Yellow 3, Pilot Officer St. John, had broken away from Cobden as he dived, in order to attack the top layer of Bf 109 escort fighters. Draper fired a short deflection burst into one which promptly half-rolled and dived away. Then, finding himself surrounded by the other Bf 109s, he climbed into cloud at 14,000 feet to evade them. When he re-emerged, Draper found himself in a good position to carry out a diving attack on the Do 17Zs. He attacked two bombers, and saw the crew of one take to their parachutes. He then flew back to the coast, taking a parting shot at a Bf 109 on the way. Pilot Officer St. John came under attack from astern by a Bf 109, but it was going too fast and over-shot. He half-rolled on to its tail, as the German fighter climbed steeply for the clouds. St. John got in a burst of fire as the Bf 109 disappeared into cloud cover. On attempting to follow, he stalled and fell away and could not regain contact.

During cloudy weather on 12 July Red Section was sent up to investigate a raid plotted fifteen miles north-east of Margate. Anti-aircraft fire from a ship under attack drew their attention to an He 111. Flight Lieutenant Malan, leading the section, opened the attack and closed in to 300 yards' range. His fire silenced the German mid-upper gunner. Sergeant Mould and Pilot Officer Stevenson followed up the attack and the bomber was reported to have crashed into the sea. On 19 July the squadron was scrambled to intercept a heavy raid on Dover, but the order had come too late and the twelve Spitfires could not engage the main force before it turned back for France. Flight Lieutenant Malan's Red Section did, however, engage two Bf 109s which were dogfighting with a single Hurricane. Malan opened fire on one German fighter from 100 yards' range, allowing the Hurricane to break away, and then turned on to the Bf 109's tail and gave it two short bursts from 75 yards' range. It began to pour smoke and dived away, but Malan had to break off as the second German fighter was about to attack him. Pilot Officer Stevenson, Red 3, then engaged this Bf 109 which dived away steeply. The Spitfire had no difficulty in holding the German fighter in the dive and Stevenson fired all his ammunition into it. It was last seen going down towards the French coast trailing smoke. Both the Bf 109s were assessed as probably destroyed.

On 24 July Flight Lieutenant Measures was posted to No. 7 Operational Training Unit as an instructor. His place as officer commanding 'B' Flight was taken by Flight Lieutenant D. P. D. Kelly, a former army co-operation pilot who had been posted to the squadron on 15 July. On the afternoon of 24 July Pilot Officer

Freeborn was leading 'A' Flight on patrol from Manston when they picked out three Do 17Zs flying low over the sea. On sighting the RAF fighters, the enemy aircraft turned for France. The Spitfires pursued them until they disappeared into cloud in the vicinity of Gravelines. The German gunners opened fire at 2,000 yards' range in an attempt to disconcert the Spitfire pilots, who held their fire until within 300 yards of the Do 17Zs. Freeborn, Pilot Officer Cobden and Pilot Officer D. Hastings all fired good bursts into the bombers and one of the Do 17Zs was seen to be disabled. On the following day 'A' Flight was sent up to intercept a raid off Dover, but once again did not have time to engage properly before the enemy withdrew. Red Leader, Flight Lieutenant Malan, fired on one retreating Bf 109 and saw his fire hit its fuselage. The other five Spitfires had no opportunity to attack.

The squadron was able to make a far better timed interception over Dover on the afternoon of 28 July. Twelve Spitfires were ordered off at 1350 hours to attack the fighter escort, leaving the bombers to the Hurricanes. On reaching 18,000 feet, the squadron met about 36 Bf 109s flying at the same level and a general dogfight followed. Flight Lieutenant Malan turned Red Section on to the tails of a formation of six or nine Bf 109s without being seen by them. He opened fire on one, which did not attempt to evade, except by making a gentle turn to the right. Malan reckoned that its controls had been shot away and switched his attack to a second Bf 109 which had turned across his nose. He finished off his ammunition in three deflection bursts and saw the fighter go down in a spiral. He was awarded one probable victory and one damaged. Pilot Officer Stevenson, Red 2, attacked a Bf 109 flying on the left of Malan's first target. It dived away towards the French coast with its engine smoking. Stevenson fired on two more enemy fighters seeing hits on both, and was then attacked from behind. He broke away and climbed to 20,000 feet. Then glycol fumes entered the cockpit and his engine began to run roughly. He let down towards Manston and, realizing that his engine was about to seize, lowered the undercarriage (this was operated by an engine-driven hydraulic pump) and carried out a successful forced-landing with a dead engine.

Pilot Officer Freeborn, leading Yellow Section, noticed a second group of Bf 109s, about fifty strong, flying above and behind the squadron. Instead of following Flight Lieutenant Malan, he climbed to engage these. Firing a 3-second burst at one from above and behind, he saw it burst into flames. His own aircraft then came under attack and was damaged, but Freeborn brought the disabled Spitfire back to base. Stevenson's No. 3, Pilot Officer St. John, followed a Bf 109 into a steep dive and saw his fire hitting it. He then checked his tail and saw four fighters coming down on him. St. John steepened his dive and evaded them in cloud.

Flight Lieutenant Kelly, leading Blue Section, turned to follow Red Section's opening attack, but then two small groups of Bf 109s dived past from above. Kelly took a snap shot at the first, without apparent effect, and engaged emergency boost to dive after the second group, closing in to 250 yards before opening fire. His target burst into flames and went down into the sea. Blue 2, Pilot Officer H. M. Stephen, attacked a second Bf 109 in this formation, registered hits on the tail and claimed it as damaged. Pilot Officer H. R. Gunn, Green 1, climbed to engage the Bf 109s flying above and fired at several of them. He was himself continually attacked from the beam, quarter and head-on by other enemy fighters. Gunn was able to get in one long burst from astern at a diving Bf 109 and saw it turn on to its back and its dive steepen. During one head-on pass, he missed colliding with his opponent by only a matter of feet. Despite the odds against him in this single-handed dogfight, Gunn escaped unharmed. Two of the squadron's Spitfires, however, failed to return. Pilot Officer J. H. R. Young was shot down and killed, while Sergeant Mould was wounded but baled out. Their opponents in this fight were the élite Jagdgeschwader 26 and Jagdgeschwader 51.

On 31 July thick haze over the Channel made interception difficult and No. 74 Squadron was the only one of five squadrons sent up to meet an afternoon raid on Dover. 'A' Flight had been ordered on patrol earlier than 'B' Flight and was able to climb to 20,000 feet over Dover. It sighted a formation of enemy aircraft out to sea, but was unable to catch up with them. 'B' Flight, still climbing for altitude at 18,000 feet, were attacked from above by about fifteen Bf 109s. Blue Section was especially hard hit; Blue 2, Pilot Officer H. R. Gunn and Blue 3, Sergeant F. W. Eley, were both shot down and killed. Blue Leader, Flight Lieutenant Kelly, tried to turn on to the tail of a fighter, but was fired at from behind and his Spitfire was damaged. He attempted to continue the combat but his aircraft was barely controllable and he returned to Manston. Green Section had evaded the Bf 109s' opening attack by carrying out a steep climbing turn to the left. Green 3, Sergeant Skinner, had become separated from the other two Spitfires and saw three Bf 109s flying 5,000 feet below him. He carried out a fast diving attack on one of these, before pulling up in a tight climbing turn. His victim went down in a shallow dive and was assessed as probably destroyed. No. 74 Squadron's opponents were again the Bf 109s of Jagdgeschwader 51.

At the end of July Malan was awarded a Bar to the DFC he had earned during the fighting over France. On 8 August he was promoted to the acting rank of squadron leader and took over command of No. 74 Squadron, Squadron Leader White having been posted to HQ Fighter Command for staff duties. Pilot Officer Freeborn was awarded the DFC at the same time. Two new pilots joined the squadron in early August: the Poles, Flight Lieutenant S. Brzezina and Flying Officer H. Szczesny, who were soon nicknamed 'Breezy' and 'Sneezy'. On 6 August the squadron lost Pilot Officer Dowding, who was posted to No. 6 Operational Training Unit as an instructor.

Early August saw a lull in fighter operations, but on the 11th No. 74 Squadron became heavily engaged again, fighting four separate combats during the course of the day. Operating from the forward base at Manston, the squadron was sent up at 0749 hours to meet a raid approaching Dover. Squadron Leader Malan led his twelve Spitfires up to 20,000 feet and then with the sun behind him flew towards Dover. He was able to surprise a formation of Bf 109s, which when attacked half-rolled and dived away. Seeing no fighters above, Malan decided to break his rule of never following a German aircraft down in a dive. He found that he could easily overtake the Bf 109 and, closing in to 200 yards' range, opened fire. The German fighter levelled off at 12,000 feet, but finding the

Spitfire still behind him, again half-rolled and dived for the French coast. Malan pursued him until within a mile of Cap Gris Nez and sent him down in flames.

Pilot Officer Hastings, Red 3, broke away from his section to go to the help of a Spitfire with a Bf 109 on its tail. He opened fire at 300 yards' range, causing the German fighter to break away. Hastings followed him round in a turn to starboard and fired again, seeing a stream of white liquid pour back from the Bf 109. He then had to evade a fighter on his tail, which he did by making a steep climbing turn to starboard at full throttle. Flying Officer W. H. Nelson, flying as Yellow 3, could not pick out a target during the squadron's initial attack. He therefore circled above the fight looking for further enemy aircraft. Sighting a group of six Bf 109s at 28,000 feet, he climbed to engage them, but before he could get into range, they spotted him and broke up. Nelson attached himself to the rearmost and, closing to 150 yards, opened fire. The Bf 109 burst into flames and Nelson turned away to clear his tail. The remaining enemy fighters were speeding away for France.

Flying Officer Mungo-Park, leading Blue Section, opened his attack with a deflection shot at a Bf 109 which crossed in front of him at 300 yards' range. He then turned in astern of it and fired again, seeing it go down smoking. At this point he was attacked from behind and had to break away. Shortly afterwards he saw a Bf 109 beneath him diving for the safety of France. He attacked it and saw his de Wilde incendiary ammunition hitting, but broke off the action as he was approaching the enemy coast. All he was able to claim was one enemy fighter damaged. His No. 2, Pilot Officer Stephen, was more fortunate, claiming two Bf 109s destroyed (unconfirmed) and one damaged. Stephen first opened fire on a Bf 109 which was trying to get on to his leader's tail. He saw its engine begin to smoke and then broke away. He climbed to 24,000 feet and engaged a lone Bf 109 in a turning fight. By throttling right back and pulling into a high 'g' turn – almost blacking out in the process as the blood drained from his head – Stephen was able to get on his tail. He fired a 3-second burst and the Bf 109 went into a flick half-roll and dived towards the sea. Not wishing to lose his height advantage, Stephen let him go. Shortly afterwards he spotted what he believed to be two Spitfires and decided to join them. When 150 yards astern of them, he realized that the fighters were Bf 109s and so attacked the rearmost. After a short burst from 200 yards the enemy aircraft 'seemed to fold up' and fell down towards the sea. The leading German fighter went into a climbing turn to evade the Spitfire, but Stephen followed and fired a 2–3-second burst into it. The Spitfire then stalled and fell away in a spin, but Stephen last saw the Bf 109 also spinning 3,000 feet below him.

Pilot Officer D. N. E. Smith, flying as Green 3, also claimed a Bf 109 as destroyed. Singling out a fighter from the high-flying German formation, he followed it down in a dive to 6,000 feet. Smith then fired a 5-second burst into it from astern and saw its starboard undercarriage leg come down, smoke pour from the engine and the German fighter begin a shallow dive. As he had to evade another Bf 109 on his tail, Smith could not see what became of this aircraft. Altogether the squadron had claimed seven Bf 109s destroyed (none of them confirmed) and four damaged. Their only loss was Pilot Officer Stevenson's Spitfire which was riddled by enemy fire forcing him to bale out. He came down in the sea off Dover and was picked up by a motor torpedo-boat.

The second combat of the day was fought over the same area at 1015 hours. Squadron Leader Malan led twelve Spitfires up to 24,000 feet and sighted small groups of Bf 109s flying in mid-Channel at a slightly lower height. Malan dived on to the tails of a pair of them, but was overshooting and so could only fire a short burst. Pilot Officer Freeborn, Yellow 1, attacked the second Bf 109, followed it down into a dive and saw fragments break away from it as his fire hit. He last saw it going vertically downwards, its radiator streaming coolant fluid. Malan, meanwhile, had climbed back to 24,000 feet and attempted to get Blue and Green Sections to form up behind him, but R/T reception was bad and he could not contact them so he carried on alone and attacked another pair of Bf 109s, firing on both of them and seeing one stream white smoke. He then evaded eight Bf 109s which dived on him, by climbing in a right-hand spiral. Heading for Dover, he spotted a formation of ten Bf 109s at 27,000 feet and tried to pick off a straggler from the formation, but as he closed the range, the leader turned in towards him, forestalling the attack. Malan went into a wide circle around the German fighters and attempted to call up reinforcements, but because of heavy atmospherics he could not contact any other member of the squadron. The only other pilot to claim in this combat was Warrant Officer E. Mayne, a 39-year-old veteran who had enlisted in the Royal Flying Corps during the First World War. In following the squadron's initial attack, he had blacked out in a sharp turn and regained consciousness at 2,000 feet above the sea off Cap Gris Nez. Ahead of him and 1,000 feet below were three Bf 109s. Mayne closed in and fired on one of them, giving it two bursts. The leader then crossed his sights and he fired into him, seeing the Bf 109 half-roll and go down. Then, as his ammunition was running short, he returned to base.

At 1145 hours eleven Spitfires, led by Pilot Officer Freeborn, were ordered up to patrol Convoy 'Booty' steaming twelve miles east of Clacton. The two leading sections, Red and Blue, were flying in fours, rather than the usual vics of three, and it had been arranged that the Nos. 1 and 3 and Nos. 2 and 4 in the formation would fight together as pairs. Freeborn sighted a formation of about forty Bf 110s flying at 4,000 feet below heavy cloud (8/10th cumulus) and dived to attack. On sighting the Spitfires, the Bf 110s, fighter-bombers from Erprobungsgruppe 210 with an escort from Zerstörergeschwader 26, formed their customary defensive circle. Freeborn fired at three Bf 110s during his initial attack and saw hits register on all of them. He then got on to the tails of two enemy aircraft, firing 3-second bursts from 200 to 100 yards' range, and saw both of them go into the sea.

Sergeant T. B. Kirk, flying as Red 4, saw the Bf 110 that he fired at roll slowly on to its back and dive inverted into the sea. He then engaged a second aircraft, seeing his fire hit and fragments fall away, but his ammunition ran out and he broke off the action. Blue 2, Warrant Officer Mayne, attacked a Bf 110 and set its port engine on fire. Blue 4, Sergeant Skinner, flying as his wingman, followed up this attack and saw the aircraft go into the sea. Mayne then attacked a second Bf 110 and thought that his fire damaged it. As he broke away upwards, the Bf 110 pulled up on to his tail.

However, Sergeant Skinner – who had in the meantime attacked two more Bf 110s – saw Mayne's danger and closed in on the German fighter, finishing off his ammunition on it; he reported that it went into the sea. His total claims for the combat were two Bf 110s destroyed, plus the one shared with Mayne and another damaged.

Flying Officer Mungo-Park attacked two Bf 110s in succession. The first dived into the sea and the other went down with one engine pouring black smoke. Flying Officer Nelson's opening attack sent a Bf 110 into the sea and this was confirmed by Warrant Officer Mayne. He then saw another fighter on the tail of a Spitfire. He closed in astern, opening fire with a deflection burst from 150 yards, and saw the Bf 110 take evasive action as his bullets struck it. Nelson, though, was himself being attacked and so had to break away; he claimed the enemy aircraft as damaged. When Pilot Officer Stephen dived in his initial attack, a Bf 110 flew straight through his sights and he was able to rake it with fire from nose to tail. He saw it burst into flames and go into the sea. He then got on the tail of a second flying about fifty feet above the water. After a short burst from 200 yards' range, it rolled over and went into the sea. He then fired on a third machine and silenced its rear gunner.

Nine of the squadron's Spitfires landed back at Manston at 1245 hours, two having been shot down in the combat. The missing pilots, both of whom were killed, were Pilot Officer D. N. E. Smith and Pilot Officer D. G. Cobden. It was New Zealander Donald Cobden's 26th birthday. The squadron's total claims in this combat amounted to ten Bf 110s destroyed, although only one of these could be confirmed. Actual German losses were four Bf 110s destroyed and two damaged. More importantly, No. 74 Squadron had broken up the attack on the convoy.

Wing Commander H. M. Stephen recalls the development of 'pairs in line astern' tactics in No 74 Squadron, which were worked out as a result of early combat experience. Formation keeping in the traditional vic required a great deal of flying skill, but also absolute concentration on the next man in the formation. Inexperienced pilots often fell behind, because quick reactions were essential to keep in position, and often aircraft skidded out in a turn. Line astern formation was much easier to fly in combat and enabled a better lookout to be kept. Once this was adopted it was more logical to fly in pairs, with a wingman watching his leader's tail. These procedures were worked out by Malan, Mungo-Park and Freeborn and adopted by No 74 Squadron. However, there was little or no exchange of information between squadrons and so these innovations had no great influence on Fighter Command's tactics as a whole during the Battle.

Just over an hour after landing from its third combat, eight of No. 74 Squadron's Spitfires were ordered to patrol Hawkinge at 15,000 feet. They were then vectored on to an enemy formation off Margate, which numbered about ten Ju 87s flying at 6,000 feet with twenty Bf 109 escorts 4,000 feet above them. Squadron Leader Malan led his Spitfires, flying in two sections of four, into the attack. He ordered Blue 1 to go for the dive-bombers, while his Red Section engaged the Bf 109s. However, Blue Leader, Flying Officer Mungo-Park, apparently did not receive this call and all the Spitfires attacked the fighter escort, the Ju 87s disappearing into cloud cover. Squadron Leader Malan saw the Bf 109 he was firing at burst into flames and go into the sea. He then regained height and engaged a group of four Bf 109s, firing his remaining ammunition into one without apparent result. Pilot Officer Freeborn got on the tail of a Bf 109 and chased it down through cloud at 4,000 feet. He fired and saw the German fighter's engine stop and fragments break away, before it dropped out of control.

Flying Officer Mungo-Park fired a 5-second burst into another Bf 109 and saw it catch fire and go into the sea. Pilot Officer Stephen reported that the first Bf 109 that he attacked crashed on the beach near the North Foreland lighthouse. He fired on a second and saw his bullets hit, but then had to turn to engage another fighter which was closing in on his tail. Within a period of little more than seven hours, No. 74 Squadron had fought four engagements with the Luftwaffe and claimed the destruction of 38 aircraft. Even allowing for the usual and inevitable inflation of these claims (the total Luftwaffe losses for 11 August exactly matched the squadron's claims), it was an impressive performance.

That No. 74 Squadron, after more than a month in action with No. 11 Group, was able to sustain such a high level of operations was indicative of the resilience that was to be a major factor in the RAF fighter squadrons' ultimate victory.

At 0555 hours on 13 August, No. 74 Squadron's twelve Spitfires were scrambled with orders to patrol Manston. They were then directed to intercept a raid over the estuary. This proved to number more than seventy Do 17Z bombers of Kampfgeschwader 2, which had failed to pick up a recall signal and so were operating without fighter escort. Squadron Leader Malan sighted about forty of the bombers flying at 3,000 feet off Whitstable, just below cloud base. The squadron broke up and carried out individual attacks, nine of the twelve pilots engaged making claims which totalled six Do 17Zs destroyed, six probably destroyed and one damaged. Squadron Leader Malan carried out a beam attack on a section of three Do 17Zs and then swung in astern of them. He fired four 2-second bursts into the No. 3 aircraft at 150 yards' range and saw it catch fire and drop towards the sea. Switching his attack to the leading bomber, Malan's fire disabled one of its engines. He fired his remaining ammunition into the third Do 17Z, but without result. Pilot Officer Freeborn first opened fire on a pair of bombers flying in close formation and was able to spray both with his bullets. He then broke away and chased a vic of three Do 17Zs. Closing to 100 yards astern, he fired a 10-second burst into one, exhausting his ammunition, and saw it crash into the water off Birchington, Kent.

Sergeant Skinner reported that his fire disabled the port engine of the first Do 17Z that he attacked. He then climbed through cloud to 5,000 feet, but seeing five fighters circling, which he identified as Bf 109s, he dived for the cloud cover. Seeing a straggling Do 17Z, he closed in and fired a 7-second burst from slightly above and astern. Two of the bomber's crew baled out, it burst into flames and dived into the sea off Eastchurch. Because visibility was poor, Skinner became lost. His engine was then overheating and so he called up Hornchurch control for homing instructions.

Flying Officer Szczesny tried to carry out a head-on attack on a vic of three Do 17Zs, but they turned away to the right so he broke away and turned in behind them. One of the bombers was out of formation, so Szczesny attacked it, seeing it jettison its bombs and then fall in flames into the sea. On trying to land after this combat, Szczesny found that his undercarriage had jammed, but he managed to make a good wheels-up landing. His fellow-countryman, Flight Lieutenant Brzezina, attacked one bomber and saw it fall towards the sea with an engine smoking. He closed in to within fifty yards of a second when there was an explosion in his cockpit and the Spitfire fell out of control. Brezezina baled out and was uninjured. Pilot Officer Hastings engaged the leader of a vic of Do 17Zs from 300 yards, but did not close in because of heavy return fire. He saw fragments break away from the bomber, and then peeled off to attack the No. 3 aircraft in the same formation. This jettisoned its bombs and dived towards the Kent coast. Hastings followed and saw it crash about four miles west of Manston.

Flying Officer Mungo-Park and Pilot Officer Stephen both fired all their ammunition into single bombers, but could claim only one as probably destroyed and the other damaged. Flying Officer Nelson attacked four different bombers, but only one was seen to be damaged. Kampfgeschwader 2 had been seriously mauled by RAF Fighter Command, its reported losses being five bombers destroyed and seven damaged; the opening raid of the Luftwaffe's vaunted 'Adler Tag' had badly misfired.

On the following day No. 74 Squadron was withdrawn to RAF Wittering, Northamptonshire, in No. 12 Group, for a rest period. On 21 August a number of new pilots was posted in to replace casualties: Pilot Officer E. W. Churches and Pilot Officer R. L. Spurdle, both New Zealanders, came from No. 7 Operational Training Unit, while Flying Officer W. D. K. Franklin, Pilot Officer A. L. Ricalton and Pilot Officer R. J. E. Boulding were former Fairey Battle light bomber pilots with No. 142 Squadron. After a week at Wittering, the squadron moved again to Kirton-in-Lindsey, Lincolnshire, and then on 9 September to Coltishall, Norfolk. By that time No. 74 Squadron had become one of only four Category 'B' Squadrons in Fighter Command, maintained at full pilot strength in order to replace a Category 'A' Squadron should this become absolutely necessary. A number of command changes were also implemented during this period. Freeborn was promoted to flight lieutenant and took over 'A' Flight, while Mungo-Park became OC 'B' Flight when Flight Lieutenant Kelly was posted away to No. 6 Operational Training Unit as an instructor. On 10 September the squadron received its first Spitfire Mk IIs and on the same day began to operate from RAF Duxford, where it was available to reinforce No. 11 Group if needed.

On 11 September No. 74 Squadron flew in a Spitfire wing from Duxford, joining No. 19 Squadron and No. 611 Squadron. Flying as the rearmost squadron, with three four-aircraft sections in line astern formation, No. 74 Squadron was intended to attack the bombers while the two leading squadrons took on the fighter escort. At about 1630 hours the squadron intercepted a formation of thirty bombers flying at 20,000 feet in the vicinity of the London docks. Squadron Leader Malan attempted to position the Spitfires for a head-on attack, but then saw fighters coming down on him and so turned in early. Attacking from the beam, Malan saw his bullets hit two aircraft. He then continued down in a fast spiral to 13,000 feet in order to evade the fighters. Climbing back to 20,000 feet in the sun, he next attacked a straggling bomber from head-on, turned, and carried out a beam attack. Its port engine caught fire, but Malan was himself attacked by a Bf 109 and had to dive away to evade it.

After following Malan into a beam attack on the bombers, Pilot Officer Hastings (Red 2) then attacked a Bf 110, seeing smoke pour from it. However, two Bf 109s were closing in on his tail and so he carried out a steep climbing turn to evade them and lost the Bf 110. Red 3, Flying Officer Szczesny, pulled in astern of a bomber and fired three short bursts at it without seeing any results. He broke away to engage two Bf 109s which were attacking other Spitfires. Then he saw a single Bf 110 and closed in behind it firing short bursts. He saw it dive and crash in flames. Red 4, Pilot Officer Churches, followed up an attack by two Spitfires on an He

111 and saw his fire hitting and the bomber's port engine pouring out smoke. He claimed it as probably destroyed.

Flight Lieutenant Freeborn, leading Yellow Section, engaged the Bf 109s diving on Malan's section. He then became separated from the main engagement and, sighting a lone Bf 110 south of London, carried out a series of attacks on it from ahead, astern and abeam. It finally crashed at Dungeness. His No. 2, Flying Officer Nelson, could take no part in the fight; his guns would not fire owing to a faulty pneumatic system. Pilot Officer St. John, after breaking away from his first attack on the He 111 formation, noticed one of the bombers straggling. He engaged it from the quarter and saw his fire hit and an engine burst into flames. He was then chased away by two fighters. Blue 1, Flight Lieutenant Mungo-Park, damaged one bomber during his initial beam attack. Picking out another target, he set its starboard engine on fire and saw it dive steeply. Pilot Officer Stephen, Blue 3, saw that the bomber he was attacking was hard hit: its undercarriage had dropped and an engine had stopped. Before he could deliver the *coup de grâce*, however, a Hurricane went in and finished it off. Stephen was then attcked by a Bf 109, but it overshot which enabled the Spitfire to get on its tail. Stephen fired a 2-second burst and saw his de Wilde ammunition hitting, but he did not want to lose height in following the German down so he broke off the engagement.

On 14 September the squadron fought a series of minor engagements, with sections intercepting individual raiders. This was to set the pattern for the following month of operations as No. 74 Squadron did not form a regular part of the Duxford Wing. At 1000 hours Blue Section intercepted a Bf 110 flying at 23,000 feet ten miles north of Happisburgh on the Norfolk coast. Blue Leader, Flight Lieutenant Mungo-Park, put his section into line astern and closed in to 200 yards to open the attack. His fire hit the starboard engine and the aircraft went down in steep diving turns, heading for cloud cover at 5,000 feet. Pilot Officer Ricalton, Blue 2, then fired a 1-second burst from 400 yards' range which appeared to hit the Bf 110. Mungo-Park made a second attack and as the aircraft disappeared into cloud, he noticed that its starboard engine was in flames. Return fire hit his Spitfire in three places, but did no serious damage. Blue 3, Pilot Officer Boulding, took no part in the combat. At 1346 hours it was the turn of Yellow Section, led by Flying Officer St. John, which intercepted a Bf 110 flying at 18,000 feet five miles north-east of Great Yarmouth. Yellow 2, Pilot Officer Draper, was able to fire a short burst from long range before it went into cloud. He followed the Bf 110 into the cloud bank, while Yellow Leader and Yellow 3, Sergeant Parkes, waited above. However, the Bf 110 aircraft did not reappear and the section reformed.

At 1400 hours Pilot Officer Draper sighted a Ju 88 flying at 10,000 feet ten miles south-west of Lowestoft, but on sighting the Spitfires, the aircraft turned eastwards and headed for cloud cover. Before it disappeared Draper fired two bursts into it. St. John flew over the cloud tops and saw the Ju 88 re-appear in a break in the clouds. He attacked, giving it a 5-second burst of fire which disabled the starboard engine, but again it disappeared in cloud and Yellow Section could not regain contact.

An hour after Yellow Section's combat, Green Section led by Pilot Officer Churches, was directed to Debenham, Suffolk, to intercept a raid. Churches sighted a Ju 88 flying at 8,000 feet and led his section in line astern into a rear quarter attack on the bomber. It was flying in and out of cloud, but Churches was able to deliver three attacks before he finally lost contact. Green 3, Pilot Officer Boulding, was able to pick up the Ju 88 again, however, and he fired four or five short bursts into it from astern. He saw it jettison its bomb load and then dive smoking into cloud. Meanwhile Pilot Officer Churches had been directed by control to investigate a 'bogey' (unidentified aircraft) in his vicinity, but it turned out to be Boulding's fighter. By then the Spitfires were low on fuel and so they landed at RAF Wattisham. At about that time, Red Section had been sent up from Coltishall to intercept a raid in the Lowestoft area. At 1530 hours they intercepted an He 111 flying at 11,000 feet just above a layer of 9/10th cloud. Flight Lieutenant Freeborn opened the attack from astern and was followed in by Red 2, Pilot Officer Spurdle. The bomber was then flying in the fringes of the cloud and was only intermittently visible. Red 3, Sergeant Kirk, followed it 25 miles out to sea before losing contact.

After this day of frantic activity the remainder of September was comparatively quiet in the Coltishall Sector. During a routine patrol off the Suffolk coast on 23 September, Sergeant D. H. Ayers had to bale out of his Spitfire about 1½ miles south-east of Southwold. An intensive sea search failed to find him and his body was not recovered until 4 October. On the afternoon of 24 September Green Section, led by Flying Officer Franklin, intercepted a Do 17Z ten miles south-west of Sheringham on the Norfolk coast. The bomber attempted to find cover in cloud, but there were sufficient gaps to allow the RAF pilots to continue the pursuit. Franklin, Pilot Officer Churches (Green 2) and Pilot Officer Boulding (Green 3) each carried out five separate attacks, before the Do 17Z escaped by diving to sea level where it disappeared in thick haze. During the latter half of September the squadron lost three of its old hands, when Warrant Officer Mayne and Pilot Officer Stevenson were posted as instructors to operational training units and Flight Lieutenant Brzezina left to take command of No. 308 Squadron, a newly formed Polish fighter unit. Four new pilots arrived at the end of the month to fill the vacancies.

October opened with an indecisive combat between Green Section and an He 111 off the Norfolk coast. The three Spitfires, led by Pilot Officer Stephen, whose award of the DFC had been announced five days before, took off from Coltishall at 1220 hours on 1 October. After seventy minutes of fruitless searching above a layer of 7/10th cloud which reached up to 10,000 feet, the Spitfires were short of fuel and about to turn for home. Stephen then saw the He 111 flying 2,000 feet above cloud and down sun from him. He carried out a quick head-on attack and then half-rolled on to the German bomber's tail; his fire hit its fuselage and port engine and the He 111 dived into cloud. The Spitfires then had to break off the combat and return to base. Pilot Officer Boulding, Green 3, landed with only five gallons of fuel remaining. Stephen was again leading Green Section on 5 October, when at 1405 hours they intercepted a Do 17Z thirty miles east of Harwich. The three Spitfires, in line astern, attacked one after the other. Green 3,

Flying Officer Szczesny, reported that as he broke away the enemy aircraft was diving towards the sea with its port engine in flames. Three days after this combat, the squadron lost two pilots during a training mission. The Spitfires flown by Pilot Officer D. Hastings and Pilot Officer F. W. Buckland, a recently joined pilot, collided and both pilots were killed.

No. 74 Squadron was again committed to the Battle in the south on 14 October, when its sixteen Spitfires flew to Biggin Hill to replace No. 72 Squadron. That unit, after a month and a half of heavy fighting, had been reduced to only seven experienced pilots, so it was essential to withdraw it to a quieter sector and assign one of the precious Category 'B' Squadrons in its place. By this stage of the Battle, the No. 11 Group squadrons were having to intercept high-flying sweeps by the Luftwaffe's Bf 109 fighters and fighter-bombers. At 1510 hours on 17 October the squadron was ordered up to intercept one of these raids, which had been detected heading for London. Squadron Leader Malan led eleven Spitfires in a climb to 26,000 feet, keeping up-sun from the fighters' reported position. He then saw AA fire towards the Thames estuary which led him to intercept about sixty Bf 109s over the Maidstone–Gravesend area. Two Bf 109s flew across the front of the squadron and Malan was able to surprise them from out of the sun. He fired on the right-hand fighter, closing in to 100 yards range, and saw it push its nose straight down suddenly to evade him.

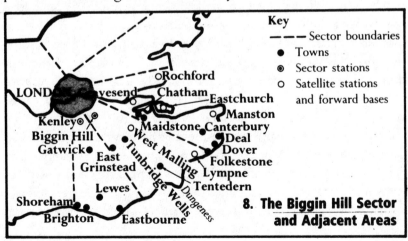

Key

— — — Sector boundaries
- Towns
◉ Sector stations
○ Satellite stations and forward bases

8. The Biggin Hill Sector and Adjacent Areas

The Bf 109's engine, fitted with direct fuel injection, continued to run during negative 'g' manoeuvres, whereas the Spitfire and Hurricane's Merlin engine, with a float carburettor, would cut under these conditions. However, it is not true to suggest, as do some accounts of the Battle, that the Bf 109s usually evaded by pushing their noses straight down, for as numerous RAF combat reports attest, their customary evasive tactic was a half-roll and dive away. This was probably because, whereas the Bf 109's engine could cope with negative 'g', its pilots found it unpleasant and so would avoid such manoeuvres unless *in extremis*.

Malan followed the Bf 109 through its unusual manoeuvre, his engine cutting and then picking up again. He fired two 4-second bursts into the diving Bf 109, finding that he had to carry out an aileron turn to keep his sights on. He then blacked out due to the positive 'g' imposed by this manoeuvre and then pulled out of his dive. Only his port guns were working during this combat and so his fire was comparatively ineffectual, but Malan saw his victim begin to smoke before he lost it in the dive; he claimed it as probably destroyed.

The second Bf 109 which crossed in front of the squadron was engaged by Flying Officer Nelson, flying as Red 2. He opened fire at 150 yards' range and saw the Bf 109 half-roll and dive. He followed it and fired three more short bursts, seeing smoke pour from its engine. At 2,000 feet the Bf 109 went vertically into cloud and Nelson pulled out to avoid hitting the ground. As Squadron Leader Malan's Red Section went in to engage the two Bf 109s, another four enemy fighters pulled in behind them. Flying Officer St. John, flying as No. 2 in Yellow Section, broke away to the left, climbed steeply and executed a semi-stall turn to bring his Spitfire on to the tail of the last of these. He began firing at 250 yards' range, but as this had no apparent effect, St. John closed right in. The enemy's slipstream was buffeting his Spitfire and he had trouble keeping his sights on the target, but he noticed smoke and then flames streaming from the Bf 109's engine. It rolled slowly on to its back and fell away downwards. St. John considered following, but on checking his mirror decided it would be unwise.

Pilot Officer Draper, Yellow 3, saw a Bf 109 cross his nose at 200 yards' range. He fired a 3-second deflection burst and saw hits on the fighter's engine, which streamed black and white smoke, but as there were more Bf 109s above him, Draper could not follow up this attack. He next saw seven Bf 109s flying southwards and got into position behind the rearmost without being seen. His fire sent it down in flames. After breaking away, he found another formation and positioned himself for an attack only to find that they were Hurricanes. Turning south towards the coast, Draper saw twelve Bf 109s flying below him. He attempted another surprise attack, but was spotted and the Bf 109s turned on him. He quickly sprayed the two leading fighters with fire, causing them to swerve away, and broke off the unequal combat. The squadron claimed a total of three Bf 109s destroyed and two probably destroyed; they lost Flying Officer Ricalton, who was shot down and killed.

On 20 October nine of No. 74 Squadron's Spitfires took off at 1405 hours with orders to rendezvous with No. 66 Squadron and patrol base at 30,000 feet. They were then directed to the Maidstone area, where they sighted about thirty Bf 109s coming in from the south at 29,000 feet. The Spitfires dived on them from 500 feet above, but were seen and the German formation split up. Half of it dived away towards Dungeness, while the remainder climbed. Flight Lieutenant Mungo-Park followed the latter and fired a 4-second burst into the rearmost fighter. It spun away and Mungo-Park saw its tail unit disintegrate. He then had to evade an attack from behind and so could not watch it any longer. Pilot Officer Draper also pursued the climbing enemy fighters and fired two long bursts into one of them. It began to go down, seemingly out of control, but Draper was attacked from behind at this moment and his oil cooler was damaged. Shortly afterwards the engine seized and he had to make a crash-landing; the machine was a write-off, but Draper was unhurt. Sergeant T. B. Kirk followed Draper and attacked another Bf 109, seeing his fire hit the fuselage and wings. He was then himself attacked and baled out of his Spitfire severely wounded. Kirk did not recover, but died the following July. Sergeant C. G. Hilken was also shot down and wounded during this combat.

The only other pilot to claim was Pilot Officer Stephen, who picked out four of the diving Bf 109s. He fired on the left-hand fighter in the formation, seeing its tail begin to break up and the cockpit canopy being jettisoned. As the other three fighters were then climbing above him, he had to break away to deal with them. In the dogfight that followed, he got on to the tail of one Bf 109 and fired a 6-second burst into it from 150 yards. Stephen saw its pilot bale out before the stricken fighter crashed into a wood.

Two days later, at 1340 hours, the squadron was ordered on to the Maidstone patrol line at 15,000 feet, in readiness for intercepting high-flying raiders. They were soon directed against several individual German fighters, but made no contact. The controller then ordered them to rendezvous with No. 92 Squadron at 30,000 feet over Maidstone, as raiders were approaching from the south and south-east. Squadron Leader Malan remained for a short time at this height, where condensation trails were forming, hoping thereby to intimidate the German fighter-bomber pilots. He then dropped to 28,000 feet, where the tell-tale trails stopped, before intercepting the Bf 109s. Nine Spitfires had taken off from Biggin Hill, but one pilot had experienced oxygen trouble and returned home with his wingman. Another two Spitfires had been unable to keep up with the formation. So when six Bf 109s were sighted at 1410 hours, they were opposed by only five RAF fighters. Going down in a fast dive from 2,000 feet above, Malan attacked the German leader. After his second burst, the Bf 109 began to smoke, but continued to dive away towards the coast, levelling off at 8,000 feet. Malan carried on firing intermittent bursts at him, but had to break off to clear ice from the inside of his windscreen. This was to be a frequently recurring problem with the Spitfire during this stage of the Battle. Eventually he saw the Bf 109 dive into the sea five miles off Dungeness.

Flight Lieutenant Mungo-Park followed a Bf 109 down, after it had half-rolled and dived. At 9,000 feet he opened fire with a 2-second burst. The Bf 109 began to smoke and its dive steepened. Mungo-Park then had to wipe ice off his windscreen before he could resume the attack. He fired another 2-second burst and followed the fighter down to 2,000 feet where it disappeared in haze and low cloud. In return for claims for two enemy aircraft destroyed, 'the squadron had lost two Spitfires. Pilot Officer Spurdle had baled out unhurt, but Pilot Officer P. C. B. St. John was killed.

On 27 October the squadron's twelve Spitfires took off at 0745 hours with instructions to rendezvous with No. 66 Squadron and patrol base at 30,000 feet. Once in the air, though, they were vectored to the Maidstone area, where they engaged some thirty Bf 109s. Squadron Leader Malan led the attack from out of the sun, but was unable to claim any damage to the enemy; shortly afterwards he himself was attacked by three enemy fighters. His Spitfire was damaged by cannon and machine-gun fire and he had to force-land at Biggin Hill. Flying Officer Nelson made sure of his victim by closing in to close range, but fragments from the enemy fighter hit his Spitfire damaging the spinner and propeller. Nelson then watched the Bf 109 crash south of Rochester. Pilot Officer Stephen drove off a Bf 109 from a Spitfire's tail and followed the enemy aircraft into a dive, firing all his ammunition into it. The Bf 109 went down in flames.

Pilot Officer Chesters fired two 3-second bursts into a Bf 109 and saw its engine stop. The German fighter, from the 3rd Staffel of Jagdgeschwader 52, made a wheels-up landing on the airstrip at Penshurst, and Chesters, short of fuel, landed beside him. Flight Lieutenant Mungo-Park found that only three of his guns were working, but he closed in to within fifty yards of a Bf 109 and fired until the ammunition ran out, seeing parts of the enemy aircraft's tailplane break away. Sergeant J. A. Scott was shot down and killed during this combat. Scott was a newly-joined pilot, formerly of No. 611 Squadron. In all, six replacement pilots from Category 'C' units were posted to No. 74 Squadron in late October.

The squadron's last combat of the month – and of the officially reckoned Battle of Britain period – was fought on 29 October. Flight Lieutenant Mungo-Park led eight Spitfires, which were instructed to join up with No. 92 Squadron at 20,000 feet over Biggin Hill. Shortly after they made contact, the other Spitfire squadron dived away to engage enemy aircraft. Mungo-Park increased his altitude to 26,000 feet and soon afterwards saw thirty Bf 109s flying about a thousand feet below. He led the Spitfires down on to them, firing two short bursts into a Bf 109, which he saw burst into flames. Continuing his dive, Mungo-Park engaged a second German fighter at 18,000 feet and followed it down in a vertical dive to 2,000 feet. The Bf 109 was pouring black smoke and, as Mungo-Park pulled out with only 800 feet to spare, he considered it certain to have crashed. Sergeant N. Morrison, flying as Mungo-Park's No. 2, saw a Bf 109 coming in to engage his leader and turned to attack it from the beam. The Bf 109 half-rolled and dived vertically. Morrison followed it down in a high-speed dive to 5,000 feet and lost consciousness when pulling out. He thought that the German fighter must have gone straight into the ground to the south of Maidstone.

Pilot Officer Spurdle followed Mungo-Park down and fired on a Bf 109, which went on to its back and spiralled downwards. He claimed it as probably destroyed. Flying Officer Nelson, Yellow 1, saw six Bf 109s circling above the Spitfires, as they went down to engage. He attacked one of these, finding that he could easily out-turn the Bf 109 at 26,000 feet. After firing a 3-second burst into the German fighter from only fifty yards' range, it half-rolled and went down to ground level. Nelson followed, firing twice more, and saw the Bf 109 crash into a field between East Grinstead and Tunbridge Wells. Pilot Officer Churches, the only other pilot to claim, broke away from the enemy fighters to engage a lone German bomber, which he identified as an He 111. He saw his fire hit the fuselage and wing root and when last seen, heading out to sea off Dungeness, the enemy aircraft was losing height. It was assessed as probably destroyed.

During its two weeks' fighting from Biggin Hill in October, the squadron had claimed thirteen enemy aircraft confirmed destroyed – all of them Bf 109s. In return they had lost three pilots killed and two wounded (one of whom was later to die). November began with further casualties. During a patrol over Dover on 1 November, Flying Officer W. H. Nelson was shot down and killed, Sergeant H. J. Soars and Flight Sergeant F. P. Burnard were both

bove: Flight Sergeant eorge Unwin of No. 19 quadron at the end of a rtie. (Wing Commander G. Unwin)

ight: Sergeant Unwin with s dog, Flash, stands by the se of one of No. 19 uadron's early Mk I itfires. Having completed s flying training, Unwin was sted to the squadron in 36 and remained with it til 1941. (Wing mmander G. C. Unwin)

Left: Sergeant S. Plzak (left) was one of four Czech pilots attached to No. 19 Squadron from No. 310 (Czech) Squadron in August 1940. (Wing Commander G. C. Unwin)

Left: Flight Sergeant Unwin, Sergeant Plzak and Sergeant B. J. Jennings relax at Fowlmere, Cambridgeshire, between sorties in September 1940. (Wing Commander G. C. Unwin)

Left: Three of No. 19 Squadron's Czech pilots at Fowlmere. Pilot Officer Frantisek Dolezal is on the left, Sergeant Stanislav Plzak in the centre and Pilot Officer Frantisek Hradil on the right (Wing Commander G. C. Unwin)

ove: Squadron Leader B. J. E. Lane (right)
posted to No. 19 Squadron in September
9 as O/C 'A' Flight and took command of
squadron following Squadron Leader P. C.
kham's death on 5 September 1940. Lane
officially assessed as a fighter pilot of
eptional ability. (Wing Commander G. C.
win)

Below: Pilot Officer Hradil stands by Spitfire
Mk I QV-I, the aircraft usually flown by
Sergeant B. J. Jennings. This was one of the
eight-machine-gun Spitfire Mk IAs, which
replaced the unsatisfactory cannon Spitfires in
early September 1940. (Wing Commander B. J.
Jennings)

Above: One of No. 19 Squadron's original Spitfire Mk Is has the engine run up test for magneto drop. The photograph was taken at Catterick, Yorkshire, during Squadron detachment in October 1939. (Wing Commander B. J. Jennings)

Left: Sergeant B. J. Jennings (left) and Flying Officer F. N Brinsden at Catterick during the No. 19 Squadron detachment in October 1939 (Wing Commander B. J. Jennings)

Above: Sergeant J. A. Potter (left) with Sergeant Jennings and an unidentified Czech pilot outside the Sergeant's Mess at Duxford, Cambridgeshire. Sergeant Jack Potter was shot down wounded near the French coast on 15 September and became a prisoner of war. (Wing Commander B. J. Jennings)

Right: Sergeant B. J. Jennings, March 1941. He wears the ribbon of the Distinguished Flying Medal. (Wing Commander B. J. Jennings)

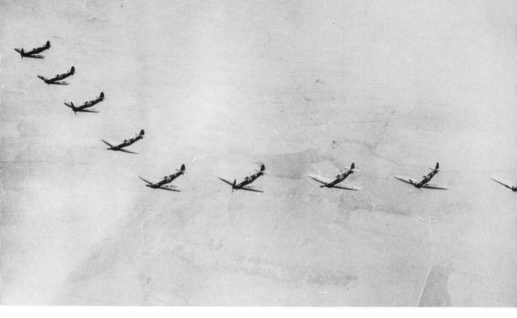

Above: The Spitfire Mk Is of No. 41 Squadron fly in immaculate formation over the Yorkshire countryside, on a sortie from the unit's station at Catterick in March 1939. (Squadron Leader R. W. Wallens)

Below: No. 41 Squadron's Spitfire Mk Is demonstrate the standard pre-war vic formation of the three-aircraft sections, whic remained the officially approved tactical unit throughout the Battle of Britain. (Squadron Leader R. W. Wallens)

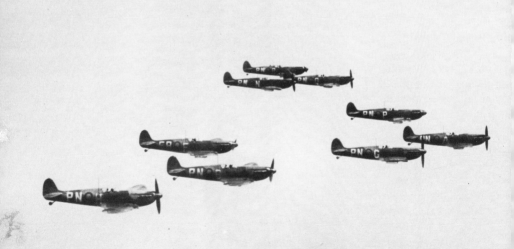

Above: No. 41 Squadron group photograph. Front row (left to right): Flying Officer W. J. 'Scotty' Scott; Flying Officer Bill Legard; Wing Commander Guy Carter (Station Commander RAF Catterick); Squadron Leader D.R.L. 'Robin' Hood; Flight Lieutenant Norman Ryder; Flight Lieutenant Stevens (Squadron Adjutant); Flying Officer Douglas Gamblen. Middle row (left to right): Unidentified; Warrant Officer Durrant (Squadron Engineer Officer); Pilot Officer J. N. Mackenxie; Pilot Officer O. B. "Buck" Morrough-Ryan; Pilot Officer Guy Cory; Flying Officer A. D. J. 'Lulu' Lovell; Pilot Officer Bill Stapleton; Pilot Officer R. W. 'Wally' Wallens. Back row (left to right): Sergeant E. V. 'Mitzi' Darling; Sergeant R. C. Ford; Flight Sergeant J. E. Sayers; Sergeant I. E. Howitt; Sergeant Robert Carr-Lewty. (Squadron Leader R. W. Wallens)

Below: Pilot Officer R. W. 'Wally' Wallens in his Spitfire 'Leaping Lena' at Catterick. He describes the emblem painted on its cowling as 'a Pterodactyl-like bird screwing the neck of Hitler's vulture'. (Squadron Leader R. W. Wallens)

Above: The wreckage of the Messerschmitt Bf 110D which fell to the guns of Pilot Officer George Bennions on 15 August. The German aircraft, from I Gruppe Zerstörergeschwader 76, came down near Barnard Castle, Durham. (Squadron Leader G. H. Bennions)

Below left: Squadron Leader G. H. Bennions DFC drawn by the artist Olive Snell at Catterick in 1942. (Squadron Leader G. H. Bennions)

Below right: Sergeant Frank Usmar of No. 41 Squadron stands by the nose of his Spitfire Mk II. He was shot down and wounded on 27 September. (Squadron Leader F. Usmar)

ove left: R. A. 'Bob' Beardsley (front) and ʳgeant T. W. R. 'Terry' Healy with a No. 41 ᵘadron Spitfire at Hornchurch. Both of these ᵒts were posted to the Squadron in ᵖtember 1940. (Squadron Leader R. A. ᵃardsley)

ove right: Squadron Leader D. O. Finlay ˢ posted to command No. 41 Squadron in

September 1940. (Imperial War Museum)

Below: Five of the surviving pilots of No. 41 Squadron at Hornchurch in December 1940. From left to right: Flying Officer J. N. Mackenzie; Flight Lieutenant A. D. J. Lovell; Squadron Leader D. O. Finlay; Flight Lieutenant E. N. Ryder and Pilot Officer R. C. Ford. (Imperial War Museum)

Left: Pilot Officer Maurice Mounsdon of No. 56 Squadron in the cockpit of h[...] Hurricane at North Weald, Essex in 1940. (Flight Lieutenant M. H. Mounsdor[...]

Below: Pilot Officer Mounsdon's Hurricane in a sandbagged revetment at North Weald. Note the lead from a trolley accumulator plugged in under the starboard wing root, ready f[...] starting. (Flight Lieutenant M. H. Mounsdon)

Above: Three of No. 56 Squadron's most successful pilots in the Battle of Britain: Sergeant Peter Hillwood (left); Flight Lieutenant E. J. 'Jumbo' Gracie; and Pilot Officer F. W. 'Taffy' Higginson. (*Fortune* magazine, via Wing Commander I. B. Westmacott)

Below: A group of No. 56 Squadron pilots, most of them veterans of the Battle of Britain, pictured in February 1941. They are (from left to right): Sergeant P. E. M. Robinson; Sergeant P. Hillwood; Pilot Officer J. Himr; Flying Officer B. J. Wicks; Flying Officer I. B. Westmacott; Sergeant Myall; Flight Lieutenant E. J. Gracie; Pilot Officer G. G. Bailey; Pilot Officer T. F. Guest; Flying Officer R. Malengreau; Pilot Officer F. W. Higginson; Squadron Leader H. M. Pinfold. (*Fortune* Magazine, via Wing Commander I. B. Westmacott)

Left: Innes B. Westmacott in 1942 when he was serving as squadron leader in Egypt. As flying officer, he was posted to No. 56 Squadron from No. 6 OTU Sutton Bridge on 3 August 1940. (Wing Commander I. B. Westmacott)

Below: A Section of No. 56 Squadron's Hurricanes takes off from North Weald in 1940. Another of the Squadron's fighters stands near the airfield perimeter. (Imperial War Museum)

Right: Pilot Officer H. M. Stephen, drawn by Captain Cuthbert Orde, was No. 74 Squadron's top-scoring pilot in the Battle of Britain. He was awarded the Distinguished Service Order in December 1940. (Wing Commander H. M. Stephen)

P.O. H.M. STEPHEN, DSO. DFC.   74 SQUADRON

Below: Flight Lieutenant J. C. Mungo-Park (left), O/C 'B' Flight, No. 74 Squadron, and Pilot Officer Stephen together formed a highly effective fighting team. On 30 November 1940 they shared in the destruction of Biggin Hill's 600th enemy aircraft. (Wing Commander H. M. Stephen)

Above: No. 85 Squadron's Hurricanes in the tightly spaced vic formation which was of more use in air displays than for air fighting. (Imperial War Museum)

Below: No. 85 Squadron's Hurricanes flying with the Sections in line astern, a much more flexible tactical formation than the vic. (Imperial War Museum)

bove: Hurricane Mk Is of No. 303 (Polish) quadron stand at readiness at Northolt, iddlesex, during the late summer of 1940. olish Institute)

elow left: No. 303 Squadron's British ommanding Officer, Squadron leader R. G. ellett (centre) and the Polish O/C 'A' Flight,

Flying Officer Witold Urbanowicz. (Polish Institute)

Below right: Squadron Leader Zdzislaw Krasnodebski was No. 303 Squadron's first Polish CO. He wears the Polish Air Force's pilot's badge in place of RAF wings on his tunic. (Polish Institute)

Above: A group of No. 303 Squadron pilots. From left to right: Pilot Officer J. Radomski; unknown; Pilot Officer J. E. L. Zumbach; Flying Officer Greschak; Flying Officer T. Sawicz; Pilot Officer W. Lokuciewski; Pilot Officer B. Mieszwa; Flying Officer Z. Henneberg; Flight Lieutenant J. A. Kent; Flying Officer E. M. Szaposznikow; Flying Officer M. Pisarek; Sergeant M. Wojciechowski; unknown; unknown; Sergeant S. Karubin; Sergeant M. Belc, unknown; Sergeant M. Brzezowski; Flight Sergeant K. Wunsche; Flight Sergeant J. Kania; Sergeant J Rogowski. (Polish Institute)

Below: One of No. 303 Squadron's pilots at cockpit readiness. The Hurricane carries the badge of No. 111 (Kosciuszko) Squadron of the Polish Air Force, No. 303 Squadron having inherited the traditions of this unit. (Polish Institute)

wounded, and the German fighters escaped unscathed. On the following day the squadron was flying in company with No. 92 Squadron, when they intercepted more than sixty Bf 109s flying at 20,000 feet over the Isle of Sheppey. The Spitfires, 4,000 feet higher than the German formation, dived into the attack, with No. 92 Squadron in the lead. The German fighters immediately scattered and headed back towards France. Flight Lieutenant Mungo-Park, at the head of No. 74 Squadron's formation, did not catch up with the diving Bf 109s until he was at 10,000 feet over Folkestone. He then fired three bursts into one of them before his windscreen iced over and he had to break off the combat.

Sergeant Skinner, Red 2, could not catch the diving Bf 109s and so climbed back to 20,000 feet where he engaged three German fighters and shot one of them down. Pilot Officer Spurdle, Red 3, followed Skinner's example and saw the Bf 109 that he had attacked crash near Ashford. Pilot Officer Churches, Yellow 2, chased a Bf 109 twenty miles out to sea before sending it diving vertically into the water. Sergeant N. Morrison, Yellow 4, used emergency boost in chasing the Bf 109s almost to the French coast. A Bf 109 then came from out of the sun and attacked him head-on, but its fire went wide. Morrison turned back and at mid-Channel met three more returning Bf 109s. With the sun behind him, he attacked one of these and saw it dive into the sea, trailing a plume of smoke.

On 5 November Flight Lieutenant Mungo-Park was awarded the DFC, Pilot Officer Stephen receiving a Bar to his DFC at the same time. The two pilots celebrated this award in style during their next encounter with the Luftwaffe on 14 November. Mungo-Park was leading twelve of No. 74 Squadron's Spitfires behind No. 66 Squadron, when a formation of more than fifty Ju 87 Stukas was intercepted off Deal at 1410 hours. Mungo-Park claimed two of them destroyed and Stephen three destroyed, with the latter's claims being matched by Pilot Officer Draper. In all, the squadron claimed fourteen Ju 87s and one Bf 109 confirmed destroyed. Pilot Officer Churches, flying as Yellow 4 on the tail-end of the squadron formation, was the only pilot not to engage the Stukas, but it was he who accounted for the Bf 109. One Spitfire was lost, although its pilot, Pilot Officer W. Armstrong, baled out unhurt, and another was damaged.

The re-appearance of the Ju 87 Stuka, which the Luftwaffe had withdrawn from the Battle in late August, provided a welcome interlude in the usual hard-fought fighter battles of November and early December. On 15 November the squadron was attacked from above by about twenty Bf 109s over Littlehampton. In the dogfight that followed Pilot Officer Draper, Sergeant L. E. Freese and Sergeant J. N. Glendinning each claimed an enemy fighter destroyed and Pilot Officer Stephen damaged a fourth. Two days later the squadron met about eighteen Bf 109s at 27,000 feet over Brighton, and Flight Lieutenant Freeborn and Pilot Officer Stephen shared in the destruction of one of them. At this time the RAF pilots often found the Germans unwilling to engage them. On 23 November the squadron found groups of Bf 109s flying above them over Dover, but they would not come down to fight. Squadron Leader Malan, however, was able to catch a pair of Bf 109s in mid-Channel and he shot one of them down. On 27 November the CO shot down another Bf 109 during an action over Chatham, and Squadron Leader H. J. Wilson, a Royal Aircraft Establishment test pilot attached to the squadron to gain operational experience, also claimed a German fighter destroyed. However, the Squadron lost Pilot Officer Chesters, who baled out of his Spitfire wounded. On 30 November Flight Lieutenant Mungo-Park and Pilot Officer Stephen were on convoy patrol off Deal, when they engaged a formation of eight Bf 109s and shared in the destruction of one of them. It was the 600th enemy aircraft to be shot down by a Biggin Hill squadron and brought No. 74 Squadron's score for November up to 27 destroyed.

The German fighters were once again reluctant to engage on the morning of 1 December, when the squadron sighted nine Bf 109s flying 5,000 feet above them at 32,000 feet to the north of Dover. Only one Bf 109 dived to attack and it was promptly shot down by Flying Officer Szczesny. On the next day the squadron followed No. 66 Squadron on patrol and were vectored to the Dover–Dungeness area. The two units then split up and No. 74 Squadron was attacked from the front quarter by small groups of

Bf 109s. The Spitfires got the better of the ensuing dogfight, claiming five Bf 109s destroyed for no loss to themselves. The squadron fought its last combat of the year on 5 December, when it met more than twenty Bf 109s in the Folkestone area. Eight fighters were claimed as destroyed by the Spitfire pilots. Flight Lieutenant Freeborn accounted for two of these, while Pilot Officer Stephen and Sergeant J. Murray each shot down one fighter and claimed a third between them. Flying Officer Szczesny, Flying Officer Boulding and Pilot Officer Spurdle all gained single victories. It was a suitable finale to a year of tough fighting in which the 'Tigers' had indeed proved to be among the Luftwaffe's more ferocious opponents.

Squadron Leader Malan's leadership of the squadron during the Battle was recognized by the award of the DSO on 13 December. Pilot Officer Stephen, its most successful fighter pilot, was also awarded the DSO – a most unusual decoration for a junior officer. Pilot Officer Draper was awarded the DFC and Sergeant Skinner the DFM. It was very largely due to Malan's qualities as a commander that the squadron had performed so well. His insistence on good discipline in the air and on the ground paid dividends, not only in victories gained, but also in the reduction of the squadron's casualties. Malan emerged from the Battle as Fighter Command's leading tactician, and his basic rules of air fighting were to be widely circulated among the operational training units and squadrons. He was the most influential (though by no means the only) squadron commander to experiment with new tactical formations, and No. 74 Squadron's sections of four fighters were to be generally adopted by Fighter Command during 1941. Malan's skill would have counted for little, however, had it not been for the courage and ability of his squadron's pilots, most notably Freeborn, Mungo-Park, Stephen and Stevenson. For it was one of the basic precepts of the RAF's new code of fighter tactics that the squadron should fly as a mutually supporting team.

NO. 85 SQUADRON

No. 85 Squadron had served as a fighter squadron during the First World War, operating over the Western Front with SE 5a scouts from May 1918 until the Armistice. During that period it had claimed 99 air victories and had been commanded by two of the newly formed RAF's legendary aces: Major W. A. 'Billy' Bishop, VC and Major Edward Mannock, VC. Disbanded in 1919 it did not re-appear until mid-1938. The squadron was then re-formed at RAF Debden in Essex on 1 June and was equipped with Gloster Gladiator biplane fighters. In common with many of the units re-formed during this period of rapid expansion, its nucleus was formed by detaching a flight from an already existing squadron – in this instance 'A' Flight of No. 87 Squadron. In September 1938 No. 85 Squadron re-equipped with Hawker Hurricane monoplane fighters and, following the outbreak of war in September 1939, took these to France as part of the Air Component of the British Expeditionary Force.

The squadron saw little action during the Phoney War period, although on 21 November Flight Lieutenant R. H. A. Lee shot down an He 111 off Boulogne for its first victory of the Second World War. Then on 10 May 1940 the opening of the German attack on the Low Countries and France ushered in a period of intense air fighting. No. 85 Squadron was in action every day, until on 20 May it was withdrawn exhausted to England to re-form. During eleven days of combat it had claimed a total of 89 enemy aircraft confirmed destroyed, but in return had lost eleven pilots killed or missing in action and a further six pilots wounded.

As one of the casualties had been the newly arrived CO, Squadron Leader M. Peacock, it fell to his successor, Squadron Leader P. W. Townsend, to train a dozen replacement pilots up to operational standard. Townsend himself was an experienced fighter pilot, having previously served as a flight commander with

No. 43 Squadron. He also had the survivors from the Battle of France, Flight Lieutenant Lee and another six battle-tested pilots, around whom to build a new squadron. Most of June 1940 was occupied with training flights from Debden, but by the beginning of July the squadron was again fully operational and was carrying out convoy patrols from the forward base at Martlesham Heath. The Debden satellite airfield at Castle Camps was also used during July and a number of night sector patrols was carried out from there but without success. For the most part too, the convoy patrols, while both arduous and monotonous, were uneventful although what action the squadron did see in July generally came during the course of these patrols.

On 8 July Flight Sergeant G. Allard, patrolling over Martlesham Heath, was directed to intercept an enemy aircraft flying off the Suffolk coast. He attacked an He 111, which was seen to go down into the sea off Felixstowe. Allard, a former aircraft apprentice at RAF Halton, had already gained ten air victories during the fighting in France. He was to become No. 85 Squadron's highest-scoring pilot before his death in an air crash in March 1941. On 9 July Allard again intercepted an He 111, but it escaped in cloud.

On 10 July both flights of No. 85 Squadron were fully occupied in providing dawn to dusk cover over an east coast convoy. 'A' Flight was commanded by Flight Lieutenant H. R. Hamilton, while the Commander of 'B' Flight was the veteran Flight Lieutenant 'Dicky' Lee. Early on the following morning the CO was scrambled to intercept a lone raider. Attacking from astern, he got in two bursts of fire at the Do 17Z, before his Hurricane was hit by return fire and its engine disabled. Townsend baled out and was picked up by a trawler, which landed him at Harwich. His damaged opponent, a bomber from 4. Staffel Kampfgeschwader 2, crash-landed on its return to base with three of its aircrew wounded.

On 12 July continuous patrols were flown from 0600 hours onwards, and at 0835 hours Blue Section caught a bomber formation attacking Convoy 'Booty' ten miles off Aldeburgh. Pilot Officer Bickerdike fired a long burst into an He 111 and saw it burst into flames and dive into the sea. Sergeant C. A. Rust opened his attack on a second He 111 with a dive from the starboard beam. His fire put the mid-upper gunner out of action and he then attacked from the port side, seeing his fire hit the bomber's port engine, which billowed smoke. The He 111 dived steeply into cloud and Rust lost contact. The third member of Blue Section, Sergeant L. Jowitt, was shot down and killed, his fighter crashing into the sea off Felixstowe. Ironically, Jowitt was the most experienced member of the section, having served with No. 85 Squadron since 1938. Their opponents were the He 111s of II Gruppe, Kampfgeschwader 53.

On 22 July Pilot Officer J. L. Bickerdike was killed when his Hurricane crashed during an approach to land at the satellite airfield at Castle Camps. The next engagement with the enemy came a week later. Flying Officer P. P. Woods-Scawen was flying as No. 3 in Blue Section, led by Flight Lieutenant Lee, during a convoy patrol off Felixstowe on 29 July. At about 1505 hours he saw a Do 17Z flying eastwards some six miles away. He broke from the section to give chase, waggling his wings to attract their

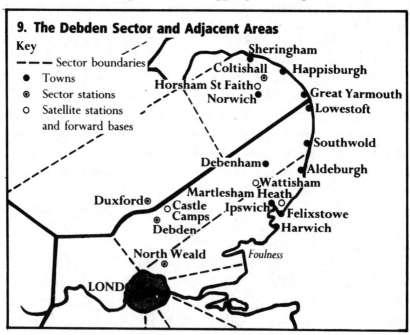

9. The Debden Sector and Adjacent Areas

Key
- — — Sector boundaries
- ● Towns
- ◉ Sector stations
- ○ Satellite stations and forward bases

Sheringham
Coltishall
Happisburgh
Horsham St Faith
Great Yarmouth
Norwich
Lowestoft
Southwold
Debenham
Aldeburgh
Wattisham
Martlesham Heath
Duxford
Castle Camps
Ipswich
Felixstowe
Debden
Harwich
North Weald
Foulness
LOND

attention, but was unable to contact his leader by R/T. Woods-Scawen opened his attack from out of the sun, firing a long burst, and followed up with quarter and astern attacks, firing off his ammunition. By this time he was nearing the enemy coast and, when four German fighters appeared, he broke off the action and returned to Martlesham Heath. His Hurricane was damaged, with bullet holes through the propeller and port mainplane. The bomber, from III Gruppe Kampfgeschwader 76, also regained its base in damaged condition, but the Gruppenkommandeur, Oberstleutnant Genth, had been killed by Woods-Scawen's fire.

On the following day Flight Lieutenant Hamilton was leading Red Section out to take up its position over Convoy 'Pilot'. *En route*, at about 1500 hours, he sighted two Bf 110s flying very low over the sea some ten miles off Aldeburgh. The Hurricanes went into line astern and gave chase, finally catching the enemy aircraft forty miles out to sea. Hamilton carried out two attacks from astern on one Bf 110 and then broke away. Flight Sergeant Allard, who two days before had been invested with the DFM, took up the attack. The Bf 110, a fighter-bomber from Erprobungsgruppe 210, hit the sea and broke up. Its companion escaped into low cloud.

On 6 August Flight Sergeant Allard was leading Yellow Section on an early morning patrol over Lowestoft, when the Hurricanes were ordered to give cover to Convoy 'Arena'. In order to find the ships, Allard had to let down through cloud to 2,000 feet. He was then ordered to climb to 10,000 feet and told that enemy aircraft were in the vicinity. With his section in line astern, Allard had completed one circle at this height before he saw a Do 17Z to his left at about 0630 hours. He turned in to approach it from the beam, his attack then developing from the quarter into a stern chase. He observed hits on the port engine before breaking away to allow the rest of the section to attack. Yellow 2, Sergeant J. H. M. Ellis, gave the Do 17Z a long burst from astern and was followed in by No. 3, Sergeant W. R. Evans. The bomber dropped through cloud until it was only a few feet above the water. The Hurricanes followed it down and Allard carried out a further beam attack, following through to the line astern position. The tail of the Do 17Z hit the sea and broke away after which the aircraft nose-dived into the sea and sank. Yellow Leader reformed his section into vic formation and returned to Martlesham Heath. Curiously, in view of the circumstances of this claim (all three RAF pilots saw the enemy aircraft go into the sea), no corresponding loss has been discovered among Luftwaffe casualty returns.

On 10 August the Debden Sector passed from the control of No. 12 Group to that of No. 11 Group, but No. 85 Squadron's pattern of operations remained unchanged, with convoy patrols being flown from dawn until dusk. At 1130 hours on 11 August Squadron Leader Townsend took off at the head of Yellow Section to patrol Convoy 'Pilot'. On arriving over the convoy he saw an unidentified aircraft flying to the east of it and turned to investigate. The aircraft disappeared in heavy, broken cloud before Townsend could reach it. So after searching for a while without regaining contact, he turned back towards the convoy. His No. 3, Sergeant C. E. Hampshire, had lost his leader and was already back over the merchant ships. There he was joined by Yellow 2, Sergeant H. H. Allgood, who had been unable to start his engine for five minutes and so had been left behind by the other two Hurricanes. The CO meanwhile, had regained contact with his original quarry some three miles to the east and identified it as a Do 17Z. He was able to fire two bursts into it, before it dived into cloud and disappeared, its starboard engine smoking. Townsend continued his search for the Do 17Z and when some thirty miles east of the convoy encountered a formation of about twenty Bf 110s circling at 4,000 feet. They turned away to the east and, after calling a warning to control, Townsend decided to return to the convoy. Unfortunately he missed the ships and made a landfall twenty miles to the south of their position. By the time that he had flown back, the Bf 110s (from Erprobungsgruppe 210) had reached the vicinity of the convoy.

Sergeant Hampshire, warned by control of the enemy aircraft's proximity, climbed through cloud to 5,000 feet. As he emerged, his Hurricane was attacked from above and behind by seven Bf 110s. Hampshire dived away and as he did so spotted a single Bf 110 flying low over the sea. He carried on down to engage it from above and behind, firing a 3-second burst. The Bf 110 dived straight into the sea and sank. Sergeant Allgood lost Yellow 3 as he entered cloud, but on emerging found himself in a position to attack a straggling Bf 110. After opening fire with a deflection shot, Allgood saw the enemy aircraft dive away and he followed it down. When he had expended all his ammunition, seeing some hits and a thin trail of smoke from the starboard engine, he broke off the attack. By now, Squadron Leader Townsend had regained contact with the main enemy formation. Picking out a Bf 110 some 200 feet below the others, he carried out a diving head-on attack. On breaking away, he was attacked from head-on by another Bf 110. The two aircraft narrowly missed a collision and Townsend carried on at high speed for the cover of the nearest clouds. On re-emerging he again tried to pick out an isolated enemy aircraft, but found most of them within the defensive circle. As his fuel was then running low, Townsend decided to return to base. It was this enemy formation that No. 74 Squadron also engaged during its third combat on 11 August.

From 13 August onwards the squadron was concentrated on the Sector station at Debden rather than operating as detached flights from Martlesham Heath and Castle Camps. Five days later it fought its first squadron-strength action of the Battle, when thirteen Hurricanes were sent up against the afternoon raid approaching North Weald. They engaged the withdrawing aircraft about ten miles east of Foulness Point at 1750 hours and became entangled with the Bf 110 escort fighters of Zerstörergeschwader 26. Squadron Leader Townsend fired a full deflection burst at a Bf 110 which crossed his nose. It went down in a vertical spiral and was thought to be out of control. He then got into a dogfight with several twin-engined fighters, before sighting a small number of Bf 109s from the top cover escort provided by III Gruppe Jagdgeschwader 51. Townsend attacked one of these in a left-hand climbing turn and reported that it spun away in flames. He was engaged by a second Bf 109, but easily out-turned it, gave it a short burst and saw the pilot bale out. He then chased further enemy fighters out to sea, but in spite of using emergency boost, could not close the gap so he finished off his ammunition in two bursts from outside effective range and turned back for the English coast.

Red 2, Pilot Officer C. E. English, attacked a Bf 110 which had dived in front of his Hurricane and saw hits on the wings. The rear gunner stopped firing and English fired the remainder of his ammunition from 200 to 300 yards' range in two long bursts. As another Bf 110 had got on his tail, he was forced to break away and could only claim his target as damaged. Sergeant H. N. Howes, No. 3 in the leading Section, broke away to follow the Bf 110 first attacked by the CO, but its dive was too steep for him to follow. On climbing back to 9,000 feet, he got on the tail of another Bf 110 and fired a 2-second burst into it. Howes followed it down and saw it crash into the sea. Having regained height once more, he dived into a circle of Bf 110s and saw his fire hit one of them. He then broke away in a climbing turn to evade an attack from behind. Reaching 15,000 feet, Howes saw a formation of bombers and finished off most of his ammunition in an attack on a straggler.

Flight Lieutenant Hamilton, Yellow 1, began to attack a Bf 110, but this was then engaged by the CO and so he switched his attention to an He 111. After a 5-second burst of fire, he saw it go down smoking and with the undercarriage dropped. On breaking away from this target, Hamilton saw a Bf 110 passing 2,000 feet below him to his right. He dived on its tail and, as its rear gunner was firing, stayed beneath the enemy aircraft's tailplane to spoil the gunner's field of fire. After a 7-second burst, Hamilton saw the Bf 110 dive towards the sea with both engines in flames. His No. 2, Pilot Officer J. E. Marshall, also singled out an He 111 for attack and opened fire at it from 250 yards' range. The mid-upper gunner stopped firing and a stream of white vapour streamed back from the bomber. Flying into this, Marshall lost sight of his target and his starboard wingtip sliced into the He 111's tailplane. The Hurricane remained airworthy, although the throttle had jammed open and a bullet had damaged its brake system and Marshall was able to bring off a successful landing on his return to Debden. The bomber was thought to have come down in the sea.

Yellow 3, Sergeant Ellis, broke away from his section and climbed in the sun before delivering his first attack. Seeing a Bf 110 outside the defensive circle formed by its fellows, Ellis dived on it from astern and saw his bullets hitting. The aircraft dived away and he lost it in haze. As Ellis climbed again, a Bf 109 turned across his nose, giving him the chance of a deflection shot. It flew right into his fire, flick-rolled several times and then went down vertically.

Flight Lieutenant R. H. A. Lee, flying at the head of 'B' Flight as Blue 1, was reported missing in action after this combat. He was last seen chasing three Bf 109s out to sea. Blue 2, Pilot Officer J. A. Hemingway, became engaged in a dogfight with a group of Bf 110s and his Hurricane's engine was hit and disabled. He began to fly back towards the coast, but the engine seized and he had to bale out. Hemingway was 1½ hours in the water before he was picked up. Blue 3, Sergeant F. R. Walker-Smith, carried out a head-on attack on a Bf 110, diving from 2,000 feet above it. He saw it glide down with both engines smoking and hit the sea about forty miles from the coast. After skirmishing with other Bf 110s, he got into position for another head-on attack. He saw his target disintegrate at about 3,000 feet before falling into the sea; one of the crew baled out.

Pilot Officer W. Hodgson, Blue 4, attacked a number of Bf 110s, but was unable to keep his sights on them as his Hurricane also was continually attacked. He climbed out of the mêlée and came down on a Bf 110. Its port engine was disabled and it dived away into the sun. Hodgson next engaged a circle of Bf 110s, but was himself attacked and so could not get in a good burst of fire. Seeing another formation of Bf 110s to the north, he dived on one of these and saw his fire knock out one of its engines. Finally, he climbed to 25,000 feet and dived on to a group of enemy aircraft, finishing off his ammunition.

Flying Officer A. V. Gowers, leading Green Section, sighted a formation of Ju 87 dive-bombers, with Bf 110 and Bf 109 escort fighters, flying twenty miles out to sea. He got into position behind one of the Ju 87s and fired two long bursts into it, seeing it pour out clouds of black smoke and dive seawards. He then turned back towards the coast, where he could see Hurricanes dogfighting with Bf 109s, but was unable to find another target. Green 2, Pilot Officer Lockhart, had been unable to keep up with the squadron formation, but on reaching the area of the combat he opened fire with a snap shot at a Bf 110 which flew across his nose. He then climbed to 20,000 feet and dived to engage another Bf 110, which he saw break away from a defensive circle. He chased it down to sea level and thought that some of his shots had hit, but it easily out-distanced him and Lockhart gave up the chase. Pilot Officer A. G. Lewis, Green 3, saw a Bf 110 leave its defensive circle and dive towards a Hurricane. He manoeuvred on to its tail and saw him dive smoking towards the sea. The total squadron claims from this combat amounted to six Bf 110s, three Bf 109s and one He 111 confirmed destroyed, plus four aircraft probably destroyed and six damaged.

On 19 August No. 85 Squadron moved to Croydon in the Kenley Sector, changing places with No. 111 Squadron. Patrols from the new airfield during the following two days proved to be uneventful and wet weather on 23 August prevented operational flying, but that night Croydon was bombed and one of 'B' Flight's Hurricanes was set alight and another two damaged by splinters. At 0758 hours on 24 August twelve Hurricanes took off with orders to patrol Dover, but within half an hour four of them landed again. They had lost contact with the squadron due to the R/T set in Pilot Officer Worrall's aircraft being left switched to transmit, thus effectively jamming all air-to-air communication between the Hurricanes. Meanwhile, the newly commissioned Pilot Officer Allard, flying as Yellow Leader in the depleted

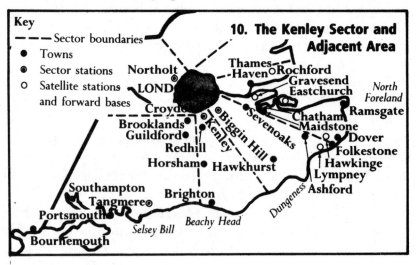

squadron formation, had spotted a stray Bf 109 over Ramsgate. The fighter was climbing to rejoin a group of about twenty-five Bf 109s flying above the Hurricanes and it was about 1,000 feet below them. Allard quickly turned to the right, dived and pulled up underneath the Bf 109, firing two short bursts. He saw it fall out of control and dive into the sea. Then he successfully evaded attacks by a number of the higher-flying enemy fighters and returned to base. Pilot Officer Lockhart's Hurricane was hit (he believed by AA fire) and he had to force-land at Hawkinge with inoperable flaps. He was slightly wounded in the ankle.

On 26 August the squadron was ordered to take off at 1450 hours and was directed to the Maidstone area, where it met a formation of eighteen Do 17Zs escorted by Bf 109s at 1530 hours. The bombers were flying at 15,000 feet in six three-aircraft vics, stepped up astern, with some thirty Bf 109s above them, flying at between 20,000 and 25,000 feet. Squadron Leader Townsend led the twelve Hurricanes into a front quarter attack on the leading bombers. After the initial onslaught, the first vic of Do 17Zs broke formation and Townsend and most of the squadron's pilots concentrated their attention on them. After a series of quarter and stern attacks, the first bomber went down in a shallow dive and was followed by Pilot Officers Allard and Worrall. It was seen to make a wheels-up landing on Rochford airfield, but before it got down a flight of Spitfires appeared and attacked it. These were fighters from No. 65 Squadron led by Flight Lieutenant G. A. W. Saunders, who claimed a half share in the kill much to the resentment of No. 85 Squadron. The four aircrew of the Do 17Z, from the 2. Staffel of Kampfgeschwader 2, survived to become prisoners of war.

The remaining two Do 17Zs of the leading vic closed formation, but further attacks from the Hurricanes caused the left-hand aircraft to break away. It dropped through the clouds heading out to sea, with one engine disabled, but then turned back and ditched in the estuary about a mile off Eastchurch. The third bomber was followed out to sea by Sergeant Howes, who fired his remaining ammunition into it. He finally saw it crash into the water about fifteen miles east of Foulness. Sergeant Ellis, whose Hurricane was hit and slightly damaged by return fire from the bombers, reported that the Bf 109 escort fighters made no attempt to come down and engage the Hurricanes and this was the general experience. Pilot Officer Hemingway broke away from the main battle and climbed to engage the German fighters. Before he could gain a favourable attacking position, his Hurricane was raked by enemy fire. The engine overheated and, thinking it about to catch fire, Hemingway took to his parachute. He landed unhurt in Pitsea Marshes and returned to Croydon the same night. The only other pilot to try and reach the fighter escort was Pilot Officer Woods-Scawen, who pulled up beneath a formation of twelve Bf 109s. He fired a 3-second burst into the belly of one of them. He saw his fire hit and the German fighter seemed to whip-stall, but as Woods-Scawen's Hurricane itself fell away in a stall he could not see what became of it.

Two days later the squadron fought with enemy fighters over the Dungeness area, claiming six Bf 109s destroyed and a Bf 110 damaged. The Prime Minister, visiting the south coast defences, was able to watch the action. Squadron Leader Townsend, seeing a formation of about twenty Bf 109s flying at 18,000 feet just above a cloud layer, led his ten Hurricanes into the attack from above and out of the sun. Just before they reached a firing position, the Hurricanes were spotted and the Germans broke away in all directions. One of them crossed Townsend's nose in a steep left-hand turn. He gave it a 2–3-second burst and the Bf 109 rolled over and dived steeply, trailing black and white smoke. Townsend picked out another fighter, but, before he could get a good burst of fire in, it dived steeply away. Even with emergency boost, the Hurricane could not catch it, but Townsend gave it one short burst from long range. His fighter was then attacked from the blind spot underneath. Fire hit the R/T set, but Townsend immediately broke away and little further damage was done.

The CO's No. 2, Flying Officer Gowers, attacked a Bf 110 and fired all his ammunition into it. He reported that it went down in a shallow dive towards the French coast. Pilot Officer Woods-Scawen opened fire on a Bf 109 from the quarter, following into the astern position. The German pilot half-rolled and Woods-

Scawen fired again. He saw the aircraft pour black smoke and go into a vertical dive towards the sea. Sergeant Walker-Smith only had the chance of a 2-second burst at a Bf 109 before it dived away into cloud. He followed it down and noticed it cross a gap in the clouds, before re-emerging and climbing again. Walker-Smith closed in behind and beneath it and saw his fire hit. As the Bf 109 went into a fairly steep dive, the Hurricane was attacked from behind and damaged. Walker-Smith broke away in a steep left-hand turn to shake off his pursuer. He then went down through cloud and saw a large explosion on the surface of the sea, which was thought to be the Bf 109 that he had attacked.

During his opening attack, Pilot Officer Hodgson was diving too fast and he overshot his target. On pulling out, he noticed two Bf 109s heading back towards France. Putting his Hurricane into a steep climb to 17,000 feet, Hodgson then came down astern of them. The two fighters saw their danger and dived away. Hodgson was only able to close to within 600 yards, which was well outside effective range. He fired a short burst at the Bf 109s, causing one of them to turn and was then able to reduce the range by turning more tightly. Meanwhile, the other Bf 109 ignored his ineffectual fire and outran the Hurricane. Hodgson fired again at the lagging Bf 109 and it turned once more, allowing him to cut the corner and reduce the range to 350 yards. The Bf 109 then slowed up as Hodgson fired his third burst. When within 250 yards, he gave the enemy fighter a long burst and it went down steeply, pouring smoke. It pulled out only a few feet above the sea. Hodgson came in fast behind and gave it a final short burst of fire, before breaking off the action five miles north-west of Cap Gris Nez.

Pilot Officer Allard was especially successful in this combat, claiming two Bf 109s destroyed. He opened his attack on one Bf 109 from 200 yards, firing two 3-second bursts while closing in to short range. It poured smoke and dived vertically into the sea off Folkestone Harbour. Breaking away, Allard then attacked a second German fighter from 250 yards' range, firing a series of short bursts into it until his ammunition was finished. He followed it down to low level and saw it hit the sea and break up. By now Allard was only five miles off the French coast and, as he turned back towards

England, he was attacked by three Bf 109s, but he evaded them with only slight damage to his Hurricane's tailplane.

On 29 August twelve Hurricanes were sent up at 1521 hours and were ordered to patrol Hawkinge at 15,000 feet. They were then brought down below cloud to only 4,000 feet, before being told to circle up again to engage enemy aircraft flying at between 15,000 and 20,000 feet. This serious mistake by the controller put the squadron at a considerable disadvantage from the outset. The Hurricanes climbed again and, as they reached 10,000 feet, Townsend saw a formation of about eighteen German bombers, escorted by thirty Bf 109s, flying just above the clouds at 7,000 feet. He immediately gave chase, edging towards the sun and keeping his height advantage, but as soon as the Bf 109 escort spotted the Hurricanes, they quickly climbed to 16,000 feet. Soon afterwards Townsend, seeing large formations of German fighters above him, turned away from the bomber formation. He had intended to climb up-sun from the large enemy fighter force, and deliver a surprise attack from above and behind them, but his plans were frustrated by a group of twelve Bf 110s which came down in a shallow dive to attack the Hurricanes. Townsend ordered his fighters to form a circle and the Bf 110s then pulled away and milled around above them. One or two of the twin-engined fighters broke away from their formation to dive past the Hurricanes. Townsend warned his pilots to keep in their circle and not try to attack these. One or two ignored his warning, however, and were immediately set upon by further Bf 110s coming down. Two Hurricanes were lost during the fight, both pilots escaping by parachute. Sergeant Ellis was unhurt, but Sergeant Walker-Smith was wounded in the foot.

After ten minutes of circling, a group of Bf 109s gave the Hurricanes the opportunity to counter-attack. Five of the single-engined German fighters dived past the squadron heading for cloud below. One of them then pulled up in a left-hand climbing turn, giving Squadron Leader Townsend the chance of a deflection shot. He fired a 5-second burst at it and saw it belch black and white smoke. The Bf 109 then stalled and went down vertically to crash north of Hastings. Flight Lieutenant Hamilton saw another

German fighter attacking a Hurricane, which escaped in cloud. The Bf 109 then began to climb to rejoin the main enemy formation. Hamilton immediately engaged it, firing a 7-second burst, and saw its engine catch fire. It then dived vertically for the sea. Sergeant G. B. Booth saw five Bf 109s beneath him and dived on to the tail of one of them. He chased it ten miles out to sea, firing short bursts, and last saw it at 500 feet, trailing thick black smoke and' continuing to lose height.

The squadron was again ordered on patrol at 1825 hours that afternoon. After following various vectors, the eleven Hurricanes climbed to 24,000 feet and circled over Dungeness. The squadron was flying with the sections in line astern and disposed in a diamond formation. At this point they were joined by a stray Hurricane and a Spitfire, which began to weave behind the flank sections. Control then warned of enemy aircraft to the north and the squadron flew in that direction. The weather made visibility extremely variable; thick haze obscured the ground and diffused the sun's light, creating a large blind spot in that direction. Seeing no enemy aircraft, Townsend began to circle to the left. At that point Pilot Officer Hodgson called a warning of enemy aircraft behind. The Hurricanes broke away steeply to the left, but Flight Lieutenant Hamilton's aircraft was hit by cannon fire. Its tail broke away and the Hurricane plunged to earth. Hamilton did not escape from it. Pilot Officer Marshall, after he heard Hodgson's warning, saw a Bf 109 appear to his right in a right-hand climbing turn. He turned towards it and fired. The fighter went into a vertical dive. Marshall followed it down to 5,000 feet, and then pulled out of his dive. The Bf 109 was last seen diving vertically into the haze, about ten miles off Dungeness. It was assessed as destroyed. The other enemy fighters dived away towards France.

In his subsequent report on this action Squadron Leader Townsend was highly critical of the action of the two stray British fighters in tacking themselves on to the rear of his formation. As he pointed out, they could not serve any useful function as weavers or rearguards, since they were on a different radio frequency from his squadron's and so could not pass on any warning, and their presence behind the squadron formation made it more difficult for the Hurricane pilots to keep a good look-out to the rear. As Pilot Officer Hodgson had become accustomed to seeing the lone Spitfire in his rearview mirror, he failed to recognize the attacking fighter as a Bf 109 until it was already within firing range. In order to prevent similar confusion in future, Townsend suggested that if straggling RAF fighters wished to join another squadron's formation, they should be instructed to attach themselves to the flanks where they could be seen clearly.

The Luftwaffe dispatched strong raids against the No. 11 Group Sector stations in Kent and Surrey on the morning of 30 August and at 1036 hours eleven of No. 85 Squadron's Hurricanes were ordered up against them as they approached the coast. At 1110 hours Squadron Leader Townsend sighted a formation of about fifty He 111s flying at 16,000 feet over the Bethersden area of Kent. They were accompanied by the usual escort of Bf 110s and Bf 109s stepped up to 20,000 feet. Townsend followed the enemy formation inland, keeping up-sun of it, until he was well ahead of them. He then led a head-on attack against the bombers, each section of Hurricanes attacking in successive waves. This tactic succeeded in breaking up the German formation, although the strong escort prevented many of the Hurricanes from following up this initial advantage by further attacks on the He 111s. After his initial attack the CO broke away beneath the bombers and turned towards the sun. He was then attacked by twelve Bf 110s and had to take evasive action, although he found that their fire was ineffectual. Climbing again, Townsend noticed two formations of Bf 110s, which he pursued. A third group of twin-engined fighters came in behind him, but did not press home their attack and turned away eastwards.

Meanwhile Townsend had singled out a Bf 110 which had broken away from one of the formations ahead of him. However, due to the distraction of the Bf 110s threatening to attack him, he misjudged his turn in behind it and had to chase the fighter from astern. He caught up with it as it crossed the coast to the west of Beachy Head and opened fire from slightly below at 200 yards' range. He then followed it down to sea level and continued the pursuit until twenty miles out to sea. When last seen it was maintaining height, with one engine smoking and so Townsend could only claim it as damaged.

As Flying Officer Gowers (No. 2, Blue Section) broke away after the head-on attack, he found a single Bf 110 and closed in astern of it. The aircraft turned steeply and headed for the coast. Gowers fired two 5-second bursts into it and saw both engines begin to smoke. The Bf 110 dived slowly towards the sea and the Hurricane followed it until it was ten to fifteen miles from land. When last seen the German fighter was at 2,000 feet, continuing to go down and with one engine disabled. Sergeant Goodman was unable to fire during the initial head-on attack. As he climbed into the sun to regain altitude he saw twelve Bf 110s pass right over the top of his Hurricane. None of the German pilots appeared to have seen him, so he turned quickly to the right, pulled the nose of his Hurricane up, and fired at one of them. Its port engine began to smoke and the aircraft broke formation, losing height as it made for the coast. Goodman then had to dive steeply away to evade the other German fighters and could not see what became of his victim. Ten minutes later he was patrolling over the coast at about 15,000 feet, when he saw a Bf 110, heading for France, 6,000 feet below him, with its starboard engine smoking. He came down on it from the rear quarter, firing a short burst which had no apparent effect, so he resumed the attack from dead astern, finishing off his remaining ammunition. Blazing fragments fell from the port engine, which began to pour black smoke. The Bf 110 turned back towards the English coast, steadily losing height. Goodman watched as it ditched in the sea about four miles off Sandgate. He could see no survivors after the aircraft sank.

Sergeant Booth climbed into the sun, after breaking away from his head-on attack. Seeing a formation of Bf 110s below him and to the left, he dived to attack one of these from ahead. He opened fire at 400 yards and continued firing until very near to colliding, before he broke away downwards. He could see his shots hitting the fuselage of the Bf 110, but did not see it go down and so claimed it as damaged.

Pilot Officer Allard selected a group of He 111s, flying on the left of the German formation, as the target for his opening head-on

attack. The bomber that he had fired at fell away from the formation and so he quickly turned in behind it to continue the attack.
Both engines began to smoke and the He 111 rolled on to its back
and went down out of control. Allard broke away and climbed to
18,000 feet in the sun. He then delivered a diving beam attack on
the leading He 111, seeing it burst into flames and go straight
down. As the German bombers turned back towards the coast,
Allard continued to harry them with diving attacks from out of the
sun until he had fired away all his ammunition. He believed that
two or three of his targets lost speed and dropped behind their
formation, but he did not claim any further definite successes.

His No. 2 in Red Section, Pilot Officer English, had difficulty
in getting his sights on a target during his head-on attack, but he
did fire at one of the tail-end bombers. He broke away downwards
and pulled up to attack another He 111 in the rear of the German
formation, giving it a full deflection shot from short range. He then
nearly collided with one of the bombers and in avoiding it found
himself in position for an attack on a Bf 110. He gave it a 6-second
burst, before pulling up into a fast turn to evade a second Bf 110
on his tail. He saw his target going down crabwise in a steep dive,
with both engines smoking. As it disappeared into cloud, he
noticed a Hurricane following it down some way behind. English
had some ammunition remaining and so engaged a stray He 111,
but he could only fire a short burst at it before he was chased off by
Bf 110s. The German twin-engined fighters had formed a number
of defensive circles above the bombers to cover their retreat.
English easily evaded his attackers by turning quickly to the left
and descending in a series of aileron turns.

Pilot Officer Hodgson, flying as Red 3, carried out a head-on
attack with his section and believed that he damaged the He 111 at
which he fired. He then climbed to 23,000 feet and dived to engage
a straggling Bf 110. He gave it a long burst, opening from the beam
and moving into line astern. The Bf 110 went down with both
engines stopped and pouring white smoke. Hodgson pulled away
and went up to 25,000 feet where he found a second Bf 110 and
attacked it with much the same result as with his first victim. He
estimated that both enemy aircraft should have crashed about five

miles to the east of Ramsgate. On gaining height once more, he saw a number of Bf 110s in a defensive circle below him. Hodgson dived through their formation and pulled up to attack one of them from below. He opened fire from about 100 yards and closed to fifty yards, seeing hits strike the Bf 110's belly. The enemy aircraft rolled over and glided down with smoke pouring from it. Hodgson then broke away, his ammunition expended, as about seven Bf 110s dived on to him. He evaded them and returned to Croydon. His Hurricane was quickly re-armed and refuelled and he was sent up again to patrol base at 25,000 feet, but the precaution proved unnecessary because no German bombers penetrated as far as Croydon on this occasion.

The only other pilot from No. 85 Squadron to claim was Flying Officer Woods-Scawen, who fired several bursts into a Bf 110. He reported that the port engine stopped and the starboard engine caught fire. The German fighter dived steeply into cloud and he lost sight of it, but he saw columns of smoke rising from the ground in the area of the combat shortly afterwards. Pilot Officer Marshall's Hurricane was badly shot up and he was forced to bale out, but he came down safely near Ashford and was unhurt. The squadron's total claims for this combat amounted to six Bf 110s destroyed, two He 111 destroyed, two Bf 110s probably destroyed and four enemy aircraft damaged. Squadron Leader Townsend considered that his opening head-on attack had been particularly effective, although the results in terms of material damage were difficult to assess.

He found that the He 111s were more vulnerable to this form of attack than the Do 17Zs engaged in the same manner by No. 85 Squadron on 26 August. He also felt that the wave attack by sections was a sound tactic, provided that the section leaders allowed sufficient time for the preceding wave to complete their attack before going in themselves. Townsend thought that it was important for the RAF fighters to break away downwards after carrying out a head-on attack, because if they climbed too soon they would present an easy target for the German escorts. He was generally scathing in his criticism of the Luftwaffe fighters, finding the Bf 110s reluctant to come down and engage below their usual operating altitude of 16,000 feet. He found that they tended to fire indiscriminately and sometimes at nothing in particular. In terms of performance, he found them about equal in maximum speed to a Hurricane using emergency boost at 5,000 feet.

The Kenley controller was slow to react to a strong Luftwaffe raid which developed shortly after noon on 31 August. Its main objectives were the Sector stations of Biggin Hill and Hornchurch, but No. 85 Squadron's airfield at Croydon was also on the target list. At 1240 hours the squadron was 'ordered to be on its toes', as Squadron Leader Townsend reported. Its state then was 'A' Flight released and 'B' Flight thirty minutes available. Within five minutes of receiving this preliminary warning, Townsend had brought the squadron to readiness. He reported this to Kenley control and was told that they did not in fact require the squadron to be at readiness, but noted its state. Only three minutes later the squadron was ordered to take off. Twelve Hurricanes were airborne at about 1251 hours; as Townsend crossed the airfield's eastern boundary, he saw bombs exploding beneath him. The CO ordered his Hurricanes to pursue the Bf 110 fighter-bombers which were retreating to the south-east, but warned them to keep a look-out for the escorting Bf 109s.

After take-off the climbing Hurricanes were sitting targets for the thirty or so Bf 109s, but none was engaged until they began to catch up with the Bf 110s. Squadron Leader Townsend easily evaded the attacks of a number of the German fighters, one of which dived below him and then began a left-hand climbing turn to regain altitude. This gave Townsend the chance of a shot at it and he saw it belch black and white smoke as it spiralled downwards. As he drew nearer to the Bf 110s, the Bf 109s became more aggressive, attacking from all directions. Townsend then saw a second formation of German aircraft, which had attacked Biggin Hill, withdrawing. One of the Bf 110s from the Croydon raiders was trailing behind and he decided to engage it, but had first to deal with a Bf 109 which barred his approach. He fired a 3-second burst into it from the quarter and it rolled on to its back and went down. A second German fighter appeared below him and very close, but before he could get his sights on it, his own Hurricane was lashed by enemy fire. He felt a blow on his left foot and was drenched with petrol from the fuselage auxiliary tank. He lost control of the fighter momentarily and it went into a steep dive. He then looked around for a place to force-land because his engine had stopped, but the country below him was densely wooded and he was becoming blinded by petrol fumes, so he decided to bale out. He landed near Hawkhurst and was admitted to the local hospital for attention to the wound in his foot.

Flying Officer Gowers was coming in behind the German formation when he saw a Hurricane under attack from two Bf 109s (probably Townsend's aircraft). He immediately delivered a beam attack on one of the enemy fighters, firing a 3-second burst. Smoke puffed from the Bf 109's engine. Gowers fired again and it dived away into the haze. Pilot Officer Worrall took off with the squadron, but soon afterwards lost contact with them because his vision was obscured by oil on his Hurricane's windscreen. He climbed to 25,000 feet and dived on the rearmost Bf 110 in the German formation. He gave it a 6-second burst of fire from within 100 yards' range and saw it going down apparently out of control as he broke away. His Hurricane was then hit by cannon fire from behind, destroying the elevator controls and knocking away the rudder bar. Worrall prepared to abandon the uncontrollable aircraft, which was on the verge of stalling. Before he could get out it was hit by a second burst of fire, and a cannon shell exploded on the pilot's seat armour plate, without penetrating it. Worrall took to his parachute and came down at Benenden, slightly wounded in the leg.

Sergeant Howes caught up with the retreating enemy aircraft in the vicinity of Biggin Hill. He picked out a group of four Do 17Zs flying to his left and saw them turn towards him. He carried out a head-on attack on the fourth aircraft, which was lagging on the outside of the formation. As he broke away, he saw his victim roll over on to its back and go down smoking. He then had to evade a Bf 109, which had got on his tail. Pilot Officer Hemingway fired at another Bf 109, which began to pour white smoke. The ten surviving Hurricanes landed back at Croydon between 1340 and 1400 hours. The German bombing had demolished a hangar and inflicted casualties, but had not impaired the station's operational effectiveness.

After a three-hour respite, No. 85 Squadron's ten Hurricanes were again ordered up at 1710 hours and directed to patrol over Hawkinge at 20,000 feet. They were then vectored on to a formation of thirty Do 17Zs with a strong fighter escort, which was approaching over the Thames estuary bound for Hornchurch. Pilot Officer Allard, leading the squadron, positioned the Hurricanes 1,000 feet above the bombers, which were flying at 16,000 feet, and between them and the sun. He then carried out a rear quarter attack on the leading Do 17Zs with his section. Opening fire on one vic of bombers, he saw a Do 17Z roll over and go down. Allard then shifted his aim to another of the leading sections, opened fire at 200 yards and broke away only when collision seemed imminent. He saw another bomber go down with one of its engines on fire. As he pulled away, a Bf 109 flew into his sights and he gave it a snap shot, without seeing any result. Allard climbed into the sun to regain height and saw that the German bomber formation had broken up and turned for home. He then carried out a number of attacks on Bf 109s, but again saw no results from them. Sergeant Evans, flying as Red 2, followed Allard in to attack the leading Do 17Zs. Opening fire on the nearest enemy aircraft, he saw his bullets hitting its port engine which began to smoke, but he was unable to follow up this attack and could only claim a Do 17Z damaged.

Yellow Leader, Pilot Officer Marshall, attacked the No. 3 aircraft in the leading section of Do 17Zs, giving it a 5-second burst of fire. The bomber dropped away from its formation, but Marshall was unable to follow up the attack because he came under fire from the fighter escort and was forced to break away. His Hurricane was hit in the rudder, but not seriously damaged. As he began to climb to 22,000 feet, he saw that the enemy formations had been scattered and were retreating to the south-east. The only German aircraft in sight were flying above 30,000 feet, and so, seeing no other targets, he returned to base. Yellow 3, Pilot Officer Hodgson, who had fallen behind his leader, got into position for a head-on attack on a Do 17Z. He saw his fire hitting it and then climbed away to engage a Bf 110. He was then attacked by Bf 109s. Hodgson out-turned one of these and saw it dive, pouring smoke. He immediately pulled round steeply to meet another two fighters which were closing in on his tail, but he had not seen a third Bf 109 sitting under his tail; its fire from short range hit the Hurricane's engine and Hodgson prepared to bale out. By now he was over the Thames Haven oil tanks and a populated area, so he decided to stay with the crippled Hurricane. He managed to keep the flames from his burning engine away from the cockpit, by carrying out a series of side-slips. Eventually he made a wheels-up landing in a field at Shotgate, Essex. During its descent, Hodgson's Hurricane was protected by the Spitfire flown by Squadron Leader J. A. Leathart, No. 54 Squadron's CO, who prevented the Bf 109s from finishing it off. The nineteen-year-old Hodgson, known to his fellow pilots as 'Ace', was later awarded the DFC. He was to be killed on 13 March 1941, in the same accident which cost Allard his life.

· Flying Officer Woods-Scawen led Blue Section ahead of the Do 17Zs and brought them into the attack from head-on. He was unable to see the result of his opening burst of fire and, after breaking away, he became engaged with the Bf 109 escort fighters. Getting into position dead astern of one of them, he gave it a 5-second burst and saw it pull up and spin away. He attacked a second Bf 109 from the quarter and it half-rolled and dived. Woods-Scawen saw it pull out and climb for height, so he lay in wait for it. Renewing his attack, he gave the German fighter a long burst from astern. It began to burn and dived away pouring out smoke. Woods-Scawen's Hurricane was then fired on by a Spitfire, but fortunately the pilot's aim was as bad as his aircraft recognition.

Sergeant Booth, flying as No. 3 Blue Section, broke away beneath the German bomber formation after delivering his head-on attack and saw a Bf 110 flying directly ahead of him. He fired on it and it dived away steeply. After falling for about 5,000 feet it rolled on to its back and continued its dive inverted. Blue 4, Sergeant Goodman, checked his rear-view mirror as his section approached the Do 17Z formation and saw a Bf 109 diving on to his tail. Calling a warning to the other Hurricanes, he had time for a shot at one of the bombers before he dived away. He reported seeing his tracer bullets going into its fuselage and claimed the Do 17Z as damaged. Shortly afterwards his windscreen became so badly obscured with oil from his engine that he had to retire from the combat.

The squadron's third combat of the day came after they had taken-off at 1917 hours. Nine Hurricanes, again led by Pilot Officer Allard, were vectored to a fighter sweep in the Dover area. About nine Bf 109s were sighted flying 500 feet above the Hurricanes at 16,000 feet. The German fighters split into two groups and the Hurricanes broke up to attack individually. Allard climbed into line astern position behind one Bf 109 flying to his left and opened fire at 150 yards' range. He reported that parts of the wing seemed to break off and the aircraft plunged down to crash in the vicinity of Folkestone. Pilot Officer Gowers pulled up beneath a Bf 109, which was turning gently to starboard. He fired a 5-second burst from 100 yards' range and saw his fire hit. He then followed the Bf 109 down to about 4,000 feet, firing a second long burst; the German fighter continued to dive vertically in flames. Pilot Officer Lewis delivered a beam attack from below, firing a 4-second burst at an opening range of 150 yards. He dived after the Bf 109 and saw it disappear into the haze off Folkestone. Flying Officer Woods-Scawen was also able to claim a Bf 109 destroyed, seeing his victim going down on fire. All of the Hurricanes returned to base safely.

Twelve Hurricanes were sent up on the morning of 1 September and at 1145 hours they intercepted twelve Bf 109s which were attacking the Dover balloon barrage. Pilot Officer Allard led a diving attack from out of the sun and he opened fire on the rearmost Bf 109 at a range of 300 yards. It broke away and headed out to sea, with Allard in pursuit. Finding it impossible to close the range, he fired a number of short bursts. The Bf 109 streamed white smoke and slowed up, allowing Allard to get within 100 yards and deliver a long burst of fire. The Bf 109 shuddered under the impact and then dived into the sea ten miles off Cap Gris Nez. As the squadron dived to attack the Bf 109s,

Sergeant Goodman's Hurricane was fired on from behind and damaged. He immediately broke away in a downward spiral and then climbed steeply into the sun, reaching a height of 22,000 feet. Seeing four Bf 109s diving across the coast to the east of Dungeness, he came down on the rearmost and fired a long burst, although only his port guns were working. The Bf 109 pulled up and then spun away towards the ground. Goodman's Hurricane was then again hit by fire from behind and he had to break away.

At 1355 hours the same day eleven Hurricanes were scrambled from Croydon and vectored to intercept a force of about 150 aircraft bound for Biggin Hill. When the Germans were sighted the Hurricanes were still 5,000 feet beneath the bombers – Do 17Zs flying at 15,000 feet, with a strong escort of Bf 110s and Bf 109s stepped up to 20,000 feet. Delay in ordering the squadron up had put the Hurricanes at a serious tactical disadvantage. In order to intercept before the bombers reached their objective, they had to climb ahead of the enemy formation, presenting the escort fighters with a perfect target, but although the Hurricanes were continually harried by Bf 110s and Bf 109s during their attempt to gain altitude, they held their formation. Allard then led them into a beam attack on the bombers. He was able to repeat this attack three more times, making use of the sun to cover his approach, although continually fired at by fighters. His Hurricane's starboard aileron was damaged by cannon fire, but he found that the aircraft remained perfectly controllable.

As repeated attacks began to break up the bomber formation, Allard was able to single out a Do 17Z which was heading back for the coast. He carried out three diving attacks from the quarter, finishing in line astern. Both engines began to smoke, one of the crew baled out, and the Do 17Z finally force-landed in the vicinity of Lydd. Allard noticed that his oil pressure was low and so brought his Hurricane into Lympne as the engine died on him. There it was attacked by a Bf 110 fighter-bomber, which aimed two bombs at the Hurricane. One of the mechanics working on the fighter was killed and a second seriously wounded. The blast from the bombs also further damaged the Hurricane.

Pilot Officer English, Red 3, was unable to keep up with the squadron formation, and so joined up with Pilot Officer Lewis in an attack on a second wave of Do 17Zs. As he broke away from his first firing pass, English was dived on by a group of Bf 110s. He evaded these and began a second attack, but enemy fighters again intervened. Two Bf 109s came down on his tail and he had to dive away into cloud to evade them. Emerging from the cloud, English spotted a straggling Do 17Z and pursued it. He fired two long bursts from quarter and astern and followed it down, seeing it crash-land in a field between Lydd and Ashford. Since, in fact, only one Do 17Z came down in this area, English's victim was most probably the aircraft also attacked by Allard.

After delivering an attack on the Do 17Zs from abeam with the squadron formation, Sergeant Evans was engaged by three Bf 109s. He manoeuvred on to the tail of one of them and gave it a 7-second burst of fire. The fighter dived straight for the ground, trailing white smoke. Evans then had to evade further attacks from other Bf 109s and so lost sight of his victim. On rejoining the main fight, he surprised a formation of ten Bf 110s and opened fire on the two leading aircraft without apparent result. He then switched his attack to the rearmost Bf 110, giving it a 5-second burst from below and abeam. It dropped away from the formation with both engines smoking, but in evading the attentions of the other Bf 110s Evans lost sight of it.

During the squadron's opening attack, Sergeant Howes saw a Bf 109 attack a Hurricane from astern. He stall-turned and, as the Hurricane began to fall with the German fighter on his tail, he fired at the Bf 109 from above and behind. At that point, Howes himself was fired on and had to break away in a steep turn to the left. He then climbed in the sun towards the bombers, taking some time to reach their height of 17,000 feet. After carrying out a beam attack and switching to line astern on the rearmost Do 17Z, Howes saw it go down smoking. As he was short of ammunition he decided to follow it down, but he had to evade an attack from a Bf 109 and lost sight of the bomber. Seeing a column of smoke rising from a wood south of Tunbridge Wells, and two parachutes, he concluded that the enemy aircraft had crashed.

The squadron's total claims for the combat were three Do 17Zs, one Bf 110 and one Bf 109 destroyed with another Bf 109 damaged. Their own losses had been severe. Flying Officer P. P. Woods-Scawen and Sergeant J. H. M. Ellis had been shot down and killed. Flying Officer A. V. Gowers baled out seriously wounded, as did Sergeant G. B. Booth, who died from his wounds the following February. Pilot Officer Lewis has to make a wheels-up landing on his return to Croydon, but was uninjured.

During a period of just over two weeks' heavy fighting, No. 85 Squadron had inflicted some heavy blows on the Luftwaffe, but in doing so had themselves suffered serious casualties. Their claims in combat during this period amounted to fifty enemy aircraft confirmed destroyed, thirteen probably destroyed and fifteen damaged. Interestingly enough, exactly half the confirmed victories were gained against Bf 109 fighters. So, although the German fighters' performance was generally better than that of the Hurricane, No. 85 Squadron had often been able to capitalize on their aircraft's greatest asset, its superior manoeuvrability. But the cost in pilots killed and wounded had been very high. Four pilots had died in action, including the two flight commanders. A further six had been wounded, among them the CO, and one of these was to die from his wounds.

So depleted was the squadron's pilot strength that on 2 September it could carry out patrols with only five or six aircraft, rather than the customary twelve. On the following day they exchanged places with No. 111 Squadron at Castle Camps, but their new airfield was still within the No. 11 Group area and so a further exchange became necessary to remove the squadron to a quiet sector where it could recoup its strength. On 5 September it flew north to Church Fenton in Yorkshire to take the place of No. 73 Squadron. Three days later it became a Category 'C' Squadron, responsible for providing replacement pilots for the units remaining in the south and meeting its Sector's minimal air defence requirements.

In order to fill the flight commander vacancies Pilot Officers Allard and Marshall were promoted to the acting rank of flight lieutenant. Squadron Leader Townsend returned to the squadron on 21 September, although he had not fully recovered from his wound and remained very lame. In accordance with Fighter Command's policy, many of the surviving experienced pilots were posted away during September to make good losses in Category 'A' Squadrons. In the following month, though, the squadron assumed a more active role. It had been decided that two Hurricane units should be selected to specialize in night fighting and the choice fell on No. 85 and No. 151 Squadrons. On 23 October the squadron moved to Kirton-in-Lindsey, Lincolnshire, and four days later fought its first combats since leaving No. 11 Group.

At about 1800 hours on 27 October a single He 111 bombed Kirton-in-Lindsey and strafed the satellite airfield at Caistor. Squadron Leader Townsend, Warrant Officer F. H. de la Boucher and Flight Lieutenant Marshall took off in pursuit and the latter caught the raider before it could disappear into cloud cover and shot it down. Five and a half hours later, Flight Lieutenant Allard intercepted an enemy bomber during a night patrol, but the engagement was inconclusive. The following night Sergeant Goodman caught another German bomber over the Humber estuary, but he could only claim it as damaged. On 7 November 'A' Flight was considered to be fully operational by night and was dispatched to Gravesend to reinforce the capital's inadequate night defences. It was joined there by 'B' Flight on 23 November.

The squadron's only other success before the end of the year, however, was by daylight. Pilot Officer Hodgson was on a test flight during the afternoon of 5 December, when he met a Bf 109 over Ashford. He chased it out to sea, before losing it in the haze, but he was credited with a 'probable'. It was not until February 1941 that the squadron gained its first night victory, Squadron Leader Townsend being the successful pilot. It then went on to become one of the RAF's most successful night fighter units of the Second World War, but its most valuable contribution to the defence of the United Kingdom had undoubtedly been made during those crucial air battles in the summer of 1940.

NO. 92 SQUADRON

Unlike many of its contemporary fighter squadrons in 1940, No. 92 Squadron was a young unit with its reputation still to be made. It had known a brief existence during the First World War, having been formed in September 1917. In July 1918 it took its SE 5a scouts to France and by the time of the Armistice the squadron was credited with 37 victories. Disbanded in 1919, No. 92 Squadron did not re-appear until after the outbreak of the Second World War. It was re-formed at Tangmere in Sussex on 10 October 1939, from a nucleus of personnel drawn from No. 601 Squadron, Auxiliary Air Force. That unit, officially the County of London Squadron, was known throughout the RAF as the 'Millionaires' Squadron' because of the rich and socially well-connected young men that it had attracted during the inter-war years.

No. 92 Squadron was to retain many of the relaxed and indisciplined ways of its Auxiliary forebear, largely due to the influence of its first CO, Squadron Leader Roger Bushell. A South African-born barrister and himself a pre-war member of No. 601 Squadron, Bushell was a fine natural leader whose strength of personality was soon to forge his squadron into a close-knit and effective fighting team. He was the first Auxiliary Air Force officer to be given command of a fighter squadron. His flight commanders were Flight Lieutenant C. P. 'Paddy' Green, a kindred spirit from the 'Millionaires' Squadron', and the elegant and debonair Flight Lieutenant R. R. S. Tuck, who already had gained a reputation in the RAF as a skilful aerobatic pilot and marksman. The lumbering Bristol Blenheim Mk If twin-engined fighters which had initially equipped the squadron, were replaced by Spitfires in March 1940 and in May they went into action over Dunkirk. It proved to be a tough initiation into the perilous business of air fighting; in only five days the squadron lost five Spitfires and their pilots killed or missing, and another pilot seriously wounded. Squadron Leader Bushell was among the casualties, becoming a prisoner of war. His exploits in captivity became legendary, culminating in the master-minding of the 'Great Escape' from Stalag Luft III in March 1944. Bushell was one of the officers to get away from the camp, but he was later recaptured and murdered by the Gestapo. Another casualty of the Dunkirk fighting was Flight Lieutenant Green, who was badly wounded in the thigh. On recovering, he took command of No. 421 Flight, the special unit formed for spotter duties in early October 1940. To balance its losses, No. 92 Squadron had claimed a total of some 35 victories and the pilots' morale remained high.

After Squadron Leader Bushell was posted missing during the squadron's second patrol over Dunkirk, Flight Lieutenant Tuck had taken over as its tactical leader in the air, but a new CO, Squadron Leader P. J. Sanders, was posted in and Tuck remained in command of 'B' Flight. Bushell was certainly not an easy CO to replace and it is clear that Sanders, though by no means an ineffec-tive or unpopular officer, found it difficult to establish his position as the new leader of No. 92 Squadron. Flight Lieutenant Green's replacement to command 'A' Flight, Flight Lieutenant C. B. F. Kingcome, was more readily accepted. A pre-war graduate of the RAF College, Cranwell, Kingcome was to become one of the RAF's foremost fighter leaders of the Second World War. He was, though, uninterested in the 'ace' concept and in accumulating a large personal score and so, in common with many other outstand-ing RAF pilots of the Battle of Britain, did not receive any great measure of publicity or recognition.

On 18 June No. 92 Squadron was transferred from Horn-church to Pembrey in South Wales. Its new station was at that time within No. 11 Group, but passed to the operational control of the newly formed No. 10 Group a month later. Originally a satellite station in the Filton Sector, Pembrey eventually became a Sector station in its own right. Its primary responsibility was for the defence of the industrial areas of Bristol, South Wales and the Midlands, both from night attack and from the small-scale raids which the Luftwaffe often carried out by day during cloudy weather. The squadron saw comparatively little action during its stay at Pembrey in July and August, and its pilots were keen to move to one of the No. 11 Group airfields. Its first encounter with the enemy since Dunkirk came on 4 July when Yellow Section (Pilot Officer H. D. Edwards, Pilot Officer C. H. Saunders and Sergeant R. H. Fokes) intercepted an He 111 and shot it down near Weston-super-Mare. In an incident reminiscent of the First World War, Edwards and Fokes landed in a field near their victim and took the wounded pilot prisoner.

On the following day Pilot Officer A. C. Bartley's Spitfire was lost, when its engine failed and he had to force-land in a bog. The pilot escaped 'practically up to my neck in mud and stagnant water', but the aircraft could not be recovered. Such incidents were part of the normally accepted hazards of flying and of course a proportion of Fighter Command's losses during the Battle of Britain were due to non-operational causes. To some degree the usual incidence of these accidents was increased by the pressures on strained and weary pilots as the Battle progressed. During August and September 1940 the Command lost 39 Hurricanes and 27 Spitfires destroyed in accidents, plus a further 98 Hurricanes and 91 Spitfires so badly damaged as to require depot level repair. These non-operational casualties represented one-fifth of Fighter Command's total losses of Hurricanes and Spitfires during the period. Fortunately, casualties among trained aircrew on the squadrons during training flights were less numerous, amounting to 48 killed and missing and eighteen injured. This represented only one in eleven of all aircrew casualties in Fighter Command, which totalled six hundred and sixty-six in August and September.

Not all of No. 92 Squadron's combats were as conclusive as that on 4 July. Flight Lieutenant Tuck, Pilot Officer R. H. Holland and Sergeant R. E. Havercroft, flying as Blue Section, intercepted a Do 17Z in the Bristol area on 8 July. All three pilots were able to fire at it, but the German aircraft eventually escaped into cloud. Two days later Red Section, led by Flight Lieutenant Kingcome, had no better success when they tried to shoot down a Ju 88 which had bombed a munitions factory only ten miles to the north-east of their airfield. Kingcome, Pilot Officer Bartley and Sergeant S. M. Barraclough all fired short bursts into the bomber, but it too made good its escape in the clouds. Pilot Officer D. G. Williams had a similarly inconclusive encounter with an He 111 when patrolling over Barry the same day. Poor weather not only provided cover for individual German raiders, but could also represent a serious hazard to the RAF's fighters. This was illustrated by an incident on 15 July, when Flight Lieutenant Tuck was returning to Pembrey from a conference at the Air Fighting Development Unit at Northolt. His Spitfire flew into storm clouds and Tuck lost his bearings. Dangerously low on fuel, he finally came out of cloud over the Cornish coast and managed to bring his Spitfire down in a wheels-up landing in a field near Liskeard. The aircraft was recovered and repaired, but Tuck was fortunate to escape, as he could so easily have crashed into high ground while flying blind in cloud.

Although No. 92 Squadron did not suffer any casualties among its pilots during July, its operations were not entirely without danger. On 17 July Pilot Officer Saunders engaged a Ju 88 over Bristol and returned to base with his Spitfire damaged by return fire from the bomber. On 24 July Red Section, led by Flight Lieutenant Kingcome, fought a conclusive action with a Ju 88 over the Bristol Channel. Red 2, Pilot Officer J. Bryson, opened the attack from astern. He fired off all his ammunition in a series of 3-second bursts, aiming at the port engine. As he broke away, he noticed that the engine was smoking and that the mid-upper gunner had ceased firing. Red 3, Flying Officer J. A. Paterson, then took up the attack, following the bomber down through cloud and firing two bursts into it. Kingcome finished the enemy aircraft off with a series of deflection bursts and the Ju 88 (from 3. Staffel Lehrgeschwader 1) was seen to crash in flames on the Devon coast. On the following day Blue Section, Flight Lieutenant Tuck, Pilot Officer Holland and Pilot Officer R. Mottram, caught another Ju 88 ten miles off Fishguard. All three pilots were able to deliver a series of attacks, but the bomber finally escaped in cloud with one engine trailing thick black smoke. On 26 July Pilot Officer Williams and Pilot Officer H. P. Hill engaged a Ju 88 near Pembroke and this too eluded them in cloud.

In addition to its daylight operations, No. 92 Squadron carried out a number of night patrols during July. Early in the month a three-aircraft section was deployed to Hullavington, Wiltshire for this duty and after this was discontinued on 10 July, night patrols were flown from Pembrey. The Spitfire, although originally envisaged as both a day and night fighter, was not well suited to night operations. In particular, its narrow-track undercarriage was less able to withstand the heavy landings which often resulted from misjudged approaches in darkness than that of the more robust Hurricane. Night landing aids were primitive; airfield lighting consisting of paraffin flares and a Chance light (a low-powered searchlight for ground illumination). And even when the hazards of night flying were accepted, the Spitfire had only a slender chance of intercepting a raider. The pilot was dependent on radioed instructions from the Sector operations room both to direct him into the vicinity of enemy aircraft and then at the end of the sortie to bring him back to base. The theory of 'cat's eyes' patrols by single-seater fighters was that daytime interception techniques could bring them to within a few miles of the night bomber and that searchlight illumination would then allow the fighter pilot to pick out his target and carry out an attack. Some early successes were obtained by this method when the bombers were operating at comparatively low levels, but against higher flying raiders, above 12,000 feet, it proved to be largely ineffective.

The pitfalls of Spitfire night operations are well illustrated by No. 92 Squadron's experience during July, in which two fighters were damaged and one totally destroyed without any successful interceptions to show for the losses. In the early morning of 22 July Sergeant Fokes overshot the flare-path at Pembrey and crashed. Four nights later Sergeant Barraclough's Spitfire was badly damaged when he landed with a burst tyre and crashed. Neither pilot was injured. On the night of 27/28 July Pilot Officer T. S. Wade was one of three pilots sent up on night patrol. 'Wimpey' Wade was a very able pilot, who became Chief Test Pilot for Hawkers after the war. In the course of his patrol over the Swansea area, the weather deteriorated with low-lying haze and 10/10th cloud obscuring the ground. Wade reported this development to his controller; however, his request to return to base was refused. Then the Spitfire's TR 9 radio became unserviceable and in Wade's words: 'while I could hear with ever-decreasing clarity the Controller's ever-increasing concern for my well-being, he could hear nothing'. Since Wade's radio was not transmitting, the position of his Spitfire could not be fixed by the usual method of HF direction finding. After flying about on a series of reciprocal courses for about an hour, Wade heard a faint instruction from the controller to steer south as an aircraft had been plotted north of base. The indication proved to be a false one and Wade gave up all hope of assistance from sector control. He selected lean fuel mixture for the engine in order to remain airborne for the maximum period, in the hope of an improvement to the weather, but after 3¼ hours he had no alternative but to abandon his Spitfire and take to his parachute. He came down safely in the vicinity of Exeter.

During the early weeks of the Battle of Britain, the hastily improvised air defences of the West Country did not always function smoothly, but the situation improved with the formation of No. 10 Group on 18 July and as the new radar station personnel and sector controllers gained in experience. Yet even as late as 13 August the greater part of No. 92 Squadron was unable to make contact with a large-scale German raid. Between 1545 and 1700 hours the Luftwaffe launched a two-pronged attack on southern England. The more westerly force struck at Portland and Southampton and were engaged by No. 10 Group fighter squadrons from Middle Wallop, Warmwell and Exeter, backed up by two No. 11 Group squadrons from Tangmere.

At 1545 hours No. 92 Squadron was ordered up and vectored south-eastwards into the combat area. The main body of the squadron was unable to intercept, but Flight Lieutenant Tuck's Blue Section, which had taken off late and operated independently, was more successful. Tuck was directed to fly to Portland Bill, but on arriving in the area he found only RAF fighters so he flew along the coast towards the Isle of Wight at 1,500 feet and then went up through cloud to 3,000 feet. On emerging, he immediately saw a Ju 88 heading south-east. Tuck ordered his section into line astern, and gave chase, but on seeing the Spitfires the German pilot dived into cloud and disappeared. Shortly afterwards, AA fire over Selsey Bill attracted his attention to a second Ju 88, which was flying at 6,000 feet. The enemy aircraft tried to climb into cloud cover 2,000 feet above, but the Spitfires headed it off. The Ju 88 then dived for sea level, with Tuck's Spitfire on his tail. Tuck's opening burst knocked out the bomber's port engine. He, Blue 2, Pilot Officer W. C. Watling, and Blue 3, Sergeant Havercroft, carried out a series of beam, quarter and stern attacks on the low-flying Ju 88, until it finally crashed into the sea forty miles south-east of Selsey Bill. On returning to the coast, they met a third Ju 88. All three Spitfires attacked it, but without apparent result.

The same three pilots were in action over Barry at 1730 hours on the following day. Flying at 15,000 feet, 5,000 feet above an unbroken cloud layer, they saw three Ju 88s in close formation 3,000 feet below them. Tuck ordered the section to carry out a head-on attack, but R/T reception was poor and they did not hear his instructions. Blue Leader therefore attacked head-on by himself, while Blue 2 and Blue 3 opened with beam attacks. Two of the bombers fell from the formation and were assessed as destroyed. Sergeant Havercroft's Spitfire was hit in the radiator and, as the engine temperature rose rapidly beyond the safety limits, he switched off and made a wheels-up landing near Aberdare. Shortly after Blue Section's interception, Green Section led by Pilot Officer A. R. Wright, were vectored on to an He 111 flying five miles north of Hullavington. Wright and his No. 2, Pilot Officer Williams, carried out a number of attacks on this aircraft as it approached Bristol and it was assessed as probably destroyed. Williams then continued to patrol the Bristol area and at 1755 hours saw another He 111 approaching from the north. He made a head-on attack and saw it jettison its bomb load as it disappeared in cloud. As a bomber of this type was reported to have crash-landed in the Bristol area at about 1800 hours, Williams claimed this as his victim.

Four days later the commander of 'B' Flight decided to take part in the fighting in the No. 11 Group area on his own initiative. Flight Lieutenant Tuck had been visiting Northolt when the station's squadrons were scrambled at lunchtime. He followed them into the air and, since he was not under the control of Sector operations, decided to patrol over Beachy Head at 15,000 feet. He soon spotted two twin-engined aircraft, which he identified as Ju 88s, making for France at low level. Tuck dived in front of them and pulled around for a head-on attack. His first burst of fire found its mark and his opponent, believed to have been a Bf 110 of Zerstörergeschwader 26, crashed into the sea. Tuck then positioned himself for a further head-on attack on the second enemy aircraft, but as he closed in its cannon fire hit his engine, forcing him to break off and head for land. It was fortunate that the damaged engine kept going until he was over Tonbridge. By then Tuck was nearly blinded by glycol fumes and decided to bale out.

On 18 August 'A' Flight moved from Pembrey to Bibury in Gloucestershire, an airfield that was better placed than the squadron's main base for the night defence of the Midlands. At about 1500 hours next day Bibury was attacked by a lone Ju 88, which damaged four Spitfires on the ground. Three Spitfires of Yellow Section scrambled and gave chase, but Pilot Officer Bartley left his flying helmet behind in his haste to get airborne. As this incorporated the R/T microphone and earphones, he had no contact with ground control and was forced to return after losing visual contact with the bomber. Flying Officers Paterson and Wade continued the chase and were vectored on to a Ju 88 flying down the Solent. Paterson carried out attacks from abeam and astern, firing off all his ammunition. On breaking away, he saw that the Ju 88's port engine had stopped and the starboard one was smoking. Paterson saw the enemy aircraft dive into the sea a few minutes later. Wade's engine had been damaged by return fire, and as he prepared to force-land it caught fire and fumes seeped into the cockpit. Wade brought the aircraft down in a wheels-up landing in a small field north of Selsey. After he got clear the Spitfire blew up and was destroyed.

Before the month was out another Spitfire was hit by return fire and written off in the ensuing crash-landing. Flight Lieutenant Tuck was on patrol over Pembroke early in the evening of 25

August, when he was vectored to intercept a Do 17Z which was reported to be attacking a ship near the St Gowan's lightship. Tuck spotted the bomber and followed it into cloud, inadvertently giving the German gunner an easy shot from below at close range. His engine was damaged, but Tuck managed to drop astern of the Do 17Z and give it a 2-second burst of fire from only twenty-five yards' range. He then broke away, as his engine was overheating badly. On coming out of the cloud, he found himself fifteen miles from the nearest land, but could only switch off his engine and attempt to glide to the shore. He was able to hold the glide long enough and crash-landed on St Govan's Head. Tuck was slightly wounded in the leg.

In view of the generally held opinion in Fighter Command that the defensive firepower of German bombers was negligible, it is interesting to note that within a period of two weeks No. 92 Squadron had lost two Spitfires destroyed and a third damaged to this cause. However, officially approved tactics required the attacking fighter to break away from an enemy bomber at 300 yards' range. Had this always been possible under combat conditions, return fire would indeed have been largely ineffective. Many pilots, though, chose to attack from much closer ranges and, as in the case of many of No. 92 Squadron's combats, poor visibility sometimes made a close approach essential.

Night operations continued to produce their toll of mishaps in August, but fortunately no pilots were lost. On the night of 27/28 August Pilot Officer F. N. Hargreaves became completely lost during a patrol from Bibury and finally baled out over Marlesford in Suffolk, on the other side of the country. Sergeant Havercroft crashed his Spitfire at Bibury when landing through ground mist on the night of 29/30 August. But the squadron's trials and tribulations on 'cat's eyes' patrols had been rewarded by one confirmed victory earlier that night. The successful pilot was Pilot Officer Allan Wright. Patrolling at 20,000 feet over Bristol, he picked up an He 111 illuminated in the searchlight beams. He turned in behind it and, just as he opened fire, his Spitfire was rocked in the explosions of a burst of AA fire. The bomber flew on, still brilliantly lit by the searchlights, and Wright was able to close in for a second attack. The searchlights then went out, but Wright spotted the glow from the bomber's engine exhausts. Flying carefully, so as not to overshoot and lose his indistinct target, he closed in for a third burst of fire. He was rewarded by the sight of his de Wilde incendiary ammunition exploding on the Heinkel's fuselage. The bomber lost speed, making it increasingly difficult for Wright to maintain his position, but he fired off his remaining ammunition in a final burst before breaking away. His fire had taken effect and the target was on fire. Its crew, from 3. Staffel of Kampfgeschwader 27, took to their parachutes and were made prisoners of war.

Although the co-ordination of the ground defences, both AA artillery and searchlights, with the fighter patrol had been poor, this night defence sortie had gone more or less according to plan, thanks in large part to the flying skill of Pilot Officer Wright. Such successes were very much the exception to the rule; a truly effective night defence of the United Kingdom was not possible before the appearance of high-performance, radar-directed night fighters.

On 8 September No. 92 Squadron's exile on the fringes of the battle came to an end and it flew to RAF Biggin Hill in Kent to relieve the Hurricane-equipped No. 79 Squadron. Its new airfield was very much in the forefront of the battle, 'a mass of bomb-scarred earth and bombed-out buildings', recalled Pilot Officer Bartley. Although the air battles were to continue with undiminished ferocity, No. 92 Squadron's move to Biggin Hill coincided with a shift in the Luftwaffe's focus of attack away from the airfields of No. 11 Group and on to London. Small-scale airfield raids were to continue, but the dangerous pressure on Fighter Command's ground organization was eased. As Air Vice-Marshal Park wrote later in September: 'Had the enemy continued his heavy attacks against Biggin Hill and the adjacent sectors and knocked out their operations rooms or telephone communications, the fighter defences of London would have been in a perilous state during the last critical phase when heavy attacks have been directed against the capital.'

It was at this time that the AOC, No. 11 Group decided to concentrate his Spitfire squadrons at Biggin Hill and Hornchurch. This would enable the high-performance Spitfire to make the first contact with the enemy formations on their approach to London and, it was hoped, distract their fighter escorts so that the way was opened for the less capable Hurricanes to attack the bombers. So far as Biggin Hill was concerned, this policy could not be implemented immediately; the damaged station could only support one operational unit and it was not until 12 September that No. 92 Squadron was joined there by its partner, No. 72 Squadron from Croydon.

Flight Lieutenant Tuck did not accompany No. 92 Squadron to Biggin Hill, since he had been given command of his own squadron. His place as commander of 'B' Flight was taken by the New Zealander, James Paterson, who was promoted to flight lieutenant. The squadron had used its period of relative inactivity at Pembrey to good effect and was now a well-knit flying team with many experienced and able pilots within its ranks. It was as well that this was so, for on the day that it moved to Biggin Hill it was designated a Category 'A' Squadron and so would be required to fight on indefinitely without prospect of relief.

On 9 September the squadron encountered the Luftwaffe's Bf 109 fighters for the first time since Dunkirk, when it was one of nine No. 11 Group squadrons scrambled to meet a series of raids on the capital during the late afternoon. Squadron Leader Sanders, at the head of the squadron, had reached a height of 26,000 feet over Dungeness when he heard a warning of 'snappers' (enemy fighters) and broke sharply to the left. He saw that Green Section behind him was under attack by Bf 109s and got in a short burst at one of them before he spun away out of his turn. This attack broke up the squadron, but Sanders then received orders from Sector control to return to base as there were 'Bandits' in its vicinity. He encountered a group of He 111s flying ten miles south-east of Biggin Hill and carried out a head-on attack against one of them. He broke away upwards and saw that his target had fallen away from the German formation. Immediately afterwards Sanders was engaged by a Bf 109, which he was able to out-turn. He fired a deflection burst and the Bf 109 half-rolled and dived away trailing smoke. Sanders followed and gave it several more short bursts of fire, before the Bf 109 went into cloud and he lost it.

Flight Lieutenant Kingcome lost contact with the rest of the Squadron, but was able to intercept the bomber formation in the vicinity of Biggin Hill. He climbed above it to attack a formation of twelve Bf 109s. After firing a short burst into the rearmost fighter, he was set upon by the others and, after firing another burst from long range, dived away into the clouds. He and the CO between then claimed two enemy fighters probably destroyed, and Squadron Leader Sanders also accounted for an He 111. In return the squadron lost Pilot Officers Watling and Saunders, who were wounded. Pilot Officer Wright's Spitfire was damaged by enemy fire, but he escaped unhurt.

The following day, 10 September, was cloudy, and the raids were on a small scale, but Pilot Officer Wade and Sergeant Fokes were vectored on to a Do 17Z of 9. Staffel, Kampfgeschwader 76 and brought it down at Gatwick in Surrey. The Luftwaffe returned in force on the 11th with three strong raids over the south-east. No. 92 Squadron was ordered up at 1520 hours and intercepted an escorted bomber force crossing the coast at Dungeness. Squadron Leader Sanders carried out a beam attack on an He 111 flying on the right of the German formation and saw its starboard engine pour out heavy black smoke. Thirty minutes later he saw a Bf 109 flying southwards at low level in the vicinity of Tonbridge and dived to engage it. After firing two short bursts he saw it crash. Flight Lieutenant Kingcome made a head-on attack on the bombers and saw an He 111 begin to smoke. Pilot Officers Wade and Williams both attacked a straggling He 111, which had also been fired on by a Hurricane. After setting its starboard engine on fire and knocking out the mid-upper gunner, the two pilots watched as the bomber crashed into a field near Lympne. Wade then landed at the airfield at Lympne to re-arm and refuel, but as neither ammunition nor petrol was available there, took off again and flew to Hawkinge where he and Williams landed.

Pilot Officer Wright became separated from the Squadron formation, but positioned himself over the Croydon area. He saw a large formation of He 111s approaching and made a head-on attack, causing a bomber to fall away from its formation smoking. He later found a straggling He 111 which he and three Spitfires from No. 66 Squadron sent down to crash in the Dungeness area. Pilot Officer G. H. A. Wellum also lost the squadron formation, but finding a damaged He 111 making its way out over the coast, he fired all his ammunition into it. He last saw it losing height with both engines disabled. Sergeant P. R. Eyles, who had taken off five minutes after the rest of the squadron, met the He 111 formation as it was crossing the coast and dived to engage them. He came in from out of the sun and attacked them from head-on. After repeating this attack, his ammunition was finished, but Eyles reported that one of the He 111s had dropped from the formation with an engine smoking. The squadron was credited with a total of six He 111s destroyed. Pilot Officer J. F. Drummond claimed a Bf 109 damaged and Flight Lieutenant Paterson a Bf 110 probably destroyed. Pilot Officer F. N. Hargreaves was shot down by fighters and killed during this action.

At 1745 hours on 11 September eight Spitfires took off on a bomber escort mission over the Channel. Flying at 16,000 feet the Spitfires saw a large formation of Bf 109s at 20,000 feet and broke up to engage them. In the ensuing combat Squadron Leader Sanders and Pilot Officer Wright each claimed a German fighter probably destroyed, but two Spitfires were lost. Pilot Officer H. D. Edwards was shot down and killed; Flight Lieutenant Paterson escaped with painful burns to the face. Courageously, he refused to allow his injuries to ground him, despite his vision being impaired.

Poor weather reduced the scale of the Luftwaffe's activities on 14 September and the actions fought that afternoon were mainly fighter-versus-fighter. No. 92 Squadron engaged about forty Bf 109s over the Canterbury area at 1830 hours. As the Germans had the advantage of height, they were able to pass over the top of the Spitfire formation and into the sun, before coming down to attack. Flight Lieutenant Kingcome, leading the 13-Spitfire formation, claimed two Bf 109s damaged and Pilot Officer Wright a third damaged. Two of the squadron's pilots were wounded. Pilot Officer H. W. McGowan, flying in the rear section, baled out of his Spitfire, while Sergeant J. Mann brought his damaged fighter back to base. The Luftwaffe's aim of drawing the RAF fighter squadrons into combat under conditions favourable to themselves had been largely achieved on 14 September. Overall, Fighter Command flew 860 sorties and destroyed only fourteen enemy aircraft. Their own losses were fourteen fighters. Little wonder that the German pilots reported that RAF fighter opposition was becoming intermittent and poorly co-ordinated and that Fighter Command was beginning to disintegrate.

The combats over the past week had none the less allowed Fighter Command to begin to take the measure of the tactical problems posed by the new phase in the Luftwaffe offensive. Air Vice-Marshal Park identified two aspects of the Germans' latest method of operation as being especially dangerous. First, he was concerned that the mass attacks of 300 to 400 aircraft, which came in two or three successive waves within an hour, did not completely swamp the defences. He was also worried that the strong Luftwaffe fighter escorts would absorb the efforts of most of his fighter squadrons, allowing the bombers to reach their objective relatively unscathed. Park planned to meet these threats by engaging the German high-flying fighter screen as early as possible, using paired Spitfire squadrons operating from Biggin Hill and Hornchurch. Hurricane squadrons from the London Sector stations would then intercept the bombers and their close fighter escorts to the east and south of London, while the squadrons from Debden, Tangmere, and sometimes Northolt, were to deal with the following waves of an attack, or harass retreating aircraft from earlier waves.

In view of the Luftwaffe's quite erroneous assessment of Fighter Command's imminent collapse, it is not surprising that the fine weather of 15 September brought about a trial of strength between the RAF's fighters and the German air forces. No. 92 Squadron was heavily engaged against massed raids both at midday and in the afternoon. At 1100 hours radar detected the build-up of the first attack and Nos. 92 and 72 Squadrons were the first units to engage the enemy shortly after they crossed the Kent coast. The Spitfires split up, some attacking the German fighter escort and others going for the bombers. Pilot Officer Holland took the leading section in to a dogfight with a group of Bf 109s flying at 23,000 feet, the same altitude as the Spitfires. He later saw a single

Bf 109 below him heading for the coast and attacked it from behind, seeing fragments fall from the wings and a thin stream of smoke come from the engine. He then spotted two more German fighters diving on him and so disengaged. Pilot Officer Williams, Green 1, dived to 15,000 feet to attack fifteen Do 17Z bombers and was able to damage two of them before fighters drove him off.

His No. 2, Flight Sergeant C. Sydney, was preparing to follow Williams, when he was attacked by two Bf 109s. One of them overshot his Spitfire as he went into a turn and Sydney was able to dive after him and get in a long burst from astern. The Bf 109 dived steeply away and was credited to Sydney as probably destroyed. The second German fighter had meanwhile got on the Spitfire's tail and its cannon fire damaged its wing, forcing Sydney to break off the combat and return to base. Pilot Officer Hill, Green 3, was also attacked by a pair of Bf 109s. He turned into their attack and fired at both of them as the range closed. One dived vertically trailing smoke. Pilot Officer Bartley chased a Do 17Z back to the coast, carrying out a series of attacks until the bomber disappeared into cloud. He next engaged a Bf 109, but this too eluded him in cloud and Bartley could only claim two German aircraft damaged. Sergeant Fokes also claimed a Do 17Z damaged. He made a head-on attack on the bomber formation and saw the aircraft that he had fired at pull up into a near-vertical climb. As he passed beneath it, he rolled the Spitfire on to its back and dived. Going down he met another bomber and fired a quick burst at it. As he was then engaged by Bf 109s, he could not see what became of these aircraft.

At 1415 hours the squadron was again scrambled and nine Spitfires climbed to 21,000 feet over Hornchurch to rendezvous with No. 41 Squadron. They were vectored south and met large formations of enemy aircraft and the two squadrons split up to attack. Squadron Leader Sanders ordered line astern formation and came down behind a group of Do 17Zs. Singling out a bomber on the right of the formation, he saw his fire hitting, one of the crew baled out and the starboard engine was leaving a heavy trail of smoke. Pilot Officer Mottram had become separated from the rest of the squadron, but climbed to 20,000 feet over the Maidstone area and dived on a number of Do 17Zs flying 5,000 feet below him. He pursued one of these until he lost it in cloud; he claimed it as damaged. Mottram went down through the clouds and patrolled their base at 6,000 feet. Shortly afterwards he saw an He 111 and carried out a series of attacks, which set it on fire; he watched it crash in a field in the vicinity of Ashford. Pilot Officer Williams was one of four pilots to gang up on a straggling Do 17Z and he saw it go down as the crew baled out. He then attacked the rearmost bomber in a ragged formation of He 111s. It broke away smoking and was set upon by a number of British fighters. Williams last saw it going down in flames into cloud over Hendon. Pilot Officer Hill joined Williams in attacking the Do 17Z and then went on to engage a further three He 111s in company with other fighters, seeing all of them go down to crash.

Flight Lieutenant Kingcome was late in taking off, as his Spitfire was found to be unserviceable and he had to change to another. He was unable to catch up with No. 92 Squadron, but joined another Spitfire formation. Climbing to 16,000 feet they met a formation of Do 17Zs and attacked them from the beam. Kingcome saw the bomber that he had singled out drop back from the formation with both engines smoking. So he turned his attention to a second Do 17Z and finished off his ammunition on it. Pilot Officer Wade decided to take on the fighter escort and fired a short burst into one Bf 109 from the front quarter at short range. He saw it going down smoking, but then had to evade attack from other German fighters.

Pilot Officer Bartley followed his leader down to attack the Do 17Zs. Approaching from the rear quarter and then closing in astern, Bartley saw his fire disable the engine of one bomber. He then carried out a head-on attack on a second formation of Do 17Zs. As he broke away downwards, his Spitfire was hit and went into a spin. He recovered from this and climbed to finish off his ammunition on a straggler, seeing it pour smoke from the engines and fuselage. The Squadron's only casualty in this combat was Pilot Officer Holland, who baled out of his disabled Spitfire slightly injured. A total of six bombers were credited to the squadron as

confirmed destroyed, two enemy aircraft were probably destroyed
and a further three damaged.

What is most striking about the accounts of these engagements
by No. 92 Squadron is that the pilots seemed totally unaware of
Park's intention that they should attack the enemy fighters rather
than the bombers. It is clear that so far as they were concerned the
earlier Fighter Command instructions to concentrate on the
bombers at all costs still held good. Another problem which these
combats illustrate was that of satisfactorily breaking up an enemy
bomber formation once squadrons had split into sections or
individual aircraft. All that individual aircraft could do was to
nibble away at the flanks of a formation, or perhaps make a solo
head-on attack in the hope of so crippling a bomber that it was
unable to keep up with its fellows. There was also a tendency for
single fighters to concentrate on lame ducks, rather than continue
to harry the main bomber formations. Two days of slight activity
followed the heavy fighting of 15 September. The only incident of
note so far as No. 92 Squadron was concerned was when Pilot
Officer Hill made a heavy landing at the end of a patrol on 16
September causing his Spitfire's undercarriage to collapse.

Heavy Luftwaffe activity on the morning of 18 September
proved to be made up in the main of fighter sweeps, which Fighter
Command would have ignored if they could have been recognized
as such sufficiently early. As it was, seventeen RAF fighter
squadrons were engaged. Ten of No. 92 Squadron's Spitfires were
sent on patrol at 0915 hours in company with No. 72 Squadron.
On reaching 20,000 feet in the vicinity of Gravesend they were
attacked head-on from out of the sun by twenty Bf 109s and the
squadron formation was split up. Shortly afterwards Pilot Officer
Bartley saw a Do 17Z and three Bf 109s flying west and closed in
on the bomber, giving it a long burst of fire. It went into a slow
dive and was seen to go into the sea off Folkestone. Bartley's
aircraft was then attacked by Bf 109s and seriously damaged; its
cockpit hood was shattered and petrol and glycol tanks punctured.
He decided to bale out, but seeing a Bf 109 coming in from the
port quarter, instead turned into this attack. The German pilot,
apparently thinking the Spitfire undamaged, sheered off. As his

engine was still running, Bartley decided to stay with his aircraft and attempt to bring it down, but as he was coming in to a field near Appledore his engine failed and he crash-landed. Pilot Officer Mottram also had to crash-land his burning fighter, but was injured in the process. After the squadron had been split up, Pilot Oficer Wade climbed to 27,000 feet over the Folkestone–Dover area and was able to surprise four Bf 109s making for home, 1,000 feet below him. He fired on two aircraft, finishing his ammunition, and saw one of them dive vertically towards the sea. It was assessed as damaged.

At 1555 hours that afternoon eight Spitfires were sent up and ordered to join No. 66 Squadron in a patrol at 30,000 feet over Tenterden. On reaching that altitude, Flight Lieutenant Kingcome, leading the squadron, found himself in cloud and decided to come down to 18,000 feet. There AA fire directed their attention to a formation of sixteen Bf 109s and the formation split up to give chase, but the German fighters disappeared in cloud before they could be brought to combat. Kingcome managed to collect three members of his scattered formation and they attacked a group of twenty Ju 88s from the starboard beam, the Spitfires in echelon peeling off to go in one after another. Flight Lieutenant Kingcome saw hits on the bomber at which he fired. He went right through the enemy formation and delivered a second attack from the opposite side, causing a Ju 88 to drop out and spiral down into cloud. On breaking away, Kingcome found a third bomber which had been disabled by an earlier attack. He gave it a burst from above and behind and saw it spin down to crash in the estuary off the Isle of Sheppey.

After delivering his initial beam attack, Pilot Officer Hill picked out a Ju 88 which had broken formation and fired a number of bursts into it as it went down. He followed it through cloud and finished off his ammunition in a last attack. The Ju 88 finally ditched in the sea seven miles off Shoeburyness. Hill, circling the wreckage, saw two aircrew in the water and guided a rescue boat to them. By 1818 hours seven Spitfires had returned to Biggin Hill and the eighth, flown by Pilot Officer J. G. Pattison, force-landed at Debden.

During cloudy weather on 19 September two Spitfires of Red Section, flown by Pilot Officers Wright and Hill, were sent up to intercept a single raider approaching Biggin Hill from the south. They made contact with it at 5,000 feet over base and both pilots were able to fire several bursts into it. However, it eluded them in cloud and was reported by the Observer Corps to have passed out to sea at 900 feet over Dover, with smoke pouring from both engines. The following day the squadron was surprised by Bf 109s when on patrol over the Folkestone–Dover area and lost two pilots killed. Squadron Leader Sanders turned into the German fighters' attack and fired a deflection burst at one of them. It half-rolled and dived steeply through 10,000 feet with Sanders in pursuit. As it began to pull up, the CO fired again. The Bf 109 half-rolled again and dived, but did not pull out. Sanders followed it down to 500 feet, firing intermittently, and saw the Bf 109 go into the sea off Dymchurch.

Pilot Officer Wade also got on to the tail of one of the attackers, but eventually lost it in cloud fifteen miles off the French coast. He observed his fire hit the Bf 109's wings, but the damage had no apparent effect on the German fighter's performance. Pilot Officer H. P. Hill and Sergeant P. R. Eyles failed to return and are believed to have been the victims of the Luftwaffe's master tactician, Major Werner Mölders, Kommodore of Jagdgeschwader 51. During a skirmish on 21 September one of the squadron's Spitfires was shot-up by Bf 109s, but its pilot escaped unhurt.

Pilot Officer J. G. Pattison was severely wounded in the thigh during a combat with Bf 109s from III. Gruppe Jagdgeschwader 26 over Gravesend on 23 September. The formation leader, Flight Lieutenant Kingcome, accounted for one of the German fighters, seeing its pilot bale out and the aircraft crash to the north-west of Dungeness. Another Bf 109 was shot down by Pilot Officer Drummond, who forced it to break away from behind a Spitfire and followed it down. It was seen to force-land north of Chatham. During its fifteen days of combat flying from Biggin Hill, the squadron had lost four pilots killed and nine wounded, out of the nineteen on strength at the beginning of the month. And, although a number of the less seriously wounded pilots returned to the squadron after short periods in hospital, losses were to continue.

On 24 September the squadron was flying in company with Nos. 72 and 66 Squadrons, when they intercepted a formation of Ju 88s with a large fighter escort south of the Thames estuary. No. 92 Squadron's Spitfires went for the bombers, but were then set upon by Bf 109s. Pilot Officer J. S. Bryson was shot down and killed. Squadron Leader R. C. F. Lister, No. 41 Squadron's former commanding officer, who had been attached to No. 92 Squadron as a supernumerary on 20 September, was again wounded in action. Sergeant Ellis brought down his badly damaged Spitfire in a crash-landing near Gravesend and was unhurt. No conclusive results were observed from the squadron's combats, but two enemy aircraft were claimed as probably destroyed and three as damaged. Later the same day Flight Lieutenant Kingcome claimed a further Bf 109 as probably destroyed, when he led the squadron on an escort mission to bombers attacking German shipping in the Channel.

It was at this time that Squadron Leader Sanders sustained burns to his hands in an accident on the ground. His replacement, Squadron Leader A. M. MacLachlan, was posted in on 26 September, but proved to be inexperienced and in any case only survived for a couple of weeks before he too retired injured. Flight Lieutenant Kingcome therefore became the *de facto* leader of the squadron and was indeed the natural choice for its commanding officer. However, peacetime attitudes to promotion and seniority died hard and it was not until after the Battle that the principle of promotion according to proven performance as a fighter leader had become well established.

No. 92 Squadron was certainly not an easy command for an officer who had yet to prove himself. They had become notorious for their contemptuous attitude towards the conventions of Service discipline. Their unorthodox dress, fast cars and wild parties were all part of the Auxiliary Air Force tradition which Squadron Leader Bushell had instilled in the squadron. Only an experienced fighter pilot, himself in tune with the squadron spirit, could hope to establish his authority over such an unruly team, and the fact that the squadron was performing effectively in the air tended to make their attitude to authority even worse.

Opinions of surviving members of the squadron differ somewhat as to whether the unit's reputation for indiscipline has been exaggerated. Squadron Leader Anthony Bartley writes: 'Indeed we were a wild and indisciplined bunch on the ground, but in the air were a self-disciplined, expert fighting unit which became one of the top scorers in Fighter Command.' Squadron Leader G. H. A. Wellum agrees that 'our reputation for being a bit on the wild side was probably right', but, he thinks that 'some of the post-war authors have used poetic licence' in describing the squadron's excesses: 'Generally speaking the pilots of 92 Squadron were a charming bunch and I would say first-class material, but I think as the Battle went on we all got a little "flak happy" and certainly towards the end I now realize that what is now known as combat fatigue was very much in evidence.'

In Group Captain A. R. Wright's view, the squadron's in-discipline and wild behaviour was probably exaggerated. After the loss of Squadron Leader Bushell 'we had a succession of almost unnoticed COs' and 'as a consequence, we worked things out for ourselves, tactics and behaviour, tending to follow the forthright personalities and abilities of Bob Tuck and Brian Kingcome. We were very successful and took pride in being known as a "bunch of individualists".'

Green Section, led by Pilot Officer Wright, was sent up during cloudy weather on the afternoon of 26 September and attacked three separate German bombers, one of which was reported by the Observer Corps to have crashed. Further heavy engagements followed on 27 September, when the Luftwaffe attempted to clear the way for its first wave of bombers by sending in fighter and fighter-bomber forces ahead of them. The plan miscarried and the main weight of Fighter Command's riposte fell on the bomber formations as they flew across Kent. No. 92 Squadron followed by No. 72 Squadron intercepted a formation of about twenty Do 17Zs and their fighter escort over Sevenoaks at 0915 hours. Kingcome led the Spitfires in an attack on the bombers from quarter ahead. He himself claimed one bomber probably destroyed and a second damaged. The squadron broke up after its opening attack and Pilot Officer Wade climbed to 20,000 feet over London, where he engaged a pair of Bf 109s. They evaded him, but on following them towards the coast, Wade saw a group of twelve Bf 110s flying over Brighton. They formed their customary defensive circle as he approached. Wade joined the circle, meeting heavy return fire. His fire disabled the engine of one Bf 110, which fell away, but Wade's Spitfire was hard hit and he had to crash-land on Lewes race course, putting the Spitfire on its back in the process.

Sergeant Bowen-Morris found a straggler from the Do 17Z formation and damaged it in attacks from astern and the port and starboard quarters. On pulling up into the sun, he lost contact with the bomber. Pilot Officer Wright, as Green 1 leading the last section in the squadron formation, saw two Do 17Zs fall away after the opening attack. He then joined a number of RAF fighters in finishing off a stray He 111. Wright's No. 2, Pilot Officer Mansell-Lewis, carried out a follow-up attack on one of the rearmost Do 17Zs, seeing it dive away smoking. His Spitfire was attacked by a Bf 109 as he pursued the bomber formation towards London. He evaded it, but his Spitfire was then hit and sustained damage to the wing and tail. This was probably from a second German fighter, although Mansell-Lewis did not see his attacker. He then returned to base and landed safely. The two Spitfires of Yellow Section, led by Pilot Officer Drummond, had remained on patrol over Biggin Hill. On seeing an escorted bomber formation, they engaged it and Drummond shared in the destruction of a Bf 110 with a number of Hurricanes. The squadron lost Flight Lieutenant J. A. Paterson and Flight Sergeant C. Sydney in this action.

At 1145 hours that morning the squadron was sent up again and engaged a formation of Bf 109s over Canterbury. The only pilot to claim was the formation's 'weaver', Sergeant T. G. Oldfield, who probably destroyed a German fighter. This pilot was killed during the squadron's third engagement of the day, which was fought over Sevenoaks at 1500 hours. Flight Lieutenant Kingcome led the Spitfires of Nos. 92 and 66 Squadrons into a head-on attack on a formation of fifteen Ju 88s, splitting them up before the fighter escort could intervene. Kingcome saw the Ju 88 that he had first fired at drop from the formation and he made a second head-on attack on another bomber, damaging this also. He next joined two other Spitfires in finishing off a Ju 88, which he saw crash in flames. Pilot Officer Bartley made two quarter astern attacks on a Ju 88, disabling its starboard engine, and Pilot Officer Sherrington reported that this aircraft crashed in the vicinity of Redhill.

Sergeant Bowen-Morris was attacking a Ju 88 from astern when two Bf 109s came down on him. He turned into their attack and they sheered away. He then resumed his attack on the bomber, in concert with a Spitfire from No. 66 Squadron, and the Ju 88 went down to crash-land in a field near Sheerness. Pilot Officer Drummond picked out a Ju 88 flying in the rear section of the German formation and followed it as it broke away. He and another Spitfire finished this aircraft off, seeing it crash in the vicinity of Tenterden. Acting Flight Lieutenant Wright, newly promoted to fill the vacancy created by Paterson's death, saw fire from his opening burst hit a Ju 88. He then followed a bomber which had broken away from the main formation and, in company with about four other Spitfires, harried it until it burst into flames and dived into the ground. He finished off his ammunition in hastening the retreat of another Ju 88, claiming it as damaged.

Most of the squadron's pilots reported that a considerable number of Bf 109s flew about 500 feet above the bombers during this engagement, but made little attempt to intervene. The only claim against an enemy fighter was made by Sergeant D. E. Kingaby, who was set upon by five Bf 109s and managed to damage one of them before he made good his escape. The squadron's victims on this occasion were the Ju 88s of Kampfgeschwader 77. The unit reported that nine of its bombers were lost, most of them being shared between several RAF fighters.

In cloudy weather on 29 September Pilot Officer Williams led Green Section in an interception of a Do 17Z over Canterbury. Williams was able to damage the enemy aircraft before its escape into cloud cover. September ended with another day of high activity. In the early afternoon the squadron joined up with Nos. 66 and 72 Squadrons and at about 1400 hours was attacked and split up by Bf 109s over Maidstone. Pilot Officer Williams then met an escorted formation of Do 17Zs and was able to claim one of them as probably destroyed. At 1617 hours the squadron was sent up again in company with No. 66 Squadron. Over Brighton they encountered an escorted bomber formation and became involved in a dogfight with the Bf 109s. Flight Lieutenant Wright disabled one of these and, following it down, saw it ditch in the sea. He was then surprised by two Bf 109s whose fire damaged his Spitfire and wounded Wright in the thigh. He brought his damaged fighter in to land at Shoreham. Pilot Officer Drummond claimed a Bf 109 probably destroyed and Sergeant Kingaby damaged another. That the serious-minded and able Wright should fall into the trap that all beginners were constantly warned against, by following down a damaged victim to see what became of it, was indicative of the effect that the strain of continuous combat was having on the squadron's pilots.

In October the Battle entered its final phase, with the Luftwaffe resorting to high-flying fighter sweeps. Rather than easing the pressures on Fighter Command's hard-pressed squadrons, the new conditions if anything exacerbated them. The month, however, began on a low key. On 4 October Pilot Officer Williams intercepted a Ju 88 above 10/10th cloud and claimed it as damaged. The following day Pilot Officer J. W. Lund became separated from the squadron formation and attacked a Bf 110 over Maidstone, firing off all his ammunition and claiming it as probably destroyed. Flying Officer Drummond, taking off ten minutes after the other Spitfires, made a solo attack on a formation of twelve Bf 109s flying at 20,000 feet over Dungeness. He fired on the rear-most fighter and saw it dive into the sea. He then saw a Henschel Hs 126 flying low over the water and engaged it, claiming it as destroyed.

During a squadron patrol over Canterbury on 9 October, the twelve Spitfires were attacked by large numbers of fighters and Sergeant E. T. G. Frith baled out severely wounded; he died in hospital eight days later. On the following day the squadron lost two more pilots, when nine Spitfires engaged a lone Do 17Z off the Sussex coast. The Spitfires' windscreens were icing up and this so reduced visibility that Flying Officer J. F. Drummond and Pilot Officer D. G. Williams collided, both crashing to their deaths. Sergeant Ellis's Spitfire was hit and he had to crash-land and the Do 17Z then eluded the remaining Spitfires. Flight Lieutenant Kingcome was able to claim one Bf 109 destroyed on 11 October, when No. 92 Squadron and No. 66 Squadron chased a large formation of Bf 109s out over the Kent coast.

Squadron Leader Tuck, visiting his old squadron on 12 October, flew with them on a morning patrol. He joined in a dogfight over the Dover area and shot down a Bf 109. That afternoon the squadron engaged about fifty Bf 109s over Rochester. Three of the German fighters were claimed as destroyed (by Flight Lieutenant Kingcome, Pilot Officer Wade and Sergeant Kingaby), but Pilot Officer A. J. S. Pattinson, who had only joined the squadron the previous day, was shot down and killed. Flight Lieutenant Kingcome shot down another Bf 109, when on patrol over Ashford on 13 October. He had begun to chase four Bf 109s which themselves were in pursuit of a formation of Hurricanes, when he saw a single German fighter coming in to attack his squadron from behind. Discovering that his R/T was unserviceable, Kingcome was unable to warn the other Spitfires, so he turned to meet the enemy fighter. He sent it down to crash in the vicinity of Ashford, but in the confusion caused by the leader's unexpected breakdown of communications, the other four Bf 109s were able to escape. On the following day Pilot Officer Holland and Pilot Officer Lund caught a Ju 88 over Ashford, but it was able to elude them in cloud and they could only claim it as damaged.

No. 92 Squadron's gallant partners at Biggin Hill, No. 72 Squadron, were withdrawn from combat on 14 October and replaced by Squadron Leader Malan's No. 74 Squadron. This tightly disciplined and brilliantly led team was in many ways the complete antithesis of the easy-going No. 92 Squadron; but while Malan looked askance at the indisciplined state of No. 92 Squadron, he was ready to acknowledge the individual brilliance of its pilots. As a fresh unit, No. 74 Squadron was able, to some degree, to ease the burden of combat flying for No. 92 Squadron, but there was no prospect of the latter's being fully rested until the Battle ended.

On 15 October it was to fight two separate actions. At 0845 hours eleven Spitfires took off with orders to rendezvous with No. 66 Squadron over base. They encountered about fifty Bf 109s withdrawing from a sweep over London and pursued them out into mid-Channel. In the ensuing dogfight Sergeant Kingaby and Sergeant Fokes each destroyed a Bf 109 and the latter also found a stray He 111 which he shot down into the sea. The Squadron lost Sergeant K. B. Parker in this action. At 1145 hours nine Spitfires were directed to intercept a force of fifty Bf 109s over Ashford. Sergeant Fokes shot down one German fighter and Pilot Officer Holland probably destroyed another, but Flight Lieutenant Kingcome baled out wounded and Pilot Officer Lund came down in the sea; he was rescued unhurt. Kingcome was the one pilot that the squadron could least afford to lose, but fortunately when No. 72 Squadron had moved from Biggin Hill, it had transferred to them one of its most experienced pilots, Flight Lieutenant J. W. Villa.

Flight Lieutenant Villa was leading No. 92 Squadron on 20 October, when it intercepted a high-flying Bf 110 east of Tunbridge Wells. The German aircraft dived to low level with the Spitfires of Nos. 92 and 222 Squadrons in pursuit and was finally brought to earth. Two Spitfires were damaged by enemy fire. Four days later Sergeant Kingaby accounted for a Do 17, when on patrol over Maidstone. Twelve Spitfires were sent up at 1250 hours on 25 October and they joined No. 222 Squadron over Rochford. Large numbers of Bf 109s were encountered to the south-west of Maidstone, flying between 20,000 and 28,000 feet. Flight Lieutenant Villa, leading No. 92 Squadron, and Pilot Officer Sherrington each shot down a German fighter, while Sergeant Kingaby damaged another. Pilot Officer Mansell-Lewis's Spitfire was damaged by enemy fire, but he force-landed on Penshurst airfield unhurt. Next day the squadron engaged about thirty Bf 109s over Tunbridge Wells at 1040 hours and, having the advantage of superior height, were able to claim two destroyed (by

Sergeant Fokes and newly promoted Acting Flight Lieutenant Holland), two probably destroyed and one damaged.

During a morning patrol on 27 October, Pilot Officer Sherrington damaged a Do 17Z over the Ashford area, and in the afternoon eight of the squadron's Spitfires had to land away from base at the end of a patrol, when ground mist covered Biggin Hill. The Spitfires of Sergeant Bowen-Morris and Sergeant Kingaby were damaged in a taxying accident on the morning of 29 October, but the month ended on a high note, when twelve Spitfires led by Flight Lieutenant Villa intercepted a similar number of Bf 110s flying over the Kenley area. Two enemy aircraft were claimed as destroyed, two probably destroyed and one damaged.

On 26 October No. 92 Squadron was given a new commanding officer, the tough Canadian Squadron Leader J. A. Kent, who had previously served as a flight commander with No. 303 (Polish) Squadron. Kent's first impressions of his new command were of a disorganized and indisciplined group, who were none the less first-rate fighter pilots, and he set about the thankless job of restoring some semblance of normal Service discipline. His efforts were deeply resented at first, but such were Kent's qualities as a leader that he eventually won the pilots over to his point of view. The new CO was leading the squadron on 1 October when they intercepted an escorted formation of Ju 87 dive-bombers over the Thames estuary at 1420 hours. Most of the Spitfires became entangled with the Bf 109s, Squadron Leader Kent and Sergeant Kingaby each destroying one fighter and Flight Lieutenant Holland, Pilot Officer Bartley and Sergeant X. de Montbon shared in destroying a third. Two pilots, Pilot Officer Saunders (who had that morning claimed a reconnaissance Bf 110 damaged) and Pilot Officer M. C. Kinder, managed to reach the vulnerable Stukas. Each accounted for one Ju 87, before they were set upon by Bf 109s. Kinder was wounded by a cannon shell, but he turned into his attacker and saw his fire hitting the Bf 109, probably destroying it. He then made for Eastchurch airfield, but was overcome by dizziness from loss of blood and had to crash-land, writing off his Spitfire. Saunders also made a wheels-up landing near Eastchurch, when his damaged engine seized up, but he was uninjured.

In November and early December the squadron's operations were characterized by an often frustrating routine of patrols and chases after elusive radar contacts, interspersed with brief periods of fast and furious combat. On 2 November Squadron Leader Kent led an attack from above and astern on a large formation of Bf 109s over Rochford. This initial advantage allowed the squadron to claim four German fighters destroyed, one probably destroyed and two damaged, Squadron Leader Kent's share being two destroyed and a 'probable'. The initiative was with the Luftwaffe on the afternoon of 5 November when the squadron was attacked by Bf 109s while on patrol north of Gravesend. Sergeant Ellis's Spitfire, flying in the rear section, was badly damaged by cannon fire, but Ellis force-landed at Gravesend and was uninjured. Pilot Officer Bartley, despite the handicaps of an iced-up windscreen, got on the tail of one of the attacking Bf 109s and shot it down. Sergeant Fokes, recently awarded the DFM, together with Sergeant de Montbon intercepted and shot down a Ju 88 on 9 November. On the following evening Biggin Hill was raided by a German bomber and one of No. 92 Squadron's Spitfires was destroyed and three others damaged. Red Section was detached from a squadron patrol on the morning of 13 November and attacked a Do 17Z which escaped damaged in clouds.

Two combats were fought by No. 92 Squadron on 15 November. At 1330 hours they met about 25 Bf 109s over the estuary and gave chase. Flight Lieutenant Villa, leading the squadron, claimed one destroyed, as did Sergeant Fokes and Sergeant Kingaby, while Pilot Officer Bartley damaged a fourth. Then at 1615 hours forty Bf 109s were intercepted over Selsey Bill. Flight Lieutenant Holland damaged one of them, while Sergeant Kingaby shot down three to give him four Bf 109s destroyed in a single day. This remarkable feat was recognized by the award of a DFM and Kingaby ended the war as one of the RAF's leading aces with 23 victories to his credit. Flight Lieutenant Holland was leading No. 92 Squadron in company with No. 74 Squadron on 17 November, when they attacked about twenty Bf 109s over Eastbourne. They could only claim two German fighters probably destroyed and three damaged, but suffered no loss apart from

Sergeant W. J. Allison's Spitfire which force-landed after its radiator was hit. Allison was unhurt. Two further combats were recorded before the end of the month. On 26 November Pilot Officer Wade probably destroyed a Do 17Z when leading Blue Section on convoy patrol. Two days later Pilot Officer Mottram probably destroyed a Bf 109, when he was acting as 'weaver' for the squadron formation.

The first week of December saw a further six Bf 109s destroyed by the squadron in three separate combats. At 1500 hours on 1 December the squadron pursued twenty Bf 109s out to mid-Channel and claimed four of them destroyed, plus two probably destroyed and six others damaged. Pilot Officer Saunders' Spitfire was damaged and he had to make a wheels-up landing. One of the confirmed victories went to Flight Lieutenant Villa, flying one of the squadron's recently-delivered, cannon-armed Spitfire Mk IBs. Opening fire at 300 yards' range, he saw the shells from his second burst hit the Bf 109 and it exploded. The next day Pilot Officer Wade shot a fighter down into the Channel. On 5 December Flight Lieutenant Wright, now recovered from his wounds, led the squadron and he probably destroyed a Bf 109, while Pilot Officer Fokes (newly commissioned) was credited with an enemy fighter confirmed destroyed. However, as the weather worsened towards the close of the year, contact with the enemy became infrequent. The hazards of bad weather were brought home to No. 92 Squadron on 7 December, when ground mist covered Biggin Hill after an afternoon patrol had taken off. Five Spitfires landed at Croydon, but two had to force-land away from an airfield and one of these crashed.

The squadron's last victory of 1940 went to Pilot Officer Fokes on 21 December. An event of equal significance was a patrol over France, which was flown at low-level by Flight Lieutenant Wright and Pilot Officer Mottram on 27 December. For Fighter Command's operations in the New Year were to take the offensive into the enemy's territory and during these missions the veterans of No. 92 Squadron soon established themselves as the Command's top-scoring unit. However, their contribution to Fighter Command's victory in the Battle of Britain was to be measured not in enemy aircraft destroyed (although the squadron's victory claims were substantial), but in their ability to continue fighting until the onset of winter at last brought them relief. Entering combat in No. 11 Group as a fresh unit in early September, No. 92 Squadron had stayed in the front line until the fighting finally petered out in late December. The Battle's final phase had been as much a test of endurance as a contest of arms and, despite losses and crises in leadership, No. 92 Squadron had fought on until the end.

NO. 111 SQUADRON

In December 1937 No. 111 Squadron became the first squadron in RAF Fighter Command to fly the new generation of eight-gun monoplane fighters, when it began to take delivery of Hawker Hurricanes to replace its Gloster Gauntlet biplanes. The squadron, based at Northolt in Middlesex, attracted considerable attention from the Press and when in February 1938 the CO, Squadron Leader J. W. Gillan, flew from Edinburgh to Northolt in 48 minutes, at an average speed of 408mph, the incident was widely publicized. Well it might have been, since the actual top speed of the initial production batch Hurricanes was only 318mph, the additional impetus having been provided by an unusually strong tailwind. Shortly after the beginning of the Second World War, the squadron moved from its peacetime station at Northolt to Acklington in Northumberland. Its first encounter with the Luftwaffe was on 29 November, when Squadron Leader H. Broadhurst intercepted and shot down an He 111 off Alnwick. Broadhurst, who had succeeded Gillan as CO in January 1939, was destined for a distinguished RAF career and he retired as an Air Chief Marshal in 1961.

In December 1939 the squadron moved to Drem in East Lothian and then yet further northwards to Wick in Caithness in February 1940. The opening of the Battle of France brought No. 111 Squadron's Hurricanes back to Northolt on 13 May. During the following week both flights operated (independently of each other) from bases in France and claimed a total of sixteen victories. The squadron was then pulled out of No. 11 Group for a brief rest period at Digby, Lincolnshire, before flying to North Weald on 30 May in time to participate in the closing battles of the Dunkirk air fighting. At the end of this campaign it moved to Croydon in Surrey, a pre-war civil air terminal which had become a satellite station in the Kenley Sector.

The squadron's first action of the Battle of Britain was fought on the afternoon of 10 July. Nine Hurricanes, led by Squadron Leader J. M. Thompson, who had succeeded Broadhurst as CO in January 1940, took off from Croydon at 1300 hours bound for the forward base at Hawkinge. *En route* the squadron was diverted to the Folkestone–Dover area, where a coastal convoy was threatened with attack. At 1340 hours the squadron engaged an escorted force of about twenty Do 17Z bombers from Kampfgeschwader 2, which were attacking the convoy; it was one of five RAF squadrons to become involved in the combat.

Squadron Leader Thompson ordered his section (Blue Section) into line astern and led Red and Yellow Sections into an attack on the rearmost vic of bombers. Thompson fired on the Do 17Z flying on the left of the formation, closing in to 100 yards' range where he noticed the effect of the bomber's slipstream. He broke away to the left and came back into the attack. At that point he saw a Hurricane collide with a bomber, both aircraft diving towards the sea out of control. The Hurricane was flown by Flying Officer T. P. K. Higgs, who crashed to his death. Thompson then attacked a second Do 17Z and reported seeing the crew of another bomber take to their parachutes. He finished off his ammunition on a Do 17Z which had already been fired on by four other Hurricanes, but could see no results from this fusilade.

Sergeant R. Carnall, flying as No. 3 in the leading section, selected the left-hand aircraft in the rearmost vic and saw his fire hit its fuselage, apparently disabling the rear gunner. He reported cross-fire from the other two bombers in the vic and his Hurricane was hit in the port wing. Seeing a Hurricane diving in a quarter attack, Carnall broke away to avoid the danger of collision. His Hurricane crashed on landing at Hawkinge, but was repairable.

Flying Officer H. M. Ferriss, Red 1, carried out a quarter attack on the three Do 17Zs flying ahead of the vic engaged by Blue Section. He picked out the right-hand aircraft, leaving the leader to his No. 3. Ferriss opened fire with a 5-second burst from 300 yards, but on breaking away could see no damage to the bomber. He next attacked a straggling Do 17Z, which several Hurricanes had already engaged, and chased it fifteen miles out across the Channel. There he saw a Bf 109 diving away ahead of him and pursued it down to sea level. Ferriss fired five short bursts into it from astern and saw it finally plunge into the water. His Hurricane was then hit by fire from astern, a splinter hitting the pilot's right leg. As he turned back towards the English coast Ferriss saw three Bf 109s on his tail. He successfully evaded about a dozen separate attacks from this trio, until they eventually broke away five miles from the Kent shore. Ferriss flew his damaged fighter to Croydon, where he picked up a replacement Hurricane and flew it to Hawkinge. Red 2, Sergeant J. T. Craig, damaged two Do 17Zs and then drove a Bf 109 off another Hurricane's tail. The squadron's claims were two bombers and a Bf 109 confirmed destroyed.

Later that afternoon at 1820 hours the squadron was ordered to patrol Hawkinge at 5,000 feet. Flying Officer Ferriss and Pilot Officer B. M. Fisher, were detached to investigate a formation of unidentified aircraft, which turned out to be Spitfires. As they rejoined the squadron, they were trailed by one of the Spitfires. This fighter then attacked Pilot Officer Fisher's Hurricane, damaging the wings and tailplane and holing the petrol tank, but Fisher was unhurt and landed his damaged fighter at Hawkinge. There were no further contacts with the enemy during the following week, although the squadron flew convoy patrols from Hawkinge on 12 July and 14 July. During the latter deployment, a Hurricane crashed and was damaged when taking-off, but its pilot, Pilot Officer A. G. A. Fisher (who was the brother of Pilot Officer B. M. Fisher), escaped unhurt. On 18 July Blue Section was scrambled from Hawkinge and intercepted an Hs 126, which was damaged but escaped. At 1820 hours the squadron joined with the Hurricanes of No. 615 Squadron to escort a formation of eighteen Blenheim bombers to Boulogne, but they met no opposition from German fighters.

No. 111 Squadron was again operating from its forward base at Hawkinge on 19 July, when at 1220 hours the Hurricanes were sent up to intercept enemy aircraft sighted in the vicinity. In fact the air raid warnings had sounded and Ju 87s were seen nearby before the order to take-off came through. The Hurricanes had climbed to 10,000 feet between Dover and Folkestone when Green 2, Pilot Officer J. H. H. Copeman, reported twenty Bf 109s flying off the coast. His section leader, Flight Lieutenant S. D. P. Connors, attempted to inform the remainder of the squadron, but apparently his call was not heard. Connors therefore led his three Hurricanes into an attack on the fighters, which he saw were themselves engaging a squadron of Defiants. Opening fire at short range from abeam, Connors saw a Bf 109 burst into flames and dive into the sea. He then shifted his aim to a second fighter, but could not press home the attack as he had to evade a number of other Bf 109s. Pilot Officer Copeman followed up his leader's attack on this fighter and saw it begin to smoke. As he neared the French coast Copeman broke away and returned to Hawkinge. The third member of the section, Pilot Officer P. J. Simpson, got on the tail of a Bf 109 and sent it down pouring smoke. His windscreen then became covered in oil and Simpson lost sight of the enemy aircraft, but Connors reported that it had fallen into the sea.

The three Hurricanes had made a timely intervention, so far as the Defiant crews of No. 141 Squadron were concerned. Overwhelmed by the Bf 109s, five Defiants had gone into the sea and a sixth crash-landed. The appearance of No. 111 Squadron's Green Section had prevented a massacre from becoming a complete annihilation. The surviving Defiant crews were immediately withdrawn to Prestwick, Ayrshire, but their sister unit, No. 264 Squadron, would have to suffer an equally severe mauling before it was finally recognized that the Defiant was totally unsuited to daylight operations.

None of the squadron's patrols over the following five days made contact with enemy aircraft. On the evening of 24 July the squadron was forced by bad weather to stay overnight at Hawkinge. It returned to Croydon at 1330 hours the following day. An hour and twenty minutes later it was scrambled from a state of 'fifteen minutes available' instead of, as was customary, being brought to 'readiness' before it was sent up. The twelve Hurricanes were airborne within fourteen minutes and were vectored on to a formation of fighters flying at 17,000 feet off Dover. They were to some extent hampered by a number of

Spitfires, which threatened to attack several of the Hurricanes. Squadron Leader Thompson reported being twice attacked by friendly fighters. Flight Lieutenant Connors saw two Bf 109s on the tail of a Spitfire and led Green Section down to engage them. As the German fighters broke away, Connors carried out a head-on attack on one. He then came in from astern, noticing that one of the Bf 109's undercarriage legs had dropped. After three more bursts of fire, Connors broke off to clear his tail and Green 3, Sergeant Carnall, continued the attack. Pilot Officer Simpson, Green 2, saw the Bf 109 belch black smoke and thought further action on his part unnecessary, as it seemed obvious that it was going to crash. However, the squadron Intelligence Officer thought differently and the claim was only recorded as damaged.

Flight Lieutenant R. P. R. Powell, Red 1, made a head-on attack on a Bf 109 and saw his fire hitting it. His No. 3, Pilot Officer R. R. Wilson, attacked four Bf 109s from astern, firing a long burst into one from 250 yards, closing to 100 yards. The Bf 109 went into a steep dive and as Wilson turned away he saw it hit the water. He then found a Spitfire on his tail and so dived to 2,000 feet, waggling his wings as a recognition signal. The Spitfire realized that he was pursuing a Hurricane and broke off. Wilson climbed back to 7,000 feet and, seeing two enemy fighters circling, attacked the rear one, seeing it flick roll and dive. Wilson could not follow it down, as he needed to ensure that the second fighter was not about to attack him. In fact it had disappeared. The only other pilot to claim was Sergeant Craig, Yellow 3, who was attacked from head-on and above by two Bf 109s flying in line astern. The leader overshot him, but the wingman was able to fire. Craig replied and believed that his fire hit the Bf 109 before it broke away. The squadron landed at Hawkinge and after further patrols from there returned to Croydon, landing at 2120 hours.

On 28 July twelve Hurricanes were ordered to take-off at 1430 hours and patrol Maidstone at 20,000 feet. They were directed from there into mid-Channel where they encountered two He 59 floatplanes carrying out air–sea rescue duties. The first was seen to have alighted on the water by Flying Officer Ferriss, who went down in a fast dive towards it from an up-sun position. Ferriss fired a long burst into it from 600 yards, closing to short range. His wingman, Pilot Officer B. M. Fisher, only fired briefly, as he had noticed that the German aircraft was marked with a Red Cross, but Ferriss's attack had already severely damaged the enemy aircraft. Fifteen minutes later Pilot Officer Wilson dived on another He 59 which he spotted flying at 1,000 feet ten miles north-west of Boulogne. Wilson flew past the floatplane without attacking it, but his No. 2, Sergeant Robinson, gave it a 5-second burst of fire and sent it into the sea in flames. Whether or not the German air–sea rescue aircraft were entitled to the protection of the Red Cross, which strictly should have been applied only to ambulance aircraft, was a moot point at the time of these attacks. However, on the following day the Air Ministry clarified the situation by stating that it did not consider that the operations of the German He 59s were 'consistent with the privileges generally accorded to the Red Cross'.

The last day of the month saw a further successful engagement for the squadron. Twelve Hurricanes had left Croydon at 0450 hours bound for Hawkinge. At 0710 hours Blue Section was sent up from the forward base and vectored towards Dungeness. Some minutes afterwards Green Section was sent after it. The Hurricanes were then ordered out to mid-Channel, with Blue Section patrolling above cloud and Green Section below. It was the latter, led by Flight Lieutenant Connors, which spotted a Ju 88 flying 500 feet below the cloud base. The Hurricanes gave chase as the enemy aircraft climbed for cover, and Connors opened the attack with a 3-second burst from dead astern, opening fire at 300 yards and closing to 100 yards. The Ju 88 carried out a series of evasive manoeuvres, turning to the left and right and alternately diving and climbing. Connors closed in to short range and fired a 1-second burst, but as no results could be seen from this he carried out two quarter attacks and finished with another from astern, exhausting his ammunition in the process. By that time both of the Ju 88's engines were pouring dense black smoke. Sergeant Carnell, Green 3, then fired off all his ammunition into the Ju 88 from astern. Green 2, Pilot Officer Copeman, went in after him and followed the aircraft down to 1,000 feet, where it disappeared into thick mist, diving vertically for the sea.

The first week of August was a quiet period for Fighter Command and No. 111 Squadron saw no further action until 11 August. At that time, though, it lost Flight Lieutenant Powell, who was posted to an operational training unit as an instructor, and Pilot Officer Simpson was temporarily detached to No. 64 Squadron, which flew Spitfires from Kenley. At 1245 hours on 11 August twelve Hurricanes left Croydon for Hawkinge, but they were later diverted to North Foreland where enemy activity had been reported. Heavy cloud hampered the squadron from the outset and Pilot Officers H. G. Hardman and A. G. A. Fisher became separated from the formation and landed at Hawkinge without engaging the enemy. At 1340 hours Flight Lieutenant Connors, Green 1, noticed fifteen Bf 109s pass over the squadron formation 3,000 feet above them at 20,000 feet. They disappeared into the sun and shortly afterwards he saw a German fighter climbing behind his No. 2, Pilot Officer Copeman. He turned towards the Bf 109 and followed it as it dived away into cloud cover. Connors then went down through a gap in the clouds and saw a destroyer under attack from Ju 87 Stukas. He attacked one of the dive-bombers' fighter escort from astern, giving it a 2-second burst and following the Bf 109 down until he saw it crash into the sea. Immediately afterwards he saw Pilot Officer J. H. H. Copeman's Hurricane spinning down to crash. The pilot was killed. Connors next attacked another Bf 109 and fired a short burst at a Ju 87, but as his windscreen had become obscured with oil he had to break off the action and land at Manston to have it cleaned.

Meanwhile, the remainder of the squadron had been instructed to patrol over Hawkinge, but *en route* they ran into a formation of about 45 Do 17Zs flying on an easterly course 200 feet above the cloud tops. Squadron Leader Thompson immediately ordered an attack by sections and, putting his own Blue Section into line astern, he closed in behind the German bombers. On his approach, Thompson flew just in the top of the clouds, until at 400 yards' range he ordered Blue Section into echelon right and pulled up underneath the rear left Do 17Z. At 100 yards he opened fire, raking all three bombers in the rearmost vic with a 5-second burst of fire. He saw a fire begin in the fuselage of the left-hand bomber, but as he was receiving intense fire from the Do 17Z's ventral gun positions he broke away downwards into the clouds. He was followed by his No. 2, Pilot Officer J. W. McKenzie. After Thompson re-emerged from the clouds, with the intention of re-engaging the bombers, he suddenly noticed that his No. 2 was no longer with him. Looking behind, he saw a Bf 109 on his tail and turned to engage it. The German fighter immediately dived away into cloud. As McKenzie failed to return from this patrol, the commanding officer concluded that he had been shot down by this enemy fighter. Thompson was by then too far behind the bombers to be confident of catching them again and so he flew to Hawkinge and landed.

On sighting the bomber formation, Flying Officer Ferriss attempted to lead 'A' Flight into position for a head-on attack, but before he could pass ahead of the bombers, they changed course towards the north-east and the Hurricanes had insufficient fuel to prolong their manoeuvring for position. Accordingly, Ferriss led his Red Section into a beam attack. Each pilot was able to fire about 800 rounds into the bombers, but they met with intense return fire and observed no damage to their targets. Yellow Section, by then only two-aircraft strong, made an astern attack on the formation. One Hurricane was seen to break away with its engine heavily smoking, and both Pilot Officer R. R. Wilson and Sergeant R. B. Sim were posted as missing in action after this combat. A fifth Hurricane was lost when Blue 3, Sergeant H. S. Newton, crash-landed his fighter when out of fuel at Boyton in Suffolk. The pilot, however, was uninjured.

For the loss of four pilots, the squadron could only claim one Bf 109 destroyed, although several more enemy aircraft had been damaged. On the following day eleven Hurricanes left Croydon for Hawkinge at dawn, but returned to base at 1330 hours and therefore missed an afternoon raid by the Luftwaffe on its forward airfield. Further sorties were flown during the afternoon and evening, but although most pilots were in the air for between six and seven hours none of them contacted the enemy.

Early on the morning of *Adler Tag*, 13 August, No. 111 Squadron was to exact its revenge for the losses of two days before, when it was one of the RAF squadrons to intercept Kampfgeschwader 2's unescorted Do 17Zs in the vicnity of Eastchurch. Twelve Hurricanes were ordered up from Croydon at 0550 hours and ordered to patrol Hawkinge below cloud. They were then vectored towards Eastchurch and told to keep a look-out for enemy aircraft returning from the direction of the Isle of Sheppey. None was seen and on arriving over Eastchurch, Squadron Leader Thompson decided on his own initiative to take the squadron above the clouds to patrol, since by then he had lost R/T contact with Kenley control. At about 0710 hours a formation of about nine aircraft was seen approaching from the east, flying in vics of three at 3,000 feet. As they were too far off to be positively identified, Thompson decided to lead 'B' Flight past them on the port beam, while leaving 'A' Flight on station above Eastchurch. On doing so, he recognized the aircraft as Do 17Zs and ordered 'A' Flight to attack them from head-on, while he led his six Hurricanes around for an astern attack. The CO changed his plans, however, when he saw a second bomber formation trailing behind the first, and he carried on to engage these Do 17Zs from ahead.

The head-on attack by six Hurricanes broke up the German formation and Thompson came in astern of one of the bombers. On breaking away from this attack, he saw a stray Do 17Z flying eastwards over Sittingbourne and fired on it from abeam and astern. The bomber disappeared into clouds with both engines smoking and Thompson considered it destroyed. On his way back to Croydon, short of fuel, he encountered another Do 17Z over West Malling, but could only give it a short burst from long range before it disappeared into cloud. Blue 2, Pilot Officer Walker, after delivering his initial head-on attack, fired on a number of bombers from the broken formation. He finally found himself in position for a head-on attack on one of them and saw this Do 17Z pull up sharply and then dive away. He lost it in haze at 1,500 feet but thought it certain to have crashed. Green Section attacked and damaged three Do 17Zs, the Section's No. 3, Pilot Officer Hardman, reporting hits on the engine of one of these.

The leading bombers had meanwhile been engaged by 'A' Flight, which approached them in line astern with the intention of making a head-on attack. However, the Do 17Zs evaded the Hurricanes by diving down through cloud. Flying Officer Ferriss, leading 'A' Flight as Red 1, followed them down on a parallel course. On emerging below cloud base, he saw their bombs falling on Eastchurch airfield and turned into the leading Do 17Zs with Red Section to carry out a head-on attack. At the same time, Yellow Section made a similar attack on the second wave of bombers. As Ferriss closed in on the Do 17Zs he saw them pull up and waver slightly in anticipation of the Hurricanes' attack. He saw no results from his opening fire, although he and the other two pilots of Red Section all gave the bombers long bursts. The Hurricanes remain in formation and set upon a straggling bomber, which was seen to stall and fall away. Ferriss then saw another lone bomber disappearing into cloud. He followed its course above the cloud tops until he reached a gap, where he lay in wait for the enemy aircraft. When it appeared, he dived to attack it from astern and saw it burst into flames. The four crew baled out, one parachute becoming caught up on the bomber's tail, before the Do 17Z crashed into the sea.

Yellow 1, Sergeant Dymond, in company with his No. 3, Sergeant Craig, opened fire when 500 yards ahead of the German bombers and at 100 yards' range broke away downwards and to the left. The two Hurricanes then climbed up to deliver an astern attack. One bomber broke away from the formation and was engaged in succession by Yellow 1 and Yellow 3. After carrying out two attacks and seeing the Do 17Z's starboard engine begin to smoke, Sergeant Dymond broke off to pursue another Do 17Z. He was able to damage this aircraft, but by that time had used up all his ammunition. Sergeant Craig stayed with the other straggling bomber and after firing his third burst into it, saw one of the crew bale out over Herne Bay. Craig drew away to give the rest of the crew a chance to abandon the aircraft, but as no more parachutes appeared he closed in for a final attack from short range, firing most of his remaining ammunition. His own aircraft was hit by return fire and he was then short of fuel, so he decided to leave the crippled Do 17Z and return to base. Sergeant Dymond's Hurricane was also damaged by enemy fire, having been hit in six places, but both Hurricanes landed safely without further damage. A third fighter was damaged when Pilot Officer McIntyre crashed on landing. The squadron's claims far outweighed these small losses, with five bombers assessed as destroyed and another five damaged.

The Luftwaffe's greatest effort of the Battle, in terms of sorties flown, came on 15 August and No. 111 Squadron was heavily committed in the defence of No. 11 Group's airfields, fighting three major engagements during the course of the afternoon. The first order to scramble came at 1454 hours and Squadron Leader Thompson led twelve Hurricanes into the air with orders to patrol Beachy Head. The squadron was then vectored towards Dover where enemy fighters were sighted at a higher altitude. In attempting to engage them the squadron broke up into sections, which fought separately. Thompson's Blue Section pursued two Do 17Zs bombers over the Thames estuary. Thompson fired all his ammunition into one of these and he saw both engines catch fire and the bomber go down to crash in the sea.

His No. 2 was Squadron Leader E. A. McNab, CO of No. 1 Squadron Royal Canadian Air Force, which was then based at Croydon but had not yet been declared operational. McNab was flying his first combat sortie with No. 111 Squadron to gain experience. He engaged the second Do 17Z, carrying out two attacks from astern and then following the bomber down. He saw it crash near Westgate-on-Sea. Green Section, led by Flight Lieutenant Connors, had followed the high-flying German fighters inland towards London, but they refused to come down to fight. Connors then saw a formation of 24 Do 17Zs to the south of Kenley and carried out a quarter attack on one of these. The German bomber dived away towards the coast, with Connors in pursuit. He fired his remaining ammunition into it from astern and saw damage to its tailplane. He last saw it crossing the coast between Bognor and Brighton, losing height; he claimed it as probably destroyed. His own Hurricane was slightly damaged.

Flying Officer Ferriss, on hearing the report of enemy fighters above, began to lead 'A' Flight up to engage them. His attention was then diverted by AA fire over Dover and, turning to investigate it, he saw a formation of 24 Do 17Zs. He ordered Red and Yellow Sections into line astern and turned in to a head-on attack. The three Hurricanes in Red Section each opened fire on one of the Do 17Zs in the leading vic, and then fired short bursts into the following three bombers. Ferris reported that a fire had started in the cockpit of the bomber that he fired into, but he was unable to continue the attack because his engine coolant system had been hit. He went down to force-land at Hawkinge, protected by the other two Hurricanes in his section.

Yellow Leader, Sergeant Dymond, made his head-on attack on the second wave of bombers with his section. Two Do 17Zs were seen to be hit and broke formation. Yellow 1 turned to re-engage from astern and set alight the German bomber's forward fuselage. He finished off his ammunition on three bombers flying in a vic and saw hits on the port aircraft. On landing at West Malling to re-arm it was found that Dymond's Hurricane had been damaged by return fire and was unairworthy. He therefore returned to Croydon in a communications Magister. Yellow 3, Sergeant Craig, attacked one of the Do 17Z which had broken formation. He gave it a 10-second burst, which sent it down with one engine on fire. Seeing a Bf 109 attacking a Hurricane, Craig went to its help, but claimed no results from his fire. He finished his ammunition in short bursts against another three bombers, claiming them as damaged. Sergeant Newton damaged a Bf 109, but his own Hurricane was also hit; he returned to Croydon and landed safely.

The squadron had scarcely time to refuel and re-arm before they were ordered to scramble again. Ten Hurricanes took off at 1705 hours, but Squadron Leader Thompson had to return because of engine trouble. The remaining fighters were vectored towards the Portsmouth area. At 1745 hours they intercepted a large force of German aircraft, consisting of Ju 88 bombers with Bf 110 and Bf 109 fighter escort, which was crossing the coast at 16,000 feet south-east of Thorney Island, Hampshire. Flight Lieutenant Connors, who had taken over the lead when the CO dropped out, engaged a Ju 88 with a short burst. He then broke away to evade an attack by Bf 109s. After shaking them off he returned to the bomber formation and fired on a Ju 88 from the rear quarter and from astern. He saw fragments fall from its port engine and the other one was smoking badly. The bomber glided down to crash five miles north of Selsey Bill.

Sergeant T. Y. Wallace, Blue 3, decided to remain above the bombers to cover his section from interference by the fighter escorts. He was attacked by a Bf 110, which he met head-on. Wallace held his fire until the range had closed to 400 yards and fired a 2-second burst. The Bf 110 went down to crash. A Bf 109 then attacked Wallace's Hurricane, but he evaded it. Sergeant Craig, leading Red Section, made his opening attack from out of the sun on two Ju 88s which had become separated from the main formation. He fired a 10-second burst into one of them and saw it go on to its back and spiral down. He attacked a second bomber which also went down with one engine disabled. Craig finally finished off his ammunition in a beam attack on a third Ju 88. He saw his tracer apparently going into the cockpit and the enemy aircraft rolled over and disappeared beneath the Hurricane. Pilot Officer A. G. A. Fisher and Flying Officer B. M. Fisher together attacked and damaged a Ju 88, but B. M. Fisher was then shot down and killed. Pilot Officer McIntyre was slightly wounded and his Hurricane badly damaged by enemy fire, but he successfully force-landed at Hawkinge. The other seven Hurricanes landed back at Croydon between 1745 and 1825 hours.

At 1850 hours nine Hurricanes scrambled on receiving an air raid warning and without waiting for instructions from Sector control. Ten minutes later Croydon was attacked by the bomb-carrying Bf 110s of Erprobungsgruppe 210, the Luftwaffe's fighter-bomber trials unit led by its Swiss-born Kommandeur, Hauptmann Walther Rubensdorffer. The German aircraft approached the airfield from the east and dived low over the hangars, their bombs hitting the main terminal building and the Rollason and Redwing companies' hangars. Fires were also started in the armoury of No. 1 Squadron, RCAF. Squadron Leader Thompson had climbed the squadron to 5,000 feet, before sighting the Bf 110s diving into their attack. He then ordered the Hurricanes into line astern as he turned to engage them, the squadron chasing the Bf 110s in a south-westerly direction. The CO selected one Bf 110 and pulled up behind it in a vertical climb, firing a 5-second burst. He saw hits on the engine and fuselage, but then as his speed dropped off he had to break away. As he was unable to climb back to the Bf 110's height of 6,000 feet, he instead engaged a Bf 109. The German fighter was on the tail of a Hurricane, which was itself chasing another Bf 109. Thompson opened fire at 200 yards' range with a deflection shot and saw hits on the wing and fuselage. As he broke away, black smoke was pouring from the Bf 109's engine. Ground observers confirmed that the Bf 110 which Thompson had earlier attacked went down to crash.

As Sergeant Wallace caught up with the retreating Bf 110s, he found that they had formed a defensive circle. After firing several bursts at a number of Bf 110s from below, he saw one of them break away. It was immediately engaged by Flight Lieutenant Connors, who gave it a long burst, and smoke streamed from its starboard engine. Wallace then closed in astern of the Bf 110 and fired two short bursts. The Bf 110 went straight into the ground to the south of Redhill. On his way back to Croydon, Wallace met and attacked a further two Bf 110s, claiming both of them as damaged. Sergeant Craig turned across Croydon airfield immediately after sighting the Bf 110s and so was in position to attack one as it pulled up from its dive. Firing from ahead and below, he saw pieces fall from the Bf 110, and ground crew at Croydon reported that it crashed to the west of the airfield. He then followed the Bf 110s and tried to break up their defensive circle by firing deflection shots from below. This proved to be unsuccessful. Shortly afterwards Craig was set upon by six Bf 109s and had to take violent evasive action to escape them. Sergeant Dymond attacked two Bf 110s from head-on while they were circling and saw one of them break away and fly south. He caught up with it in the vicinity of Redhill and saw it crash in flames. No. 111 Squadron claimed four of the Croydon raiders as destroyed, a further four damaged and one Bf 109 escort fighter destroyed. In fact Erprobungsgruppe 210 had lost six Bf 110s, including that of their commander who was killed, and one Bf 109. No. 32 Squadron's Hurricanes from Biggin Hill had also engaged the Bf 110s during their withdrawal.

On 16 August ten of No. 111 Squadron's Hurricanes left Croydon for Hawkinge at 0900 hours. They were ordered to patrol the forward base at 15,000 feet, as the build-up of a series of Luftwaffe raids on coastal and inland airfields was detected by radar. Taking off at 1150 hours, the squadron intercepted a large formation of Do 17Z bombers crossing the coast over Dungeness at 10,000 feet. Ignoring the fighter escort of Bf 109s, the squadron dived to attack. Blue, Red and Yellow Sections came in at the bombers from head-on, while Green Section opened their attack from astern. Squadron Leader Thompson selected the extreme left-hand bomber of the German formation and opened fire on it at 600 yards, closing to 100 yards. He saw hits on the Do 17Z and, as he broke away downwards and turned, the bomber spiralled down from its formation. Thompson followed it and saw it crash south of the main Ashford to Redhill railway line.

The other two Hurricanes of Blue Section followed the commanding officer into his attack in line-astern formation. Pilot Officer Walker, Blue 2, on breaking away saw a Bf 109 on a Hurricane's tail and went to his comrade's assistance. He gave the German fighter a 3-second burst from astern at 200 yards. It went spinning down to the ground and crashed in flames. Walker's Hurricane was then attacked by five Bf 109s. Four of them broke away, leaving the fifth sitting on the British fighter's tail. Walker was able to out-turn it, but on reaching a good firing position against the Bf 109, he found that oil on his windscreen made it impossible to take accurate aim. Sergeant Newton, Blue 3, picked the three leading Do 17Zs for his head-on attack and closed in to short range before firing a 2-second burst into one of them. He was certain that his shots had damaged the bomber, and another pilot reported that he saw it crash.

Flight Lieutenant Connors, leading Green Section, fired on a Do 17Z from astern and damaged it, but was himself attacked by seven Bf 109s. While evading them, he had the chance of one shot at a German fighter, but could see no results. His own fighter however, was damaged in the combat. Flight Lieutenant G. R.

McGregor of No. 1 Squadron, RCAF, who flew with No. 111 Squadron on this patrol, could see no results from his fire. It was his first experience of combat. Sergeant Carnall was shot down and baled out wounded. Flight Lieutenant H. M. Ferriss (newly promoted to fill the flight commander vacancy) was killed when his Hurricane crashed head-on into a Do 17Z. Red 3, Sergeant Craig, was unable to get into position for a head-on attack and so broke away to the right and came in again from the German formation's beam. After carrying out three of these attacks, he saw the crew of a bomber bale out. He was then chased away by Bf 109s and lost sight of the enemy formation in haze. Yellow 1, Sergeant Dymond, saw no results from his opening attack from head-on, but after delivering a second attack from astern, he saw hits on one of the Do 17Zs. He finished off his remaining ammunition in firing from abeam of the bomber formation.

Dymond's No. 2, Sergeant Wallace, experienced heavy return fire during his head-on attack on the bombers. On breaking away, he climbed to engage the fighter escort, but found himself greatly outnumbered and was driven away to the south. He later regained contact with the enemy aircraft during their withdrawal. Chasing a Do 17Z, Wallace engaged it near the French coast and saw it trailing smoke as it lost height. At that moment six Bf 109s came in to attack the Hurricane from astern and so Wallace had to break away from the bomber and dive to sea level. As he made for Dover, one Bf 109 stayed on his tail despite Wallace's evasive twists and turns. The Hurricane was twice hit by enemy fire, before Wallace turned unexpectedly into the Bf 109's attack. This gave him the chance for a head-on burst of fire from below, as the Bf 109 pulled up to disengage. Wallace's shots found their mark and the German aircraft dived straight into the sea.

Flight Lieutenant Ferriss's death showed how dangerous the head-on attack, which No. 111 Squadron had made its speciality, could be, even when delivered by a very experienced pilot. The closing speeds of fighter and target were so high that there was only a brief opportunity for accurate sighting and firing. The Hurricane, which was an extremely steady gun platform, was better suited to this type of attack than the Spitfire, but such tactics could only be employed routinely by a highly trained and well-led squadron and were the exception rather than the rule during the Battle. This was simply because many of the RAF fighter squadrons had been so diluted by inexperienced replacement pilots that they lacked the necessary skill to bring off this difficult opening gambit successfully. However, there can be no doubt that it was by far the most effective form of squadron attack since it almost inevitably broke up the bomber formation and thus allowed individual fighters to pick off straggling bombers during follow-up attacks. For, as already stressed, one of the great weaknesses of the RAF's tactical fighter formations in 1940 was that they tended to break up into single aircraft, after the formation had made its initial attack. If at that stage the enemy bomber formation was unbroken, it was very difficult for the RAF fighters to find a worthwhile target.

In the early afternoon of 18 August No. 111 Squadron was scrambled in defence of its Sector station at Kenley, the intended target of the Croydon raiders three days earlier. The twelve pilots had been brought to cockpit readiness before the order to take-off came through at 1305 hours. They were initially told to patrol base at 20,000 feet, this was then changed to 5,000 feet and then to 3,000 feet. Once airborne, a formation of Do 17Zs (the 9. Staffel of Kampfgeschwader 76) were seen at 50 feet approaching Kenley. Flight Lieutenant Connors, Green 1, leading the squadron, ordered the Hurricanes into line astern and went in to attack. He got into position behind the leading Do 17Z in a vic of three and opened fire. When Connors broke away, his No. 2, Pilot Officer Simpson, followed up the attack and reported that the bomber's starboard engine was in flames. Simpson's Hurricane was then hit and he had to force-land, getting down safely on the golf-course at Woodcote Park, near Epsom in Surrey. Flight Lieutenant S. D. P. Connors was seen to break away safely from the bombers, but shortly afterwards he was shot down in flames and killed. It was thought that he had been hit by AA fire from Kenley. Green 3, Sergeant Wallace, reported attacking and destroying a Do 17Z from astern. He also fired on two other bombers, seeing his tracers going into them, and leaving them apparently in difficulties.

Sergeant R. Brown led Blue Section in astern of Green Section, picking out the right-hand Do 17Z in the German formation, but as he opened fire, his Hurricane flew into the Kenley AA barrage and he broke away to the east of the airfield. He next attacked one of the retreating Dorniers from the beam, seeing hits on its fuselage, before making beam and quarter attacks on a third bomber. This he lost sight of for a short period, but he then saw a Do 17Z crashing into a field near Biggin Hill airfield and believed it to have been the aircraft he had attacked. It proved to be that of Oberleutnant Rudolf Lamberty, which was carrying 9./KG 76's Staffelkäpitan Hauptmann Joachim Roth. Brown finally finished his ammunition off on a fourth Do 17Z, which was probably not one of the Kenley raiders since he reported that it jettisoned its bomb load when attacked. His fire hit the bomber's fuselage and Brown was able to claim two Do 17Zs damaged and a third destroyed from this very successful combat.

Brown was impressed by the bombers' tactics, as their low flying among trees and high-tension cables made interception very difficult and forced the RAF fighters to break away upwards, exposing their vulnerable undersides to enemy fire. The No. 3 of Blue Section, Sergeant Newton, had in fact been shot down and wounded by fire from one of the bombers. He was, however, able to claim a Do 17Z destroyed in return, although by some oversight his report was not made until he rejoined the squadron on recovering from his injuries in early October.

Sergeant Craig, Red 2, was the only member of his section to engage the bombers, as the other two pilots could not pick out the camouflaged Do 17Zs from the countryside over which they were flying. He attempted to carry out an attack on the formation during its run up to Kenley, but was forced to turn aside by the AA barrage. He then pursued two Do 17Zs which were flying towards Biggin Hill and saw one of the bombers shoot down a Hurricane (most probably Newton's) before a second British fighter shot down a Do 17Z in flames. Craig continued to chase the surviving bomber, seeing his fire hit it several times. His own Hurricane was hit by one bullet, but remained serviceable. The Do 17Z finally evaded Craig and he returned to Croydon. Yellow 1, Sergeant

Dymond, reported that he attacked a Do 17Z from astern and that it crashed near Biggin Hill. This was the bomber previously fired on by Sergeant Brown. Dymond went on to attack a second Do 17Z, which he claimed as badly damaged.

Sergeant Deacon, flying as Yellow 3, was shot down and injured after claiming a Ju 88 as destroyed. His victim may have been one of the bombers of II. Gruppe Kampfgeschwader 76 which attacked West Malling. During the combat over Keniey, a number of Do 17Zs sneaked through to Croydon hitting a hangar and destroying one of No. 111 Squadron's Hurricanes on the ground and damaging another.

A new flight commander, Flight Lieutenant H. S. Giddings, was posted in from No. 615 Squadron on 18 August and at 1700 hours he led eight Hurricanes on patrol over Maidstone. They sighted a number of Bf 109s and chased them into cloud, Giddings' Hurricane being slightly damaged during the skirmish. The loss of both experienced flight commanders within two days was a blow to the squadron. On 19 August No. 111 Squadron was ordered to the quieter No. 11 Group Sector of Debden (changing places with No. 85 Squadron) in order to give it a chance to recover its strength, but the depleted squadron was still required to carry out operational patrols. At dawn on 24 August nine Hurricanes left for the forward base at Martlesham Heath. The squadron was scrambled at 1525 hours with orders to patrol Chelmsford at 20,000 feet. AA fire over North Weald attracted their attention to the bombers.

Flight Lieutenant Giddings took Red Section in to attack a formation of He 111s flying at 15,000 feet, but saw no results from his fire. His No. 3, Sergeant Wallace, saw a number of Bf 109s diving from 22,000 feet to engage the Hurricanes so he broke away from his section and climbed to meet them head-on. The German fighters split up, but he got a 2-second burst into one of them and saw his tracers going into the enemy aircraft. He was unable to follow its progress because his Hurricane was attacked by six Bf 109s and he had to evade them in cloud.

Sergeant Dymond led Yellow Section in a head-on attack and turned to make three further attacks from astern on the He 111 that he had picked out. He saw the bomber's port engine catch fire and the flames spread quickly to the wing centre-section and fuselage. Two of the crew baled out and the bomber (from III. Gruppe Kampfgeschwader 53) crashed near the De La Haye reservoir. Sergeant Brown was to have led Blue Section, but Blue 2 and 3 failed to take off after the scramble order and so Brown attached himself to Yellow Section. On seeing a group of Bf 109s coming in to attack the Hurricanes from astern, he broke away to engage them. One Bf 109 was damaged by Brown's fire and their attack on Yellow Section was thwarted.

On 25 August Flying Officer D. C. Bruce returned to the squadron, having been detached on an air navigation course in early July. He was promoted to the acting rank of flight lieutenant and took command of 'B' Flight. Bruce was in action with the squadron on the following day. Nine Hurricanes had left Debden at dawn to fly to Martlesham Heath, and at 1500 hours they were scrambled to intercept a strong raid on the No. 11 Group Sector stations north of the Thames. A formation of about fifty Do 17Zs, escorted by a hundred Bf 110s and Bf 109s was sighted over Maldon on the Essex coast, heading inland. Flight Lieutenant Giddings led his own Red Section, followed by Blue and Green Sections, into a beam attack on the bombers. The Hurricanes were then pounced upon by the German escort fighters and had to seek refuge in the clouds. Flight Lieutenant Bruce, after firing a short burst at a Do 17Z, found a Bf 110 on his tail. His Hurricane was hit in the wings and fuselage, but Bruce was able to turn into his attacker and give it a 2-second burst from head-on. The aircraft fell in the vicinity of Marks Tey. Pilot Officer Simpson's Green Section was attacked by Bf 110s and Bf 109s as it went in to attack the bombers. Simpson and Green 2, Sergeant Wallace, broke away downwards and met a stray Do 17Z flying just above the clouds at 12,000 feet. Wallace carried out a head-on attack against it and Green 1 followed this up with an attack from abeam. The bomber plunged into the clouds and Simpson followed, seeing it crash near Great Bentley. Sergeant R. F. Sellers' Hurricane crashed near Martlesham Heath and the pilot was slightly injured, but otherwise the squadron escaped without casualties.

The squadron continued to operate at a strength of nine Hurricanes, instead of its full complement of twelve. On 30 August it was ordered to its forward base at Martlesham Heath and then directed to intercept four bombers approaching from the east at 4,000 feet. For once it seemed that the odds would be in the Hurricanes' favour. Flight Lieutenant Giddings saw three aircraft, which he took to be Ju 88s, flying at 3,000 feet, and went into the attack. Fortunately, he then noticed that the aircraft were marked with RAF roundels and he ordered the Hurricanes to break off. His intended targets were in fact Blenheim Mk If twin-engined fighters of No. 25 Squadron. Later, No. 111 Squadron was ordered to Manston in Kent and at 1710 hours they engaged about forty Bf 110s which were escorting a formation of Do 17Z bombers.

Flying Officer B. H. Bowring, flying in Red Section, saw a Bf 110 on his leader's tail and gave it a 2-second burst of fire. He then had to turn into the attack of a formation of Bf 110s. When he looked around, he saw the Bf 110 that he had fired at diving for the French coast and trailing smoke. Bowring's Hurricane was damaged by enemy fire. Sergeant Dymond, Yellow 1, attacked the right-hand aircraft in a formation of five Bf 110s. He saw hits on its starboard engine and the aircraft broke formation and dived. Dymond followed, giving it a second burst of fire, but another fighter was on his tail and he had to break away. On climbing back to 15,000 feet, Dymond was engaged from head-on by a Bf 110. He turned on to its tail and fired a 2-second burst, without seeing any hits. Yellow 2, Sergeant Craig, damaged a Bf 110 with a 7-second burst, but after breaking away from this attack had insufficient speed to regain contact with his target. The squadron made no claims for enemy aircraft destroyed in this combat, but in return for one Hurricane slightly damaged had damaged three Bf 110s.

On the last day of August, No. 111 Squadron carried out an especially successful interception, turning back a raid which was bound for Duxford. Nine Hurricanes were scrambled at 0810 hours and intercepted a force of thirty Do 17Z bombers escorted by forty Bf 110s over Hildersham. While Red Section, augmented by Sergeant Wallace from Blue Section, took on the bombers, the other two sections covered them from attack by the Bf 110s. Flight Lieutenant Giddings led Red Section in astern of the Do 17Zs and picked out the leader of the rearmost vic, closing in from 300 yards to eighty yards and firing off all his ammunition. As the Hurricanes opened their attacks, the Dorniers jettisoned their bomb loads into open fields. Giddings reported that the port engine of the Do 17Z that he had attacked was on fire. The bomber was later reported to have crashed in flames.

Flying Officer Bowring, who had taken off as Red 2, was lagging behind when the squadron launched its attack and so Sergeant Wallace moved up from Blue 2 position to take his place. Wallace fired a 5-second burst into one of the rearmost Do 17Zs and then broke away as he saw Bf 110s coming in astern. He thought that his victim was out of control and claimed it as probably destroyed. The enemy formation then turned back towards the coast. Wallace gave chase, but was a long way behind and below them after his evasive break-away manoeuvre. As he neared the coast, a Bf 110 dived in front of him and Wallace gave it a short burst, before having to evade several more fighters diving to engage him.

Pilot Officer J. R. Ritchie, Red 3, made his opening attack on the left-hand Do 17Z in the rearmost vic, firing a long burst and seeing his fire hit. It was assessed as probably destroyed. Flying Officer Bowring had meanwhile engaged the Bf 110 escorts, carrying out a head-on attack on one which broke away and appeared to be damaged. He then got into a dogfight with the twin-engined fighters, which continued until they broke away to head back to the coast. Bowring chased after them and picked out a Bf 110 which had broken away from the main formation. He attacked it from the beam and saw it dive away with both engines smoking. After finishing off his ammunition, Bowring landed at Martlesham Heath; his Hurricane had been slightly damaged by enemy fire. Sergeant Craig was shot down in combat with the Bf 110s and baled out injured.

As Sergeant Wallace chased the stragglers from the abortive Duxford raid out to sea, he saw a dogfight at 14,000 feet off Clacton between some twenty to thirty Bf 110s and the Hurricanes of No. 257 Squadron. The German aircraft were in a defensive circle, while the Hurricanes were attacking them head-on in line astern. Wallace saw one of the Hurricanes go down in flames. He climbed up-sun into position for an attack on the Bf 110s' circle and dived into it, attacking three aircraft in quick succession from head-on. He saw hits on all three targets. One of the Bf 110s dived away, giving Wallace the chance of a 3-second deflection burst and he saw it going down pouring thick black smoke. As the fight was by that time breaking up and he was short of fuel, Wallace returned to Debden. Pilot Officer R. Atkinson, who had become separated from Blue Section, also joined in this combat. He accompanied the No. 257 Squadron Hurricanes and delivered a head-on attack on a Bf 110, firing a 2-second burst and seeing hits on its fuselage. The squadron's overall performance in this engagement had been most efficient, for not only were the bombers deflected from their target, but two enemy aircraft had been destroyed, three probably destroyed and a further three damaged.

No. 111 Squadron was operating from the Debden satellite airfield at Castle Camps on 2 September, when at 1230 hours nine Hurricanes were sent up with instructions to rendezvous with No. 46 Squadron's Hurricanes over Rochford at 15,000 feet. Ten minutes later the Hurricanes intercepted a formation of more than twenty He 111s flying in vics of five at 15,000 feet and escorted by Bf 110s and Bf 109s. Flight Lieutenant Giddings led Red Section in a head-on attack on the He 111s and was followed in by Yellow and Green Sections. As they engaged, they were set upon by the escort fighters. Flight Lieutenant Giddings' Hurricane was damaged and he force-landed at Detling, where he was caught on the ground by a heavy German raid. His No. 3, Pilot Officer Ritchie, likewise came down with a damaged Hurricane at Rochford. Red 2, Flying Officer Bowring, turned quickly after his opening attack and found a Bf 110 on his tail; it broke away and Bowring gave it a steady burst of fire, seeing hits. He finished his ammunition on a Bf 109, but saw no results from this attack.

Yellow 1, Sergeant W. L. Dymond, was missing after this action and it is thought that he was shot down by fighters over the estuary. Sergeant Hampshire, Yellow 2, opened his attack on a Bf

110 and followd it around in a turn, giving it a 7-second burst of fire. At that moment, his Hurricane's engine unexpectedly cut out and, thinking the aircraft was hit, Hampshire broke off. In fact it was undamaged. He was therefore only able to claim a probable victory, although his aircraft was covered with oil from the enemy fighter. Sergeant V. H. Ekins, Yellow 2, saw his fire hit an He 111 and the engine started to smoke. He was then attacked by a Bf 109, which he shook off. Flight Lieutenant Bruce, who led Blue Section, saw an He 111 crash into the sea and this was credited to the squadron rather than to an individual. Bruce next pursued a Bf 110, which he damaged before he was forced to break away to evade an attack from a Bf 109. Blue 2, Pilot Officer Simpson, saw his opening fire hit an He 111, but his fighter was then attacked and damaged by a Bf 109 and he returned to base. Sergeant Brown, as Blue 3, the last pilot to attack the bombers, saw hits on an He 111 in the leading vic. He was also able to fire on the following two sections of bombers, before breaking off his attack downwards. On climbing behind the bombers, he found himself in position for a quarter attack on a Bf 109, which was seen to be damaged.

On 3 September No. 111 Squadron was sent back to Croydon to replace No. 85 Squadron, which had suffered serious losses and needed to be relieved immediately. No. 111 Squadron itself was not back to full strength, although since moving to the Debden Sector it had fought well with nine Hurricanes instead of the usual twelve. At dawn on 4 September only eight Hurricanes were available to deploy to the forward base at Hawkinge. When the order to scramble came through at 0900 hours one of these could not take off and so the squadron formation was further reduced to seven aircraft. They engaged large formations of German aircraft five miles to the east of Folkestone, but before the Hurricanes could reach the bombers they were surrounded by the fighter escorts.

Flight Lieutenant Giddings, leading the squadron, fired a 2-second burst into a Bf 109 as it dived away from him. His aircraft then stalled at high speed and he spun down for 2,000 feet. On regaining control, Giddings chased the German formation and came up astern of two Bf 109s. He was able to shoot both of them down in flames. Continuing the pursuit, Giddings himself was surprised by an attack from behind. His Hurricane was hit by a cannon shell and oil streamed over his cockpit canopy. He half-rolled and dived away to evade his attacker and then had to force-land at Staplecross, Sussex. Red 2, Flying Officer Bowring, turned on to the tail of a Bf 109 and fired a 6-second burst into it, but a second fighter had got into a firing position behind him and his Hurricane was hit. As he broke away to evade this attack, he saw the first Bf 109 dive into the sea in flames.

Shortly after the start of the dogfight, Sergeant Wallace saw a Hurricane pilot bale out at 15,000 feet. He therefore attempted to protect the helpless pilot while he descended to about 8,000 feet, as several Bf 109s were trying to fire at the parachute. Wallace himself was then attacked by the fighters, but he managed to out-turn them. Shortly afterwards, when he was climbing to regain height, Wallace was set upon by six Bf 109s. While avoiding their attacks, he managed to fire several bursts into them from close range and saw one pilot take to his parachute. Wallace broke away from these fighters and, after evading another formation of Bf 109s over Hawkinge, returned to base and landed. Despite Wallace's efforts to protect him, the parachuting Hurricane pilot, Pilot Officer J. Macinski, was killed. Flight Lieutenant D. C. Bruce also failed to return from this combat. Pilot Officer Simpson, flying as No. 3 in Blue Section, saw a Bf 109 he had fired at go down in flames and this was claimed as destroyed. In all, five Bf 109s were claimed as destroyed by the squadron and a further five as damaged.

Eight Hurricanes were sent up at 0950 hours on the following day to intercept a raid approaching Biggin Hill. Red Section, led by Flying Officer Bowring, attacked the bombers from out of the sun. Bowring shot down a Bf 109, probably destroyed another and damaged a Do 17Z, but his Hurricane was damaged by cannon fire. Sergeant Ekins, Red 3, also probably destroyed a Bf 109. However, Blue and Green Sections, following astern, failed to engage. Blue 1, experiencing oxygen trouble on approaching the bombers at 15,000 feet, had to dive to a lower altitude and the other

Hurricanes followed him. Sergeant F. H. Silk force-landed after this combat and was wounded.

Flying Officer Bowring again led No. 111 Squadron on 6 September, when five Hurricanes were sent up to patrol base and were then directed to intercept forty Ju 88s approaching Kenley. He and his No. 2, Sergeant L. J. Tweed, climbed to 18,000 feet and dived in a head-on attack on the bombers. The three Hurricanes of Blue Section climbed to 20,000 feet to engage the Bf 109 escorts. Red Section's opening attack separated one Ju 88 from its·formation and Bowring finished this straggler off. He then had to break off the action, as his windscreen was smashed by a bullet. Sergeant Tweed had to crash-land his damaged Hurricane and was injured. After Blue Section's dogfight with the Bf 109s broke up, Pilot Officer Simpson saw a formation of about twenty Bf 110s over Lympne. He attacked the rearmost aircraft and damaged it and then, his ammunition expended, was driven off by Bf 109s.

That afternoon Squadron Leader Thompson led nine Hurricanes on patrol over Maidstone and the Thames estuary at 20,000 feet. Haze and smoke made visibility poor, but Sergeant Hampshire spotted a formation of bombers at 12,000 feet. He was, however, unable to inform the CO because of R/T problems. Shortly afterwards the Hurricanes were attacked from above by Bf 109s and Flying Officer Bowring was shot down and wounded.

The Luftwaffe's first raid on London on 7 September, which opened a new phase of the Battle, caught RAF Fighter Command unprepared. No. 111 Squadron's base at Croydon was well placed to defend the capital, but a series of contradictory instructions from Sector control robbed the Hurricanes of their initial advantage. Nine Hurricanes, led by Squadron Leader Thompson, were ordered to take off and patrol Maidstone at 20,000 feet. They were next ordered back to base and brought down to 10,000 feet, before finally being told to climb back to 20,000 feet. The interception was made over Croydon, where three large formations of Bf 110s were circling (apparently waiting for the bombers to return). Squadron Leader Thompson led Red Section in a beam attack. He, Sergeant Ekins, flying as Red 3, and Sergeant Brown as Blue 3 all got in good bursts at enemy aircraft, but without apparent results. Sergeant Wallace, who had earlier landed at base to refuel, joined another squadron and was able to chase the raiders well out to sea. He was then attacked by a Bf 109. His Hurricane's engine was badly damaged, but Wallace regained the Kent coast before baling out, injured, over Ashford.

This was the squadron's last combat in No. 11 Group during 1940, for on 8 September it exchanged places with No. 605 Squadron at Drem. Squadron Leader Thompson was posted to HQ, No. 11 Group and replaced by Squadron Leader A. J. Biggar. No. 111 Squadron then became a Category 'C' Squadron and lost many of its experienced pilots in postings to Category 'A' units. A further move northward to Dyce in Aberdeenshire was made on 12 October, with 'A' Flight being detached to Montrose, Forfarshire. A number of brushes with individual raiders took place during the autumn and winter months. The only conclusive success came on 13 November, when Yellow Section (Pilot Officer Simpson, Sergeant O. Kucera and Sergeant M. J. Mansfeld) intercepted an He 111 off Aberdeen and shot it into the sea. No. 111 Squadron, as RAF Fighter Command's senior Hurricane unit, had made a major contribution to the tactics of air fighting during the Battle by their adoption of the technique of the head-on attack. That they were able routinely to carry out such a very demanding evolution is a tribute both to the standard of pilot training and to the quality of leadership of the squadron.

NO. 303 (POLISH) SQUADRON

On 2 August 1940, No. 303 (Polish) Squadron was formed at RAF Northolt, Middlesex. Thirteen Polish officer pilots, eight Polish NCO pilots and 135 Polish ground staff reported to the station on that day to join the skeleton British staff who had been preparing for their arrival for the past fortnight. Two Polish fighter squadrons were to become operational in RAF Fighter Command during the Battle of Britain: No. 302 Squadron, which formed at Leconfield, Yorkshire, on 13 July 1940, and No. 303 Squadron. The former unit was the first to see action, shooting down a Ju 88 bomber off Hull on 20 August. But it was No. 303 Squadron that was to have the greater share of combat during the Battle, operating within No. 11 Group from 30 August to 10 October. The personnel for these much-needed reinforcements of Fighter Command's slender resources were drawn from more than 8,000 former members of the Polish Air Force (aircrew and groundcrew), who had escaped to Britain by late July. Many of the pilots had flown in combat during the Battles of France and Poland, and 141 of them were to engage in operations in the Battle of Britain, either with the two Polish squadrons or while serving with RAF fighter units.

In view of Fighter Command's critical shortage of trained pilots it is surprising that the Poles were initially regarded with some distrust by senior officers. Dowding thought that their morale would have suffered from the experience of defeat in Poland and France – a suspicion that was very soon dispelled. However, there were practical problems in the integration of the Poles into RAF Fighter Command. Trained pilots though they were, there were many features of the Hurricane with which they were unfamiliar (for example, its retractable undercarriage and eight-gun armament), but as their training progressed it became apparent that the Poles had no more trouble in learning how to operate the new generation of fighter aircraft than had their RAF comrades. A more intractable problem was their almost complete ignorance of English. Since the RAF's fighter direction system relied on ground-to-air radio-telephone communications, poor understanding of English was thought, not unreasonably, to be a serious handicap. Although there were no completely satisfactory short-term solutions to this problem, it was partly overcome by ensuring that every patrol was led by one of the squadron's RAF officers. Interpreters were available for briefing on the ground and two of the RAF officers spoke French, which the Poles understood much better than English.

In addition, of course, the Poles were given intensive instruction in English. In this respect, the RAF's relatively simple and standardized R/T procedures were an advantage, because if the key code-words (such as 'Angels', 'Vector', 'Buster') and numerals were memorized and understood, the Poles could at least pick up the gist of the controllers' instructions. Considerable scope for misunderstanding and confusion none the less remained, and the reluctance of Fighter Command's senior officers to commit the Polish squadrons to action was quite understandable. Events were to show that their worries were much exaggerated.

Sergeant Jan Kowalski remembers the ground training given in RAF R/T procedures with some amusement. This was carried out on the football pitch at RAF Station, Uxbridge in Middlesex. He recalls that pilots were mounted on tricycles, which were fitted with R/T, compass and speed indicators. The view ahead was largely obscured by a wooden shield pierced by a small eye-piece. Thus equipped, the pilots were directed into 'interceptions' from an 'operations room' mounted on top of the football stand. This surrealistic training procedure allowed them to master the basics of the RAF control system before they practised interceptions in the air. Jan Kowalski's conversion to the Hurricane proceeded with very little difficulty. He was an experienced pilot who had flown fighters in Poland and then instructed on multi-engined aircraft in France. 'After four take-offs and landings with Squadron Leader Kellett on the Master,' he recalled, 'I went off in the Hurricane and enjoyed every minute of it.'

No. 303 Squadron was organized on much the same lines as a standard RAF fighter squadron. The main difference was that the command positions were duplicated, so that the RAF commanding officer and RAF flight commanders had Polish officers as understudies. Thus Squadron Leader R. G. Kellett, the British CO, shared command with Squadron Leader Z. Krasnodebski. 'A' Flight was led by the Canadian Flight Lieutenant, J. A. Kent, and Flying Officer Z. Henneberg. Henneberg was superseded by the more experienced Flying Officer W. Urbanowicz, who joined the squadron later in August from No. 145 Squadron RAF with which he had gained his first air victories in the Battle of Britain. 'B' Flight was commanded by Flight Lieutenant A. S. Forbes, whose Polish counterpart was Flying Officer W. Lapkowski. Most of the original pilots were former members of the Polish Air Force's No. 111 Kosciuszko Fighter Squadron or No. 112 Fighter Squadron, of the 1st Air Regiment, Warsaw. No. 303 Squadron was to adopt the emblem of the former unit.

Training began with dual instruction on the Miles Master and within a week all the pilots had flown solo in the Hurricane. R/T communication was practised constantly and on 12 August the squadron began formation flying. A number of minor accidents occurred during this period, but there were no serious casualties. The Poles became increasingly restive as the training sorties continued with seemingly no prospect of action. On 24 August the squadron began to fly defensive patrols over Northolt, but made no contact with the enemy. The AOC, No. 11 Group, Air Vice-Marshal Park, had suggested that the Poles could be usefully employed in providing cover for the inland airfields, while their squadrons were on the ground refuelling, but the station commander at Northolt, Group Captain S. F. Vincent, was reluctant to declare the squadron fully operational until there was an improvement in the Polish pilots' command of English.

No. 303 Squadron's first action of the Battle came unexpectedly on 30 August, when the six Hurricanes of 'B' Flight were carrying out an interception exercise with Bristol Blenheim bombers over the St. Albans area at 1635 hours. There they sighted an escorted formation of German bombers flying eastwards at 14,000 feet and already under attack from RAF fighters.

Flying Officer L. W. Paszkiewicz tried to contact his formation leader by R/T and then flew ahead of the Hurricanes waggling his wings to attract attention. However, the other five fighters remained with the Blenheims and escorted them to safety. Paszkiewicz then broke away to engage the German formation. He saw a twin-engined aircraft flying at the same level as his Hurricane and banking towards it. When the two aircraft were almost head-on, the German pilot noticed the RAF fighter and dived steeply away. Paszkiewicz followed it down and closed in astern as it levelled off. He opened fire at 250 yards, aiming at the fuselage, and then at 100 yards switched his aim to the starboard engine. As he broke off, he reported that the engine had stopped and had caught fire. A second Hurricane went in to the. attack and Paszkiewicz saw a crew member bale out. As he closed in again for a final short burst, he realized that it was already done for and saw it crash in flames. The other Hurricane was almost certainly that of Pilot Officer B. J. Wicks of No. 56 Squadron. Since Wicks identi-fied the victim as a Bf 110 (most probably rightly) and Paszkiewicz claimed a Do 17Z, the combat resulted in two separate victory claims rather than a shared victory being recorded. It had, however, demonstrated that No. 303 Squadron was both ready and eager for action and the following day the unit officially became operational.

It was 'A' Flight that met the enemy on the last day of August, when its six Hurricanes were on patrol east of Biggin Hill at 16,000 feet. At 1825 hours Squadron Leader Kellett saw a large formation of Do 17Zs ahead of him, escorted by Bf 109s on the flanks and above. He led his fighters into the attack, flying in line astern formation and from out of the sun. They achieved complete surprise. The CO closed in on three of the escort fighters with Red Section and, selecting one of them, fired several bursts into it. He saw the Bf 109 swerve from side to side and pull up its nose into a steep climb. It then burst into flames, turned on to its back and fell away in a vertical dive. Sergeant S. Karubin, Red 2, fired on a second Bf 109 and followed it down as it dived. When it levelled out, he resumed his attack from 200 yards' range. The German fighter dived away once more, trailing smoke. Karubin gave it a final burst and watched as it fell in flames. The third pilot in Red Section, Sergeant E. M. Szaposznikow, fired on another Bf 109 and followed it as it carried out a half-roll and dived away. When the fighter levelled out, he fired again and it rolled on to its back and fell earthwards trailing clouds of smoke.

Yellow Leader, Flying Officer Henneberg, climbed to engage four Bf 109s, which were flying above the Hurricanes and threatened to attack them. He followed them in a south-easterly direction and when one of them dropped below the others Henneberg attacked it, opening fire at 300 yards and giving it three bursts of fire. It went into a vertical dive and fell into the sea six miles off Newhaven. Yellow 2, Pilot Officer M. Feric and Yellow 3, Sergeant K. Wunsche, did not follow Henneberg, but attacked lower-flying Bf 109s. Both pilots saw their targets going down in flames.

The Poles' first combat at full squadron strength was fought on 2 September. Twelve Hurricanes were on patrol at 19,000 feet near Dover at 1750 hours when they were attacked by nine Bf 109s. Sergeant J. Rogowski, flying as rearguard in the squadron formation with Sergeant J. Frantisek, saw the German fighters diving out of the sun and turned to meet the attack head-on. The Bf 109s then scattered and dived away towards France. Rogowski pursued one of them, giving it four bursts of fire. He saw its engine catch fire and it crashed into the sea ten miles off the French coast. Sergeant Frantisek engaged the two Bf 109s that passed nearest to him. One of these broke away and got on to the tail of Yellow 1, Flying Officer Henneberg. Frantisek followed and fired repeated short bursts at close range; he saw it go down to crash. Henneberg, who had escaped this attack unscathed, was intent on pursuing another German fighter. He followed it over the Channel and eight miles into France, before heavy ground fire forced him to break off the attack. He left the Bf 109 badly damaged, but still flying.

Yellow 2, Pilot Officer Feric, sent a Bf 109 diving vertically off the French coast, but as his windscreen was covered with oil, he could not see what became of it and so claimed a probable victory.

The Hurricane's engine then began to smoke and vibrate badly. Feric, flying at 10,000 feet, immediately switched it off and glided back to the English coast. Sergeant Rogowski saw his predicament and covered the vulnerable Hurricane until Feric carried out a successful forced-landing in the vicinity of Dover.

During a morning patrol on 3 September, the squadron was attacked by two Bf 109s over Dungeness. The Hurricanes flown by Flying Officer Henneberg and Sergeant S. Wojtowicz were damaged. The latter pilot had to force-land and was slightly wounded. Nine Hurricanes left Northolt at 1415 hours the same day and patrolled the Maidstone–Dover area. Numerous friendly fighters were seen, but the only pilot to contact the enemy was Sergeant Frantisek. He was acting as rearguard when the squadron dropped from 22,000 feet to investigate a formation of aircraft flying at 8,000 feet above cloud. They were identified as Spitfires. Frantisek then went below the cloud and saw a solitary Bf 109 flying beneath him. He dived to within 100 yards' range before opening fire, aiming at the cockpit. He believed that his 2-second burst must have killed the pilot, as the Bf 109 dived gently until it hit the sea and sank.

At 1505 hours on 5 September nine Hurricanes of No. 303 Squadron, led by Squadron Leader Kellett, intercepted a formation of about 35 Ju 88s, escorted by Bf 109s, over the Thames estuary. The bombers' target was the Thameshaven oil storage tanks. Red Section took on the close fighter escort, but a further twelve Bf 109s dived on the Hurricanes. In evading this attack Yellow Section lost the bomber formation and took no further part in the action, but the three Hurricanes of Blue Section were able to pass beneath Red Section and reach the Ju 88s. Squadron Leader Kellett, flying as Red 1, singled out one Bf 109. He gave it several short deflection shots before getting into position for a longer burst from below and astern. The Bf 109 caught fire and spun down, covering Kellett's Hurricane with its oil. While looking for the other fighters in his section, he saw another Bf 109 and fired several deflection shots at it. He saw his de Wilde incendiary ammunition hit the engine cowling and the Bf 109 dived vertically, trailing smoke. Sergeant Karubin, Red 2, claimed two Bf 109s shot down in flames. The third pilot in Red Section, Sergeant Wunsche, saw a Bf 109 diving at high speed on Squadron Leader Kellett's Hurricane. Wunsche pulled in behind it at only 60–70 yards' range and fired all his ammunition. The fighter rolled on to its back, its cockpit a mass of flames, and fell slowly towards the water.

Blue 1, Flight Lieutenant Forbes, led his section towards the Ju 88s, which were flying in vics of three. He selected the left-hand aircraft in the rearmost vic and attacked from astern. He broke away and came in again from the front starboard quarter, before finally attacking again from astern. One of the bomber's engines was in flames, but Forbes had to break off the combat at that point because a Bf 109 had got on to his tail. However, Flying Officer Lapkowski (Blue 2) reported that Forbes' victim had fallen from the formation trailing such tremendous clouds of smoke that the bomber had become invisible. He was confident that it had been destroyed and on the strength of his evidence Forbes claimed accordingly. Lapkowski himself fired at the leading Ju 88 in the last vic from only 150 yards' range and after breaking away came in for a second attack from the same range. Both engines of the Ju 88 caught fire and it dived from the formation. Lapkowski's Hurricane then came under attack from a Bf 109 and its engine was hit. As flames reached the cockpit, Lapkowski rolled the Hurricane on to its back and baled out. He broke his left arm in the process and also suffered burns to his face and leg. Frantisek, Blue 3, had broken away from the section before it reached the bombers, in order to attack a Bf 109 which was firing at a pilot who had just baled out of his Spitfire. He quickly shot the German fighter down and rejoined the other two Hurricanes in their attack on the rearmost vic of Ju 88s. Selecting the right-hand bomber, he claimed this as destroyed, but his own Hurricane was damaged by enemy fire during the combat.

Nine Hurricanes were sent up from Northolt at 0840 hours on 6 September and after following various vectors, they intercepted large formations of enemy aircraft over Sevenoaks. Squadron Leader Kellett reported that it was the largest German formation he had seen, covering an area twenty miles by five. Kellett positioned the squadron for an attack on the front quarter of a Do

17Z formation. But before this could be delivered the Hurricanes were engaged by the German escort fighters and only two RAF fighters reached the bombers. Kellett saw his opening burst cause a Do 17Z's engine to smoke. He turned to attack again from the rear quarter and the bomber's engine caught fire. Kellett's Hurricane was then hit by fire from a fighter and he dived away to evade it. On pulling out, he discovered that the Hurricane was barely controllable. It was flying right wing low and Kellett had no elevator control and very little response from the rudder, but he was able to bring it in to land at Biggin Hill without lowering the flaps.

Red 2, Sergeant Karubin, also claimed a bomber shot down, but his Hurricane was then shot down and he escaped slightly wounded. Sergeant Wunsche, Red 3, saw two Bf 109s come out of the sun to attack a Hurricane. As the first of these broke away, Wunsche turned to attack the second, which was by then firing into the Hurricane. He fired a 4-second burst and saw the Bf 109 go down in flames. The Hurricane also fell out of control. Wunsche went into a right-hand turn, thinking that the first Bf 109 could have got on to his tail, but there was no sign of it. A Bf 109 then attacked him from head-on and the two fighters circled each other seeking an advantage. After one-and-a-half turns the more manoeuvrable Hurricane was on the Bf 109's tail and Wunsche gave it two long bursts, finishing off his ammunition. The aircraft's engine was hit and it broke away trailing black smoke. Wunsche finally circled round an RAF pilot in his parachute until he saw that he was safely down, before returning to base.

The Polish CO, Squadron Leader Krasnodebski, was leading Yellow Section into the attack, when his Hurricane was hit by fire from German fighters. The Hurricane immediately began to burn and Krasnodebski had to bale out, but he was badly burned before he could get free. Yellow 2, Flying Officer Urbanowicz, was attacked from the starboard side by a Bf 109. He was able to out-turn it and opened fire from 200 yards with a 3–4-second burst. The Bf 109 went down vertically with its engine on fire. Urbanowicz made another attempt to get at the bombers, but once more the German escort fighters intervened. After evading them, he heard the order for the squadron to land and returned to base.

Pilot Officer Feric, Yellow 3, became engaged in a dogfight with the escort fighters, in which Spitfires also took part. Seeing one Bf 109 break away upwards, Feric pulled his Hurricane up into a head-on attack against it. The Bf 109 burst into flames and fell away to the ground.

Flight Lieutenant Forbes, leading Blue Section, found that he was receiving very little over his R/T because of heavy interference, and was unable to contact the formation leader. Thus handicapped, he followed the leading sections into their attack. He saw large numbers of fighters come down to head off the Hurricanes and picked out one coming in from below and to port of the RAF formation. This he fired at from 200 yards, seeing smoke and flames appear from the engine. He was about to fire again, when he realized that another fighter was behind him and so he broke away. He found it difficult to pick out a second target because the German fighters consistently out-climbed the Hurricane, but he eventually got on the tail of one, which was intent on attacking a Hurricane. He gave it a short burst and saw hits in the cockpit area. The Bf 109 flicked on to its back and fell out of control. But by that time Forbes was being attacked from behind and bullets smashed through his cockpit canopy hitting the armoured wind-shield and piercing the fuselage fuel tank. Petrol poured into the cockpit, fortunately without igniting, but Forbes was blinded by the fumes. He dived to a lower altitude and feeling faint turned his oxygen supply full on. Having selected a field in which to force-land, he found that on sliding back his cockpit canopy (standard procedure before coming down, as it facilitated a speedy exit), even greater quantities of fuel poured in on him. He therefore decided to land with the canopy closed. The effects of the petrol fumes impaired Forbes' judgement and he overshot his approach, crashing into a bank beside the field. The Hurricane was wrecked, but Forbes escaped with slight injuries. Sergeant Frantisek, No. 3 in Forbes' section, fired at a Bf 109 from the rear quarter and it dived away with the engine on fire. Two fighters then attacked Frantisek's Hurricane, damaging it in the tail, but he was able to shake them off and return to Northolt.

In this combat No. 303 Squadron had been caught at a serious disadvantage by superior numbers of escort fighters attacking from above. Consequently they had suffered serious casualties, losing three Hurricanes destroyed and a further two damaged, but of the four pilots wounded in this action, only one (Squadron Leader Krasnodebski) was seriously injured. The squadron's claims for enemy aircraft destroyed, which amounted to two bombers and five fighters, were highly creditable under the circumstances. Later that day a sixth Hurricane was damaged in the course of an airfield defence patrol. The squadron took off at 1310 hours and landed 45 minutes later without contacting the enemy. However, the engine of Flight Lieutenant Kent's Hurricane caught fire in the air and he had to carry out a quick force-landing back at base, fortunately without injuring himself. A third squadron patrol in defence of Northolt was flown between 1725 hours and 1910 hours in company with No. 1 Squadron RAF, but it was uneventful. At 1745 hours, though, Flying Officer W. Januszewicz went into action over Lenham in Kent with No. 1 Squadron, RCAF. (Confusingly, both No. 1 Squadron, RAF and No. 1 Squadron, RCAF were operating in the Northolt Sector at this time). Januszewicz attacked three Bf 110s, but was then shot down by a Bf 109. He escaped uninjured.

On the afternoon of 7 September No. 303 Squadron flew in company with No. 1 Squadron, RAF to intercept the Luftwaffe's raid on London, which was to open a new phase of the Battle. In contrast to most of the RAF squadrons operating that day, the Polish unit was able to carry out an effective attack on the bombers, claiming substantial victories. At 1620 hours eleven Hurricanes took off, led by Flight Lieutenant Forbes, and were followed five minutes later by No. 1 Squadron, RAF. Forbes took the Poles up to 24,000 feet, determined to avoid a repetition of the combat of the day before, when No. 303 Squadron lost the tactical initiative through lack of height. No. 1 Squadron's Hurricanes were flying at a lower altitude, ahead and to starboard of the Polish squadron.

At about 1700 hours Forbes saw a formation of forty Do 17Z bombers flying northwards at 20,000 feet. Its fighter escort, of some fifty Bf 109s flying at between 25,000 and 30,000 feet, were already in combat with Spitfires, and when No. 1 Squadron went in to attack the rear of the bomber formation they drew off the remaining unengaged fighters. This created the ideal conditions for a successful attack by No. 303 Squadron. AA fire had already loosened the Do 17Zs' defensive formation and when No. 1 Squadron attacked them from behind they wheeled to the east exposing their flank to attack. No. 303 Squadron quickly redeployed from vic formations in line astern, to sections in line abreast formation. The Hurricanes then dived into the attack, coming from a position almost up-sun from the Germans and at high speed. The bombers had just begun to turn away from the squadron when it slashed into them. 'They were easy meat,' reported Flight Lieutenant Forbes.

Forbes' opening burst of fire hit the starboard wing and engine of a Do 17Z and he fired again into the cockpit area. The bomber fell sideways out of formation and glided down to hit the sea. On breaking away, Forbes' Hurricane was hit and he was slightly wounded in the leg. Both the glycol engine coolant and hydraulic systems were punctured, but Forbes nursed the crippled fighter back to Northolt where he carried out a normal landing. Pilot Officer J. K. N. Daszewski brought down one bomber and probably destroyed another, before his Hurricane was hit and caught fire. He managed to bale out of the blazing fighter, but was seriously wounded. Pilot Officer Pisarek claimed a Bf 109 shot down before he was attacked from behind. His Hurricane went down in a spin, but he was able to bale out and landed safely.

Flying Officer Henneberg attacked the Do 17Z formation, but then his Hurricane's engine began to falter and he dropped back astern where he was set upon by three Bf 109s. Fortunately his engine picked up again, and he was able to outmanoeuvre one of the German fighters. His fire caused it to begin to smoke, but Henneberg was then himself threatened from behind and had to break away. He next attacked a formation of Bf 109s from astern and sent one of them down in flames. His Hurricane was slightly damaged during this combat. Flying Officer Paszkiewicz opened his attack on the bombers from very close range and saw his target burst into flames and go down. He finished his ammunition on a second bomber, which also caught fire and both of its engines were disabled. From Paszkiewicz's account it was assessed as destroyed although not seen to go down.

Pilot Officer Lokuciewski shot down one bomber and was attacking another, when two Bf 109s drove him away. Sergeant E. M. Szaposznikow fired two bursts into a Do 17Z, which caught fire and fell to earth. He dived after it to make sure that it was finished. On climbing back, he met a Bf 109 which he also sent down in flames. Pilot Officer Zumbach claimed two bombers as destroyed, firing from close range at both targets; both Do 17Zs were seen to fall to earth. Sergeant Wojtowicz also accounted for two of the bombers and reported that both caught fire and went down. Flying Officer Urbanowicz picked out a bomber that had broken away from the main formation for his first attack, opening fire at 300 yards' range. The Do 17Z quickly rejoined its companions, but Urbanowicz closed in for the kill and saw it crash to earth in flames. His next target was a Bf 109, which he fired on from close range. Its engine began to smoke, but Urbanowicz could not see what became of it, as he had to evade another German fighter. By that time he was low on fuel and so he landed at Detling, returning to Northolt at 1950 hours.

No. 303 Squadron's total claims for the combat on 7 September were ten Do 17Z bombers and three Bf 109 fighters destroyed, with a further two of each type probably destroyed. This was a very high score indeed, amounting to more than a quarter of the Luftwaffe's actual losses in combat on that day. In fact the claims for Do 17Z bombers destroyed are very difficult to substantiate from reported German losses. Only three bombers of that type were destroyed and a further three damaged on 7 September and they appear to have been involved in at least three different actions. However, the possibility of incorrect identification makes if difficult to be dogmatic about relating claims to losses; confusion between the Do 17Z and Bf 110 was especially common. There is certainly no evidence to suggest that No. 303 Squadron's claims were any more exaggerated than those of other RAF fighter squadrons, although language difficulties may have made the job of the Intelligence Officer in cross-checking claims more difficult. We do, however, have the testimony of the Northolt station commander, Group Captain S. F. Vincent, as to the integrity of the Poles' combat claims.

Vincent was one of that select band of station commanders who continued to fly on operations. He recalls in his autobiography *Flying Fever* how he became uneasy about the validity of No. 303 Squadron's high claims and decided to find out for himself whether they were genuine. Accordingly he accompanied the squadron on one of its interception patrols and, after seeing the Poles in action, returned fully satisfied that their claims were indeed made in good faith.

The combat of 7 September gives a good illustration of one unusual, if not unique, feature of No. 303 Squadron's fighting tactics. This was their use of close-range fire against the bombers. They would generally fire only a brief opening burst at between 200 and 150 yards' range, primarily with the object of unsettling the bombers' gunners. They would then close to very short range, so that the bomber's cockpit or engine (depending on the point of aim) filled the gunsight. A series of short bursts would be fired until the Hurricanes broke away at point-blank range. Pilot Officer Zumbach's Combat Report for 7 September estimates the firing range against his first target as fifty yards and that for his second as only thirty yards. Such close-range fire had the effect of cutting great chunks out of the bombers and was reckoned generally to disable them in one attack. Another characteristic of No. 303 Squadron was that all the pilots were aware of the need for mutual support. There are frequent references in the squadron's reports to pilots going to the aid of comrades under attack and of Hurricanes circling parachutes to prevent the helpless pilots from being machine-gunned.

Flight Lieutenant Kent was leading the squadron on 9 September when they joined up with No. 1 Squadron, RCAF and intercepted the enemy over Beachy Head at 1800 hours. About forty bombers appeared from out of the sun, heading southwards for France. Flight Lieutenant Kent watched No. 1 Squadron, RCAF to see how they would attack, with the idea of co-ordinating his tactics with theirs but he lost sight of them in the sun and so turned towards the bombers to attack on his own account. Only the leading section of Hurricanes was able to catch up with them and swarms of Bf 109s came down to attack the squadron. Kent picked out a straggler and chased it into cloud, seeing his fire hit its starboard engine before he finally lost sight of it. Going below cloud and circling, Kent saw another aircraft flying at 1,000 feet towards France. As he closed in to attack, the aircraft (most probably a Bf 110) dived to 500 feet and carried out a series of gentle evasive turns. Kent's fire silenced the rear gunner and then set the starboard engine alight. The aircraft turned back towards the English coast, with Kent's Hurricane flying alongside. At this point a Bf 109 came out of the clouds and began a quarter attack on the Hurricane. Kent turned to meet it and the Bf 109 sheered off and escaped. The Bf 110 had meanwhile gone into the sea about ten miles off Beachy Head. During Kent's initial attack on the bombers, he was attacked from behind and above by two or three Bf 109s. These were kept off his tail by Flying Officer Henneberg, Red 3, who was weaving behind him.

Pilot Officer Zumbach joined up astern of a fighter which he misidentified as a Hurricane. When he was within fifty yards' range, he recognized it as a Bf 109 and gave it a 2-second burst. As the fighter caught fire, Zumbach was distracted by a second Bf 109 coming in from astern. He began to dogfight with this fighter, but was then attacked by four more Bf 109s. Putting the Hurricane into a tight turn, Zumbach fought off repeated attacks. One of the Bf 109s gave him the opportunity for a burst of fire at 150 yards' range and it dived away smoking. He finally evaded the others by diving into cloud. On emerging over France he was disorientated and thought he was over England. AA fire brought his mistake home to him and he retreated over the Channel landing at the first available airfield.

Sergeant Frantisek saw a Bf 109 attacking a Hurricane ahead of him and fired into it from the starboard beam at 150 yards' range. It began to burn and the pilot prepared to bale out, but Frantisek fired again into the cockpit area and saw the German collapse. The Bf 109 crashed in flames. At about the same time, Frantisek saw a

Hurricane going down in flames and its pilot baled out. This was Sergeant Wunsche, who was wounded in the back and arm; a Spitfire circled around his parachute to protect him as he descended. Frantisek next picked out an He 111 for attack, but was engaged by two Bf 109s and had to dive into cloud to evade them. After seven minutes he re-emerged and very nearly collided with an He 111. He opened fire at it from close range and saw its cockpit area disintegrate and both engines catch fire. The Bf 109s again forced him to take cover in cloud. He flew out to sea before climbing out of the clouds. His Hurricane was then hit by cannon fire from a Bf 109. His port wing fuel tank was holed and the Hurricane's radiator was also hit. Two Spitfires came to his rescue, shooting down one of his attackers. With his engine rapidly over-heating, Franitsek regained the coast and force-landed to the north-east of Brighton.

The squadron's claims for this combat totalled one He 111, one Bf 110 and two Bf 109s destroyed, plus one fighter probably destroyed and a bomber damaged. Most of the pilots were unable to engage, because the initial interception had come too late and the Hurricanes had insufficient altitude.

Twelve Hurricanes were scrambled at 1530 hours on 11 September, with Flight Lieutenant Forbes in the lead. They were followed by the Hurricanes of No. 229 Squadron, which had relieved No. 1 Squadron, RAF two days earlier. The enemy was intercepted over Horsham, Sussex thirty minutes later. It comprised a formation of about fifty He 111s flying at 16,000 feet with an escort of Bf 110s and Bf 109s and another formation of Do 17Z bombers. The Hurricanes were directed across the front of the German formation, but one of the keen-eyed Polish pilots, Flying Officer Paszkiewicz, saw them flying six or seven miles away to the right and called out a warning to Flight Lieutenant Forbes. As the Hurricanes wheeled round to attack, Forbes' Blue Section was overtaken by the rest of the squadron. He dived to engage the bombers, seeing the crew of one bale out before he attacked. Forbes closed in to short range before opening fire and the bomber's port wing and engine sheered right off. He was so near that he had trouble avoiding a collision and the enemy aircraft's slipsteam was throwing his Hurricane about. Selecting a second target, Forbes got in a good burst from 100 yards' range, seeing hits on the port engine and cockpit areas, but then his own fighter was hit and Forbes was wounded in the arm and thigh. He dived away steeply to ground level and began to make his way back to Northolt, but he was overcome by faintness and landed at Heston instead.

Blue 2, Sergeant Frantisek, was attacked by German fighters before he could reach the bombers. He turned sharply on to the tail of a Bf 109, opened fire from 150 yards' range and saw it burst into flames. He then went into cloud and on coming out found himself in position for an attack on a straggling He 111 which he sent down into the sea. On his return he met and attacked another Bf 109, which he left smoking and on fire, but as he was by then out of ammunition and short of fuel, he broke off the combat before seeing what became of it. Flying Officer Paszkiewicz, seeing No. 229 Squadron's Hurricanes carry out a head-on attack against the bomber formation, led his Green Section into the fighter escort above them. Green 2, Pilot Officer Lokuciewski, attacked a pair of Bf 109s and shot one of them down in flames. He later encountered a stray Do 17Z and set it on fire, seeing one of the crew bale out.

Red Section was able to engage the He 111s before the escort fighters could intervene. Red 3, Sergeant Brzezowski, reported that the bomber he fired at burst into flames and fell to earth. He broke away when he saw tracer bullets flying past his cockpit. On recovering from his dive, he noticed a straggling He 111 and attacked it. The bomber burst into flames and one of the crew took to his parachute. A Hurricane was also going down in flames at this time and Brzezowski, seeing the pilot bale out, circled round him as he descended. By now his Hurricane's engine was running roughly and throwing oil, so he prepared to bale out, but as the engine had not caught fire, he determined to stay with the fighter for as long as possible and managed to reach Croydon safely. Two Hurricanes were lost in the combat, Flying Officer A. Cebrynski and Sergeant S. Wojtowicz both being killed.

As Flying Officer Henneberg led Yellow Section towards the German bombers, they were attacked by four Bf 109s, but before the Hurricanes could involve them in a dogfight the enemy fighters dived away into cloud cover. Shortly afterwards Henneberg carried out a beam attack on a single Bf 109 and set it on fire. He then had to evade further enemy fighters. Finally he engaged an He 111, which was making its way back to France. His fire disabled both of the bomber's engines and it force-landed near the coast. Pilot Officer Zumbach, Yellow 2, found a Bf 109, which he believed to have been already damaged, heading back over the Channel. He sent it down in flames. Joining forces with two other Hurricanes, he next attacked a group of five Bf 110s, but the RAF fighters ran out of ammunition and had to break off the fight before any conclusive result could be claimed. Zumbach, finding himself short of fuel, landed at Biggin Hill. Yellow 3, Sergeant Szaposznikow, picked out two Bf 110s flying behind the German bombers and attacked both of them in succession, claiming them as destroyed. In return for the loss of two pilots killed and a third wounded, No. 303 Squadron claimed seven bombers, three Bf 110s and five Bf 109s destroyed. The pilots also reported that the bomber formations had split up and numerous bombs were jettisoned over wooded country.

During the heavy fighting on 15 September No. 303 Squadron was twice in action. At 1120 hours Flight Lieutenant Kent took off with twelve Hurricanes in company with No. 229 Squadron. They were directed towards a large enemy formation flying south-east of London, but this had completed its bombing and was able to escape. A second force was sighted withdrawing to the south and the two Hurricane squadrons gave chase, overtaking the rearmost enemy aircraft in the vicinity of Folkestone. A series of individual actions were then fought between Hurricanes and German fighters. Flight Lieutenant Kent and several other pilots had only brief skirmishes with the retreating enemy and were unable to claim. Flying Henneberg overtook a Do 17Z and set its engine ablaze before he was driven off by Bf 109s. He then chased an enemy fighter out to sea and shot it down. Sergeant Wojciechowski also claimed a Bf 109 destroyed, before joining forces with Sergeant Andruszkow to send down another Do 17Z in flames. Pilot Officer Zumbach accounted for one of the fighters that had attacked Flying Officer Henneberg. Pilot Officers Feric and Pisarek each claimed Bf 109s destroyed and Sergeant Frantisek shot down a Bf 110. The squadron's only casualty, Pilot Officer Lokuciewski, was firing on a Bf 109 which he saw burst into flames, when his Hurricane was hit from behind by a cannon shell. Although wounded in the leg, he flew his damaged fighter back to Northolt and landed.

Squadron Leader Kellett, who was that day awarded the DFC, led nine Hurricanes into the air at 1420 hours. Operating independently, they were at first ordered to patrol base at 20,000 feet. On reaching 6,000 feet, however, they were vectored towards Gravesend and at 18,000 feet they sighted the enemy approaching from east-south-east. A large formation of Do 17Z bombers was flying at the same level as the Hurricanes, with a close escort of Bf 110s and Bf 109s stepped up to 25,000 feet. The CO wheeled into the attack, but Red and Yellow Sections were slow to follow him. He therefore led Blue Section against the bomber formation's front quarter. As the other six Hurricanes followed up this initial attack, Kellett saw the bombers turn away eastwards and a second RAF squadron came in from the opposite flank. Kellett fired at a Do 17Z from very close range and saw hits on the engines and forward fuselage. He was then set upon by three Bf 110s and his Hurricane was damaged by their fire. He dived away and evaded them in cloud. On climbing back towards the fight, he met a single Bf 110. His Hurricane easily out-turned the twin-engined fighter and Kellett fired two good bursts into its starboard engine from the rear quarter. The Bf 110 fell away into the clouds with its wing in flames.

The other members of Blue Section also succeeded in bringing down enemy aircraft. Flying Officer W. Zak, Blue 2, destroyed a Do 17Z and Blue 3, Sergeant Wojciechowski, claimed a Bf 109. Flying Officer Urbanowicz, leading Red Section, claimed two Do 17Zs destroyed and Pilot Officer Feric a Bf 110 destroyed. Two Hurricanes were lost. Sergeant M. Brzezowski was shot down and killed, while Sergeant Andruszkow baled out over Dartford and was unhurt. Several Hurricanes were damaged by enemy fire, but returned safely to base.

Ten Hurricanes of No. 303 Squadron were sent up at 1505 hours on 17 September in company with No. 1 Squadron, RCAF. They were directed to patrol north of Biggin Hill at 20,000 feet and then became split up while investigating various formations which turned out to be other RAF fighters. Large numbers of German fighters were eventually seen flying over the Thames estuary at 27,000 feet, but the Hurricanes were unable to reach them. The only pilot to make a claim was Sergeant Wojciechowski who saw a number of Bf 109s attacking a Hurricane formation and joined in the combat. He fired on two Bf 109s and reported that the second fell away in flames. He then evaded the other German fighters in cloud. The following day saw a similarly confused combat. Twelve Hurricanes took off at 1220 hours and joined up with No. 229 Squadron. They were ordered to patrol south of Biggin Hill at 25,000 feet, where they met a Do 17Z on reconnaissance. Eight of the Hurricanes pounced on the hapless German aircraft and it crashed ten miles to the south of West Malling, three of its crew being seen to bale out. Numerous RAF fighters were also patrolling in the area and two of the squadron's Hurricanes were damaged in attacks by these aircraft. Shortly after the Dornier was engaged, Sergeant Frantisek saw a Bf 109 heading for the coast and he gave chase. He fired two bursts into it and saw it go into the sea in flames. Frantisek's splendid fighting record had been recognized by the award of the DFM only the day before. He was, in fact, a Czech but having escaped to Poland in 1938 he had remained with Polish units ever since.

On the morning of 23 September, Flight Lieutenant Kent led a wing of three Hurricane squadrons on patrol. It comprised twelve fighters of No. 303 Squadron, together with No. 1 Squadron, RCAF, and No. 229 Squadron. They were directed to patrol south of Biggin Hill and then towards the Thames estuary. Formations of high-flying Bf 109s were sighted and twelve German fighters dived on the Hurricanes from astern. Flight Lieutenant Kent's Red Section pursued them as they dived away. Kent finally caught up with one Bf 109 fifteen miles off the French coast and shot it down into the sea. On making his way back to land he came upon a low-flying twin-engined aircraft which he identified as a French 'Potez' (it was more probably a Focke-Wulf Fw 58.) He attacked and saw his fire hit, but his engine was then running roughly and he broke off the fight, leaving the enemy aircraft damaged. Red 2, Sergeant Szaposznikow, gave chase to a Bf 109, which he had seen attack an isolated Hurricane from another squadron (No. 229 Squadron's 'weaver' was in fact shot down). Szaposznikow opened fire from below and astern at 300 yards' range and used up all his ammunition. The Bf 109 crashed in mid-Channel.

The order for No. 303 Squadron to scramble at 1630 hours on 26 September interrupted a visit to Northolt by His Majesty King George VI. Squadron Leader Kellett led twelve Hurricanes of his own squadron and those of No. 229 Squadron towards Guildford, Surrey. They were then directed towards Portsmouth and saw a raid approaching from the south. Its objective was Supermarine's factory at Woolston, which was heavily bombed before the Hurricanes could intervene. As the bombers turned away from their target, Kellett carried out an attack on the rear quarter of the German formation. It was not a satisfactory interception because as Kellett reported, the squadron was too late on the scene and at too low an altitude. For this reason it was impossible for No. 303 Squadron and No. 229 Squadron to attack as a wing. The leading fighters had to fly at full speed to catch up with the bombers and inevitably their formation became strung out and the sections came into action piecemeal, rather than in a cohesive wing formation.

Seeing a small force of Bf 109s guarding the rear of the enemy formation, Squadron Leader Kellett decided to attack these, hoping thereby to clear a path to the bombers for the following sections. He picked out the leading fighter and followed it into a dive. His fire caused the fighter's engine to burn and Kellett saw it crash into the sea. He then found that his throttle had jammed in the fully open position and by the time that he had rectified this fault it was too late to rejoin the combat. The other two pilots in his section had carried on to attack the He 111s and Sergeant Andruszkow claimed one of these destroyed. The following sections chased the bombers out to sea and Sergeant Frantisek crossed the French coast before breaking off the combat. None of the Hurricanes was lost and in general the squadron's pilots reported that the Bf 109s seemed reluctant to press home their attacks. However, three of the RAF fighters were damaged in this combat and Sergeant M. Belc and Flying Officer Januszewicz had to make a forced-landing.

The squadron's claims amounted to nine He 111s destroyed, one He 111 probably destroyed and four Bf 109s destroyed. In fact the Germans lost only one He 111 and two Bf 110s from this mission, with a further He 111 being seriously damaged. Furthermore, the raid halted Spitfire production at Woolston during a critical phase of the Battle, although an alternative source of supply was by then available from the Castle Bromwich shadow factory.

No. 1 Squadron, RCAF led No. 303 Squadron in an interception of thirty He 111s with Bf 109 escort over the Horsham area at 0920 hours on 27 September. Flight Lieutenant Forbes, leading the Polish Squadron as Blue 1, lost contact with the Canadians shortly afterwards. He saw an He 111 break away from the main formation and dive towards the coast. Giving chase, Forbes fired all his ammunition into the bomber and saw it crash in flames. Flying Officer Henneberg, leading Red Section, followed the leading two sections towards the bombers. He then saw two Bf 109s flying to his right and turned to engage them. After firing three bursts into one of them, it burst into flames and fell to earth. His own fighter was then hit and smoke filled the cockpit, so Henneberg dived away and made his way back to Northolt. His No. 2, Flying Officer Feric, attacked and shot down a Bf 109. He then gave chase to the bombers and saw the aircraft that he had fired at crash between Croydon and Gatwick. Feric's Hurricane was damaged by return fire.

Flying Officer Urbanowicz's Yellow Section was attacked by Bf 109s. After skirmishing with them, Urbanowicz saw a formation of Bf 110s in a defensive circle with a Bf 109 escort above it. One of the twin-engined fighters broke away and he chased it and shot it down. He attempted to engage another Bf 110, but was attacked by two Bf 109s. He shot one of these down and, short of ammunition, decided to break off the action. The squadron had lost two pilots killed: Flying Officer L. W. Paszkiewicz and Sergeant T. Andruszkow. Flying Officer Zak was also shot down, but baled out with burns on his face and hands. The Polish pilots claimed four bombers, four Bf 109s and one Bf 110 destroyed, plus a Bf 109 probably destroyed and an He 111 damaged.

Six of the squadron's Hurricanes were once more in action that afternoon. They were ordered to take-off at 1515 hours and rendezvous with No. 1 Squadron, RCAF over base. Soon afterwards Flight Lieutenant Kent saw a formation of about fifteen Ju 88s with an escort of thirty Bf 109s approaching London from the south-east. The Hurricanes gave chase as the enemy aircraft turned away for home, but even when using emergency boost could not overtake them before reaching the coast. Flight Lieutenant Kent got to within 100 yards of one Ju 88 and his Hurricane was slightly damaged by return fire. After aiming a long burst at the bomber's starboard engine from only 75 yards, Kent S-turned above the Ju 88 as it fell towards the sea. It hit the water and quickly sank, allowing only one of the crew time to get clear. Red 2, Flying Officer Urbanowicz, accounted for a further two of the bombers, while Sergeant Szaposznikow shot down a Bf 109.

The squadron's next two combats took place on the afternoon of 30 September. At 1315 hours twelve Hurricanes were sent up from Northolt on their third patrol of the day. They followed No. 1 Squadron, RCAF and No. 229 Squadron in a wing formation, which was directed towards Dungeness. The squadron was at 14,000 feet when a formation of about thirty Do 17Z bombers with an escort of Bf 109s was sighted above them. As the wing formation did not attack, the Poles broke away and climbed in pursuit of the enemy. They chased them out over the Channel, but were harried by the fighter escort and most of the Hurricanes were unable to reach the Do 17Zs. Sergeant Karubin, flying as Red 2, shot down one of the Bf 109s, but his section was effectively headed off from the bombers. Yellow Section, led by Flying Officer Urbanowicz was, however, able to reach the Do 17Zs and their attack caused two of the bombers to drop from the formation.

Pilot Officer J. Radomski, Yellow 2, joined a Spitfire (believed to be flown by Sergeant Beardsley of No. 41 Squadron) in finishing off one of these aircraft. While returning to the coast his engine exploded. Radomski switched off and glided back to make a wheels-up landing on the beach near Lydd. Meanwhile, Urbanowicz was attacking another Do 17Z as it headed towards France. He had fired three bursts without any visible effect on the bomber, when a pair of fighters appeared above it. Thinking that they were RAF aircraft, Urbanowicz joined up astern of them. He then recognized them as Bf 109s and was able to make a surprise attack on both from close range. His fire was effective and they crashed into the sea. Urbanowicz was then free to resume his attack on the Do 17Z. He followed it over the French coast and saw it attempt to land and crash in the process.

Two hours after returning from its third patrol, the squadron was scrambled again. Ten Hurricanes left Northolt with orders to rendezvous with No. 1 Squadron, RCAF and No. 229 Squadron, but the two flights became separated during the climb and neither was able to join up with the wing formation. 'A' Flight were attacked by Bf 109s, but escaped without casualties as they were able to take cover in the clouds. Flying Officer Urbanowicz managed to shoot down one of the attackers. 'B' Flight likewise was broken up before they could get into action against a bomber formation sighted south-east of Croydon. Sergeant Belc broke away from the flight to protect a Hurricane pilot from another squadron, whom he saw bale out, but later rejoined the flight. Sergeant Frantisek should have flown with 'B' Flight's Blue Section, but he had difficulty in starting his engine and so took off late. Before he could rejoin the other Hurricanes, he was attacked by six Bf 109s which went into a circle with Frantisek in the centre. Undaunted, Frantisek fought his way out of this predicament and in doing so accounted for one Bf 109 shot down in flames and a second probably destroyed.

No. 303 Squadron was sent up to patrol a line from Kenley to Brooklands in company with No. 1 Squadron, RCAF at 1315 hours on 1 October. They encountered large formations of German fighters but as Sector control had advised them of a bomber formation to the east they did not attack. Flight Lieutenant Kent, leading nine Hurricanes behind the Canadian squadron, saw a low-flying formation which he took to be bombers. Accordingly he dived to engage them, expecting No. 1 Squadron, RCAF to deal with the Bf 109s. As Kent later pointed out in his autobiography, *One of the Few*, a serious problem with two or more squadrons operating as a wing was that they were usually on different radio frequencies and could only communicate with each other via Sector control. There were therefore frequent cases of poor co-ordination between units because of this. (It was, though, a limitation confined to the TR 9 HF radios, as the VHF sets had a choice of available frequencies.)

On this occasion, Kent found that not only had the Canadians not realized what he was doing, but his own squadron had been left behind when he dived. The position was forcibly brought home to him when he saw tracer bullets flashing past his Hurricane. Turning in to the attack he found himself alone with a group of Bf 109s. Kent pulled the Hurricane into a tight circle and then straightened out to attack about eight German fighters ahead of him. He saw one of them hit by his fire, but had to break off to evade further attacks from behind. Finding himself within range of a second Bf 109, Kent sent it down with its engine in flames. Shortly afterwards the German fighters began to withdraw, presumably because they were short of fuel. Kent followed them and counted 38 Bf 109s in the formation.

The Battle had entered its final phase in early October, with German daylight activity being largely confined to fighter sweeps and nuisance raids by fighter-bombers. At 1140 hours on 5 October No. 1 Squadron, RCAF led the Poles into an interception over Rochester. About sixty German fighters then became involved in a running battle with some forty RAF fighters, which extended southwards to the Channel. Over Lympne the Hurricanes ran into fifteen Bf 110s which had formed a defensive circle at 20,000 feet with numerous single-engined fighters above them. The RAF fighters were able to break up this circle, despite the efforts of the Bf 109s to fend them off. Unusually, the entire combat lasted for over an hour.

As the action began, Squadron Leader Kellett saw small numbers of Bf 109s emerging from the clouds at 25,000 feet, some 7,000 feet above the Hurricanes. Putting the squadron into line astern, the commanding officer went in to attack a group of about seven German fighters. He got in a good burst from the front quarter against one of them, but then lost it in the confusion of the massive dogfight that had developed. Most of the squadron's claims, however, were made against the Bf 110s and their escorts encountered later in the combat. Flying Officer Henneberg, leading Yellow Section, began an attack on one of the Bf 110s, but then had to shake a Bf 109 off his tail. He next saw a Bf 110 making for the coast and caught up with it. After he had fired two bursts, its starboard engine caught fire and the fighter dived into the sea. After evading further attacks from Bf 109s, Henneberg returned to base. The squadron's total claims amounted to four Bf 110s and four Bf 109s destroyed, plus three enemy aircraft damaged. They lost Flying Officer W. Januszewicz, who was shot down in flames and killed.

Shortly after midday on 6 October a single German bomber took advantage of extensive cloud cover to carry out an attack on Northolt. Sergeant A. Siudak was killed during the bombing and his aircraft was completely destroyed, a second Hurricane being badly damaged. Siudak had fought particularly well on the previous day, claiming two Bf 109s destroyed and sharing with a Spitfire in the destruction of a Bf 110.

At 1320 hours on 7 October No. 303 Squadron took off from Northolt leading No. 1 Squadron, RCAF and thirty minutes later they intercepted a force of about fifty Bf 109s flying to the south of London at between 25,000 and 30,000 feet. Small groups of German fighters dived to attack the Canadian squadron and were driven off southwards by No. 303 Squadron. Sergeant Belc caught up with one of these and sent it down in flames south-west of Redhill. Further Bf 109s were engaged over the coast and both Flying Officer Pisarek and Flying Officer Szaposznikow claimed victories. At the end of the fight Pilot Officer B. Mierzwa landed by mistake on a decoy aerodrome at Borstal near Chatham. He crashed on attempting to take-off from there, but escaped from the wreckage unhurt.

The action of 7 October was No. 303 Squadron's last combat of the Battle of Britain, as it was withdrawn to RAF Leconfield, Yorkshire, on 11 October. However, in the course of an otherwise uneventful patrol on 8 October it lost the gallant Czech pilot, Sergeant Josef Frantisek, who crashed to his death in unexplained circumstances at Ewell in Surrey. With a total of seventeen victories to his credit, Frantisek was not only No. 303 Squadron's most successful pilot, but he was also one of RAF Fighter Command's top-scorers in the Battle of Britain. No. 303 Squadron's record during the Battle was equally distinguished. In four and a half weeks in combat it had been credited with 126 enemy aircraft destroyed, for the loss of eight of its own pilots killed. It was an achievement unequalled by any other RAF fighter squadron. Despite the RAF commanders' initial misgivings, the decision to reinforce Fighter Command with No. 303 (Polish) Squadron had been triumphantly vindicated. Not only were the Polish exiles shown to be pilots of great skill and courage, but they were imbued with a hatred of the enemy which inspired them to exceptional feats of arms.

APPENDIX
RAF Fighter Squadrons
of the Battle of Britain

UNIT	AIRCRAFT	COMMANDING OFFICERS	SECTORS
No. 1 Squadron	Hurricane	Sqn Ldr D. A. Pemberton, DFC Sqn Ldr M. P. Brown, DFC	Northolt Wittering
No. 3 Squadron	Hurricane	Sqn Ldr S. F. Godden Sqn Ldr G. F. Chater, DFC Sqn Ldr A. N. Cole	Wick Turnhouse
No. 17 Squadron	Hurricane	Sqn Ldr R. I. G. MacDougall Sqn Ldr C. W. Williams Sqn Ldr A. G. Miller	Debden Tangmere
No. 19 Squadron	Spitfire	Sqn Ldr P. C. Pinkham, AFC Sqn Ldr B. J. E. Lane, DFC	Duxford
No. 23 Squadron	Blenheim If	Sqn Ldr L. C.. Bicknell Sqn Ldr G. F. W. Heycock Sqn Ldr C. H. A. Colman	Wittering Middle Wallop Tangmere
No. 25 Squadron	Blenheim If Beaufighter	Sqn Ldr W. W. Loxton Sqn Ldr H. M. Mitchell	North Weald Debden, Wittering
No. 29 Squadron	Blenheim If Beaufighter	Sqn Ldr E. R. Bitmead Sqn Ldr S. C. Widdows, DFC	Digby
No. 32 Squadron	Hurricane	Sqn Ldr J. Worrall Sqn Ldr M. N. Crossley, DFC	Biggin Hill Usworth
No. 41 Squadron	Spitfire	Sqn Ldr H. R. L. Hood Sqn Ldr R. C. F. Lister, DFC Sqn Ldr D. O. Finlay	Catterick Hornchurch
No. 43 Squadron	Hurricane	Sqn Ldr C. G. Lott, DSO Sqn Ldr J. V. Badger, DFC Sqn Ldr C. B. Hull Sqn Ldr T. F. D. Morgan	Tangmere Usworth
No. 46 Squadron	Hurricane	Sqn Ldr J. R. Maclachlan Sqn Ldr A. R. Collins Sqn Ldr A. M. Gaunce, DFC	Digby North Weald
No. 54 Squadron	Spitfire	Sqn Ldr J. A. Leathart Sqn Ldr D. O. Finlay Sqn Ldr T. P. R. Dunworth	Hornchurch Catterick

UNIT	AIRCRAFT	COMMANDING OFFICERS	SECTORS
No. 56 Squadron	Hurricane	Sqn Ldr G. A. L. Manton Sqn Ldr H. M. Pinfold	North Weald Middle Wallop
No. 64 Squadron	Spitfire	Sqn Ldr N. C. Odbert Sqn Ldr A. R. D. MacDonell	Kenley Church Fenton Coltishall
No. 65 Squadron	Spitfire	Sqn Ldr H. C. Sawyer Sqn Ldr A. L. Holland Sqn Ldr G. A. W. Saunders	Hornchurch Turnhouse
No. 66 Squadron	Spitfire	Sqn Ldr R. H. A. Leight Sqn Ldr A. S. Forbes, DFC	Coltishall Kenley, Biggin Hill
No. 72 Squadron	Spitfire	Sqn Ldr R. B. Lees Sqn Ldr A. R. Collins Sqn Ldr E. Graham	Usworth Biggin Hill Church Fenton Coltishall
No. 73 Squadron	Hurricane	Sqn Ldr J. W. C. More Sqn Ldr M. W. S. Robinson Sqn Ldr A. D. Murray	Church Fenton Debden
No. 74 Squadron	Spitfire	Sqn Ldr F. L. White Sqn Ldr A. G. Malan, DFC	Hornchurch Wittering Kirton-in-Lindsey Coltishall Biggin Hill
No. 79 Squadron	Hurricane	Sqn Ldr J. H. Hayworth	Usworth Biggin Hill Pembrey
No. 85 Squadron	Hurricane	Sqn Ldr P. W. Townsend, DFC	Debden, Kenley Church Fenton Kirton-in-Lindsey Biggin Hill
No. 87 Squadron	Hurricane	Sqn Ldr J. S. Dewar Sqn Ldr T. G. Lovell-Gregg Sqn Ldr R. S. Mills, DFC	Filton
No. 92 Squadron	Spitfire	Sqn Ldr P. J. Sanders Sqn Ldr A. M. MacLachlan Sqn Ldr J. A. Kent, DFC, AFC	Filton Pembrey Biggin Hill
No. 111 Squadron	Hurricane	Sqn Ldr J. M. Thompson Sqn Ldr A. J. Biggar	Kenley Debden Turnhouse, Dyce

UNIT	AIRCRAFT	COMMANDING OFFICERS	SECTORS
No. 141 Squadron	Defiant	Sqn Ldr W. A. Richardson Sqn Ldr E. C. Wolfe	Turnhouse Biggin Hill
No. 145 Squadron	Hurricane	Sqn Ldr J. R. A. Peel	Tangmere, Dyce
No. 151 Squadron	Hurricane	Sqn Ldr E. M. Donaldson Sqn Ldr J. A. G. Gordon Sqn Ldr H. West	North Weald Digby
No. 152 Squadron	Spitfire	Sqn Ldr P. K. Devitt	Usworth Middle Wallop
No. 213 Squadron	Hurricane	Sqn Ldr H. D. McGregor Sqn Ldr D. MacDonald	Filton Tangmere
No. 219 Squadron	Blenheim If Beaufighter	Sqn Ldr J. H. Little, DFC	Catterick Kenley
No. 222 Squadron	Spitfire	Sqn Ldr H. W. Mermagen, AFC Sqn Ldr J. H. Hill	Kirton-in-Lindsey Hornchurch
No. 229 Squadron	Hurricane	Sqn Ldr H. J. Maguire Sqn Ldr A. J. Banham Sqn Ldr F. E. Rosier	Wittering Northolt
No. 232 Squadron	Hurricane	Flt Lt M. M. Stephens, DFC Flt Lt A. W. Pennington-Leigh	Wick Turnhouse
No. 234 Squadron	Spitfire	Sqn Ldr J. S. O'Brien Flt Lt C. L. Page Sqn Ldr M. V. Blake	St. Eval Middle Wallop
No. 238 Squadron	Hurricane	Sqn Ldr C. E. J. Baines Sqn Ldr H. A. Fenton	Middle Wallop St. Eval
No. 242 Squadron	Hurricane	Sqn Ldr D. R. S. Bader DSO, DFC	Coltishall Duxford
No. 245 Squadron	Hurricane	Sqn Ldr E. W. Whitley, DFC	Turnhouse Aldergrove
No. 247 Squadron	Gladiator	Flt Lt G. F. Chater Flt Lt P. St. G. O'Brian	St. Eval
No. 249 Squadron	Hurricane	Sqn Ldr J. Grandy	Church Fenton Middle Wallop North Weald
No. 253 Squadron	Hurricane	Sqn Ldr T. P. Gleave Sqn Ldr H. M. Starr Sqn Ldr G. R. Edge, DFC Flt Lt R. M. B. Duke-Wooley	Kirton-in-Lindsey Turnhouse Kenley

UNIT	AIRCRAFT	COMMANDING OFFICERS	SECTORS
No. 257 Squadron	Hurricane	Sqn Ldr D. W. Bayne Sqn Ldr H. Harkness Sqn Ldr R. R. S. Tuck	Northolt Debden North Weald
No. 263 Squadron	Hurricane	Sqn Ldr H. Eeles	Turnhouse
No. 264 Squadron	Defiant	Sqn Ldr P. A. Hunter, DSO Sqn Ldr G. D. Garvin	Duxford Kirton-in-Lindsey Hornchurch
No. 266 Squadron	Spitfire	Sqn Ldr R. L. Wilkinson Sqn Ldr D. G. H. Spencer Sqn Ldr P. G. Jameson, DFC	Digby Wittering Hornchurch
No. 302 (Polish) Squadron	Hurricane	Sqn Ldr W. A. J. Satchell Wg Cdr M. Mumler (Polish CO)	Church Fenton Northolt
No. 303 (Polish) Squadron	Hurricane	Sqn Ldr R. G. Kellett Sqn Ldr Z. Krasnodebski Sqn Ldr W. Urbanowicz (Polish COs)	Northolt Church Fenton
No. 310 (Czech) Squadran	Hurricane	Sqn Ldr G. D. M. Blackwood Sqn Ldr A. Hess (Czech CO)	Duxford
No. 312 (Czech) Squadron	Hurricane	Sqn Ldr F. H. Tyson Sqn Ldr J. Ambrus (Czech CO)	Speke
No. 501 Squadron	Hurricane	Sqn Ldr H. A. V. Hogan	Middle Wallop Biggin Hill, Kenley
No. 504 Squadron	Hurricane	Sqn Ldr J. Sample, DFC	Wick, Catterick Northolt, Filton
No. 600 Squadron	Blenheim If Beaufighter	Sqn Ldr D. de B. Clarke Sqn Ldr H. L. Maxwell	Biggin Hill Hornchurch Catterick
No. 601 Squadron	Hurricane	Sqn Ldr M. Aitken, DFC Sqn Ldr W. F. C. Hobson Sqn Ldr E. F. Ward Sqn Ldr Sir A. Hope	Tangmere Debden Filton
No. 602 Squadron	Spitfire	Sqn Ldr A. V. R. Johnstone DFC	Turnhouse Tangmere
No. 603 Squadron	Spitfire	Sqn Ldr E. H. Stevens Sqn Ldr G. L. Denholm, DFC	Dyce Hornchurch

UNIT	AIRCRAFT	COMMANDING OFFICERS	SECTORS
No. 604 Squadron	Blenheim If Beaufighter	Sqn Ldr M. F. Anderson	Biggin Hill Middle Wallop
No. 605 Squadron	Hurricane	Sqn Ldr W. Churchill DSO, DFC Sqn Ldr A. A. McKellar DSO, DFC	Turnhouse Kenley
No. 607 Squadron	Hurricane	Sqn Ldr J. A. Vick Sqn Ldr A. W. Vincent	Usworth Tangmere Turnhouse
No. 609 Squadron	Spitfire	Sqn Ldr H. S. Darley Sqn Ldr M. L. Robinson DSO, DFC	Middle Wallop
No. 610 Squadron	Spitfire	Sqn Ldr A. T. Smith Sqn Ldr J. Ellis, DFC	Biggin Hill Usworth
No. 611 Squadron	Spitfire	Sqn Ldr J. E. McComb Sqn Ldr E. R. Bitmead	Digby Duxford, Ternhill
No. 615 Squadron	Hurricane	Sqn Ldr J. R. Kayll, DSO, DFC	Kenley, Turnhouse Northolt
No. 616 Squadron	Spitfire	Sqn Ldr M. L. Robinson Sqn Ldr H. F. Burton, DFC	Church Fenton Kenley, Coltishall Kirton-in-Lindsey
No. 1 Squadron Royal Canadian Air Force	Hurricane	Sqn Ldr E. A. McNab, DFC	Kenley, Northolt Turnhouse Wick

In addition to the above listed Squadrons, Nos. 421 and 422 Flights were formed during the Battle for Spotter duties; Nos. 235, 236 and 248 Squadrons flew Blenheim fighters with Coastal Command; Nos. 804 and 808 Squadrons of the Fleet Air Arm carried out air defence sorties; the RAF's Fighter Interceptor Unit carried out night' patrols and No. 7 Operational Training Unit (not officially a participant) fought several combats with enemy aircraft.

BIBLIOGRAPHY

MANUSCRIPT SOURCES
Public Record Office:
AIR 27/252   No. 19 Squadron Operations Record Book
AIR 50/10   No. 19 Squadron Combat Reports
AIR 16/142   Trials of Cannon Spitfire Fighter
AIR 4/58   Pilot's Flying Logbooks, Squadron Leader B. J. E. Lane
AIR 27/424   No. 41 Squadron Operations Record Book
AIR 27/428   No. 41 Squadron Operations Record Book Appendices
AIR 50/18   No. 41 Squadron Combat Reports
AIR 4/49   Pilot's Flying Logbooks, Squadron Leader H. R. L. Hood
AIR 27/528   No. 56 Squadron Operations Record Book
AIR 27/534   No. 56 Squadron Operations Record Book Appendices
AIR 50/22   No. 56 Squadron Combat Reports
AIR 27/640   No. 74 Squadron Operations Record Book
AIR 27/644   No. 74 Squadron Operations Record Book Appendices
AIR 50/32   No. 74 Squadron Combat Reports
AIR 27/703   No. 85 Squadron Operations Record Book
AIR 50/36   No. 85 Squadron Combat Reports
AIR 27/743   No. 92 Squadron Operations Record Book
AIR 27/748   No. 92 Squadron Operations Record Book Appendices
AIR 50/40   No. 92 Squadron Combat Reports
AIR 4/34   Pilot's Flying Logbooks, Squadron Leader R. H. Fokes
AIR 27/866   No. 111 Squadron Operations Record Book
AIR 50/43   No. 111 Squadron Combat Report
AIR 27/1663 No. 303 Squadron Operations Record Book
AIR 27/1659 No. 303 Squadron Operations Record Book Appendices
AIR 50/117   No. 303 Squadron Combat Reports
AIR 16/334   HQ, Fighter Command Tactical Memoranda
AIR 16/99   Fighter Command Attacks, 1939

PRINTED SOURCES
Adam, Wing Commander Ronald. *Readiness at Dawn*. Gollancz, 1941
Air Ministry *Pilot's Notes: Spitfire IIA and IIB Aeroplanes, Merlin XII Engine* (Air Publication 1565B). July, 1940
— *The Origins and Development of Operational Research in the Royal Air Force* (Air Publication 3368). HMSO, 1963

Baker, E. C. R. *The Fighter Aces of the RAF, 1939–1945.* Kimber, 1962
Bartley, Squadron Leader A. *Smoke Trails in the Sky.* Kimber, 1984
Brookes, A. J. *Fighter Squadron at War.* Ian Allan, 1980
Collier, Basil. *The Battle of Britain.* Batsford, 1962
— *The Defence of the United Kingdom.* HMSO, 1957
— *The Leader of the Few.* Jarrolds, 1957
Collier, Richard. *Eagle Day.* Hodder & Stoughton, 1966
Cynk, Jerzy B. *History of the Polish Air Force, 1918–1968.* Osprey, 1972
Deere, Group Captain A. C. *Nine Lives.* Hodder & Stoughton, 1959
Dowding, Air Chief Marshal Sir Hugh. *The Battle of Britain* Dispatch published
as a supplement to the *London Gazette*, 10 September 1946. HMSO
Ellan, B. J. (Squadron Leader B. J. E. Lane). *Spitfire.* Murray, 1942
Fiedler, Arkady. *Squadron 303.* Peter Davies, 1942
Forrester, L. *Fly For Your Life.* Muller, 1956
Green, William. *Aircraft of the Battle of Britain.* Macdonald/Pan, 1969
— *The Augsburg Eagle.* Janes, 1980
Halley, J. J. *Famous Fighter Squadrons of the RAF.* Hylton Lacey, 1971
Halliday, Hugh. *No. 242 Squadron: The Canadian Years.* Midland Counties
Publications, 1982
Irving, David. *The Rise and Fall of the Luftwaffe.* Wiedenfeld & Nicholson, 1973
Johnson, Group Captain J. E. *Wing Leader.* Chatto & Windus, 1956
Jones, Wing Commander Ira. *Tiger Squadron.* W. H. Allen, 1954
Keith, Group Captain C. H. *I Hold My Aim.* Allen & Unwin, 1946
Kent, Group Captain J. A. *One of the Few.* Kimber, 1971
Mason, F. K. *Battle over Britain.* McWhirter Twins, 1969
McKee, Alexander. *Strike From the Sky.* Souvenir Press, 1960
Orange, Vincent. *Sir Keith Park.* Methuen, 1984
Page, Geoffrey. *Tale of a Guinea Pig.* Pelham Books, 1981
Price, Alfred. *Battle of Britain: The Hardest Day.* Macdonald & Janes, 1979
— *Blitz on Britain.* Ian Allan, 1977
— *The Spitfire Story.* Janes, 1982
— *World War II Fighter Conflict.* Macdonald & Janes, 1975
Quill, Jeffrey. *Spitfire.* Murray, 1983
Ramsey, Winston G. *The Battle of Britain: Then and Now.* After the Battle, 1980.
Rawlings, John. *Fighter Squadrons of the RAF and their Aircraft.* Macdonald, 1969
Reid, J. P. M. *Some of the Few.* Macdonald, 1960
Revell, Alex. *The Vivid Air.* Kimber, 1978
The Royal Canadian Air Force Overseas: The First Four Years. OUP, Toronto, 1944
Shaw, Michael. *Twice Vertical: The History of No. 1 (Fighter) Squadron, RAF.*
Macdonald, 1971
Shores, C. and Williams, C. *Aces High.* Spearman, 1966
Spurdle, Squadron Leader Bob. *The Blue Arena.* Kimber, 1986
Sutton, Barry. *The Way of a Pilot.* Macmillan, 1942

Sutton, Squadron Leader H. T. *Raiders Approach*. Gale & Polden, 1956

Tidy, Douglas. *I Fear No Man: The History of No. 74 squadron, RAF*. Macdonald, 1972

Townsend, Peter. *Duel of Eagles*. Weidenfeld & Nicholson, 1970

— *Time and Chance*. Collins, 1978

Wakefield, Kenneth. *Luftwaffe Encore*. Kimber, 1979

Walker, Oliver. *Sailor Malan*. Cassell, 1953

Wallace, G. F. *Guns of the Royal Air Force, 1939–45*. Kimber, 1972

— *RAF, Biggin Hill*. Putnam, 1957

Wood, D. and Dempster, D. *The Narrow Margin*. Hutchinson, 1961

Wykeham, Peter. *Fighter Command*. Putnam, 1960

Wynn, H. (ed.). *Fighter Pilot: A Self-Portrait by George Barclay*. Kimber, 1976

Wynn, Kenneth G. *A Clasp for 'The Few'*. Auckland, New Zealand, 1981

Zumbach, J. *On Wings of War*. Deutsch, 1975

INDEX